MONTH-BY-MONTH GARDENING

TENNESSEE & KENTUCKY

Quarto is the authority on a wide range of topics.

Quarto educates, entertains and enriches the lives of our readers—enthusiasts and lovers of hands-on living.

www.quartoknows.com

© 2013 Quarto Publishing Group USA Inc.
Text © Judy Lowe 2013

First published in 2013 by Cool Springs Press, an imprint of Quarto Publishing Group USA Inc., 400 First Avenue North, Suite 400, Minneapolis, MN 55401 USA. Telephone: (612) 344-8100 Fax: (612) 344-8692

quartoknows.com
Visit our blogs at quartoknows.com

Cool Springs Press titles are also available at discounts in bulk quantity for industrial or sales-promotional use. For details contact the Special Sales Manager at Quarto Publishing Group USA Inc., 400 First Avenue North, Suite 400, Minneapolis, MN 55401 USA.

Library of Congress Cataloging-in-Publication Data

Lowe, Judy.
  Tennessee & Kentucky month-by-month gardening : what to do each month to have a beautiful garden all year / Judy Lowe.
      p. cm.
  Includes bibliographical references and index.
  ISBN 978-1-59186-578-0 (softcover)
  1. Gardening--Tennessee--Handbooks, manuals, etc. 2. Gardening--Kentucky--Handbooks, manuals, etc. I. Title. II. Title: Tennessee and Kentucky month-by-month gardening.

  SB453.2.T2L67 2014
  635.09768--dc23

                    2013026164

Acquisitions Editor: Billie Brownell
Design Manager: Brad Springer
Layout: Danielle Smith

Printed in USA

MONTH-BY-MONTH GARDENING

TENNESSEE & KENTUCKY

What to Do Each Month to Have a Beautiful Garden All Year

JUDY LOWE

COOL SPRINGS PRESS
Home and Garden Experts™

Dedication

To my sons, Carlyle and David, for their support and belief that Mom writes the best garden books ever.

Acknowledgment

A book is never the work of just one person. It takes the efforts of many people. I, along with all the readers who gain needed information from this book, owe a debt of gratitude to Billie Brownell, the best and most conscientious editor anyone can imagine, and I would like to thank Tracy Stanley, Brad Springer, and all the other folks at Quayside who labored over locating just the right photos and made sure we were grammatically and horticulturally correct all the way through.

Contents

Introduction

Does it really matter whether you prune a shrub in September or December? Or whether you plant basil in late March when it first becomes available at a garden center, or wait until May or June? Yes, it does. Timing can make all the difference between success and failure.

For example, no matter how perfectly you prune your azalea, if you do it in September or February, you're pruning it at the wrong time of year, and there will be a penalty for that: the shrub won't bloom in April, since the flower buds were cut off when you pruned it. The right time to prune spring-flowering shrubs such as azaleas—if pruning is needed at all—is right after the plant finishes flowering. At that time, the shrub hasn't yet begun forming any flower buds for the next year, so there aren't any for you to cut off. And when you're planting the ever-popular basil, it pays to remember that basil loves heat. It won't grow well until spring temperatures have warmed up during the night as well as the day. Plant basil while temps are still chilly, and the plant will just sit there, not growing at all.

Timing issues often come up for beginning gardeners and those who have moved to Kentucky or Tennessee from another state. You may wonder: When are the best times where you live to plant, prune, fertilize, renovate a lawn, and so forth? The timing may have been different where you lived previously.

This book answers timing questions and more. It explains why two neighbors living side by side might fertilize their lawns in different months. (It has to do with the kind of grass grown.) And it explains when houseplants simply don't need fertilizing, so you can save your time and money. It also gives you the how-to information you need in order to do the right thing at the right time: how to prune a tree or a rosebush, raise vegetables from seed, and construct a water garden. Our goal is to provide the information that will make you a success.

INTRODUCTION

Tennessee and Kentucky are wonderful places to garden. Why?

- We have a long growing season.

- Our winter temperatures are mostly moderate.

- We generally receive ample rainfall throughout the year.

- Many different kinds of plants grow here.

It's easy to be a successful gardener here—provided you follow a few basic guidelines: paying attention to climate, evaluating the conditions in your yard, choosing the right plant for the right spot, and providing what plants need to grow and thrive (soil, water, nutrients, and oxygen).

HOW CLIMATE AFFECTS YOUR GARDEN

"What zone does it grow in?" That's a question that all homeowners and budding gardeners learn to ask about plants. For years, the U.S. Department of Agriculture has divided the country into zones based on their average annual minimum temperatures. For zone 6, it's minus 10 to 0 degrees Fahrenheit. For zone 7, it's 0 to 10 degrees. For zone 8, the average low is 10 to 20 degrees. Our zones in Kentucky and Tennessee range from 6a to 8a.

It's important to realize that these zones are just a guide, not necessarily the final word on what plants will or won't live through the winter. For one thing, they're averages. If your county is considered to be in zone 7, that doesn't mean that some winter the temperature might not dip below 0—and kill any plants that can't tolerate such cold.

Low temperatures aren't the only factor that determines which plants grow well in our region. Heat tolerance has to be considered too. Some plants—those with gray leaves and many needled evergreens, for instance—don't mind our winter temperatures but can't tolerate our summer heat and humidity. To help measure heat tolerance, the American Horticultural Society (AHS) publishes

the AHS Plant Heat Zone Map, which you can check out at http://www.ahs.org/gardening-resources/gardening-maps/heat-zone-map. In general, though, heat tolerance of particular plants is the kind of thing that's learned by experience, by reading local or state-specific garden books and articles, and by asking lots of questions of experienced gardeners, agricultural extension agents, and knowledgeable garden center personnel. A few plant tags do list heat zone, but not many.

KNOW YOUR YARD

You may occasionally find that weather conditions on your property aren't what they are at the official weather station in your county or even in your next-door neighbor's yard. Conditions may even vary within your yard. An area can be wetter, drier, warmer, or colder than the surrounding area. Areas with differing weather conditions are called microclimates.

There's nothing mysterious about microclimates—you have probably already observed them. For example, plants growing next to a building or wall are more protected and often bloom earlier than those in a more exposed spot.

Some other factors that create microclimates include:

- Good-sized bodies of water, such as lakes, moderate temperatures somewhat for adjacent land. Winter temperatures may not be quite as low as they are farther from the water. Spring frosts end earlier, and fall frosts arrive later.

- Cities are warmer than rural areas. Buildings and paved surfaces absorb heat in the day and radiate it into the air at night.

- Cold air flows downward. A valley (or even a dip or the bottom of a hill in your yard) may be as much as 10 degrees Fahrenheit cooler than the top of the slope. Frosts will penetrate these low-lying areas later in spring and earlier in fall, affecting plants that grow there.

You can see why it's important to be aware of not just the weather and climate in your county, but also the specific conditions in your yard. This awareness helps you choose the right plants for the right places. Instead of buying a plant and then figuring out where to put it in your yard, it's better to analyze the conditions—soil, sun, shade, and water—in the parts of your yard where you want to plant and then select plants that thrive in those situations.

SUN AND SHADE

Most of us recognize when our yards are in full sun or shade. But few spaces are in all sun or all shade all the time. And not many of us are able to gauge accurately how sunny or how shady a particular spot is. Mostly, we guess. And we set ourselves up for failure when we guess wrong and plant a tree, shrub, or perennial plant that needs either more or less sun than is available.

Here's the moral: take time to watch an area to be sure how many hours it's in the sun and how many hours it's in the shade. Full sun is at least eight hours of direct sunshine. Partial sun is about six hours of direct sunlight. Part shade is five or fewer hours of morning sun. Morning sun is mildest and considered best for plants. Afternoon sun is hotter and brighter. You may want to count every hour of afternoon sun as two for the purpose of deciding whether a sun-loving plant will be happy in a particular site.

Naturally, you'll find some in-between areas—dappled shade, where dots of sun peek through at certain times of the day, and areas that don't get much direct sun but are actually quite light because tree limbs that block some of the sun start 20 feet up, so plenty of light can shine through. All these situations call for trial and error. Don't think that you have to depend only on hostas, ferns, dogwoods, and azaleas in shade. Try some plants that like partial shade or even partial sun and see how they fare. You may be surprised.

Of course, you don't have to live with the current conditions in your yard. If there's too much sun, plant trees or large shrubs or put up a fence, trellis, or arbor to create some shade. When there's too much shade, consider removing trees that are not in good shape or "weed" trees such as box elder

and mimosa. Or consult an arborist about thinning a tree or removing some of the lower limbs to let light through.

SOIL

Soil—dirt, if you will—is often the part of gardening that beginners don't think much about. And that causes many failures that could have been prevented. Soil isn't as exciting as plants are; soil doesn't grow or bloom. But it's the foundation for everything you grow. The condition of the soil is often mirrored by the condition of the plant growing in that soil.

Soil is more complex than it looks to the eye. It's made up of mineral particles, organic material, air, and water. It's also teeming with life—earthworms, tiny insects, and microorganisms that break down organic matter (mainly plant residues that are decomposing).

What do you need to know about soil? The most important aspects of soil for gardening purposes are what type of soil is in your yard—and how quickly it drains—and what its pH is (the measure of its acidity or alkalinity). If given a choice, we all want to have deep, fertile soil that we can dig into with our hands. Unfortunately, few of us in this region have that type of soil naturally.

Soils are classified by their texture—sand, silt, or clay—but most soils are made up of all three. The easiest way to find out what type of soil is in your yard is to call the soil conservation service office in your county. (Look in the phone book under the government listings, or online under your county's name and the words "soil conservation.") Most counties have a book listing all the parcels of land in the county, classified by soil type.

Here's a test you can do at home to determine your soil type:

1. Put a trowel of loose soil (remove all rocks and stones) in a glass canning jar.

2. Add 2 cups of water, put the lid on, and shake the jar.

■ *How big is the area you want to improve with soil amendments? First measure the area and you'll have a better idea of what quantity amendments you'll need.*

3. Get a ruler. After one minute, measure the bottom layer, which is sand. Write that number down.

4. After one hour, measure the layer that's above the sand. That's silt. Make a note of that number.

5. Twenty-four hours after you first shook the jar, measure the top layer, which is clay. Write that number down.

6. Divide the depth of each layer by the total depth of the settled soil, and then multiply that number by 100. This gives you the percentage of each soil type within your soil.

Sandy soil is fast-draining, but it doesn't hold water or nutrients. Clay is just the opposite: it drains slowly and holds water and nutrients. It also warms up slowly in spring and is hard to

dig. Fortunately, the solution to sandy or loose, rocky soil (which doesn't hold moisture at the roots of plants, where they need it) and also to clay (which can hold so much water it drowns plants) is the same: amending the soil with organic matter.

For clay, the best organic materials are compost (see pages 216–218 for instructions regarding how to make compost), fine bark (such as Nature's Helper), rotted sawdust, cocoa hulls, rotted leaves, aged mushroom compost, well-rotted manure, and gypsum. Avoid peat moss, which can hold too much moisture. You may be surprised to learn that you should also avoid amending clay with sand, unless you can add enough coarse sand (the recommended kind) to equal one-fourth or more of the volume of the soil. Except in small beds, this is a huge amount of coarse sand. Lesser amounts of sand tend to pack in between clay particles, creating a sort of cement. To improve clay soil, spread a

■ *Spread compost, fine bark, or other soil amendments several inches thick over the soil's surface, then till it in.*

layer of the organic matter 2 to 3 inches thick on the surface and dig or till it into the top 8 inches of the soil.

For sandy or other very loose soils, you can hardly add too much organic matter to the soil. Start with a layer 3 to 4 inches thick if you can. Good soil amendments for fast-draining soils are compost, humus, spaghnum peat moss (moisten thoroughly first), rotted leaves, well-rotted manure, aged mushroom compost, rotted sawdust, cocoa hulls, and seaweed.

Because of our hot summers, amending the soil is an ongoing process. You will need to repeat it at least every few years. Yearly additions are even better in beds that are dug up each spring, such as those used for vegetables and annual flowers.

You can also grow your own soil amendments. In the vegetable garden and on cleared land that you plan to plant next year, you can sow seeds of green manure crops in the fall and till the crop under in the spring to improve the soil. This increases the amount of humus in the soil. Rye, buckwheat, alfalfa, sweet clover, and cowpeas are good green manure crops.

A popular no-dig, no-till way of improving the soil is layering it with organic materials. This type of sheet composting is sometimes called lasagna gardening. The bottom layer is four to six sheets of thoroughly wet newspapers. On top of that is a layer of brown materials, such as shredded fall leaves, straw or hay, eggshells, tea bags, sawdust, or wood ashes (the latter two in small amounts only). The third layer is made up of green materials: kitchen scraps, grass clippings (not treated with herbicides), plants and plant trimmings from the yard or garden, coffee grounds, manure (a small amount, but *never* from dogs, cats, or humans), or seaweed. Keep alternating layers in this order till you have a pile about 2 feet tall. Plant plants right in the pile, which will provide nutrients to the plants as it decomposes.

IS YOUR SOIL ACIDIC OR ALKALINE?

Another aspect of soil that matters to plants—and determines which plants will grow well in your yard—is its pH. The pH scale ranges from 0 to 14, with the lower numbers indicating acidity and the higher numbers alkalinity. Most plants prefer slightly acidic to neutral soil, about 6.5 to 7.0, although they may grow in soils 5.5 to 7.3.

How do you know whether your soil is acidic or alkaline? Have it tested. Garden centers sell porta-ble kits that give you a quick reading, but a more accurate assessment is available by taking samples of the soil in your yard and sending them to your state Extension service's lab for analysis. Call your county's Extension office to get a soil-testing box

HOW TO WATER YOUR PLANTS

1   *Prepare your watering tools by attaching the watering wand or hose nozzle to the hose and making sure that the water flow control is set to "off." It sounds basic, but if the water turns on and the nozzle is pointed at you, you'll be "inconvenienced," to say the least!*

2   *Turn on the water source. If you're using a spray nozzle, you won't need to turn the water on all the way. Remember to turn off the water when you're done! If you leave the faucet on, the pressure can build up inside the hose and the hose might burst.*

3   *Use the watering wand to water at the base of the plant. Direct the water into the soil next to the plant. If you spray the plant's leaves or fling water around, you waste water and increase the chances that fungal or bacterial diseases on one plant will spread, via water, to another plant. Watering wands with gentle water breakers are the best tools for hand watering because they slow the flow of water hitting the ground and keep the soil from splattering. Count to ten while watering each plant.*

and instruction sheet. Look online to find the address and phone number of your local office. (See https://utextension.tennessee.edu/pages/offices.aspx for Tennessee and http://www.ca.uky.edu/county for Kentucky.)

Some plants need acidic or alkaline soils. It pays to seek out those plants if you have soil that falls into either range. (See a partial list of plants on pages 222 and 223.)

The problem comes when soil is *extremely* acidic or alkaline. This can make some nutrients in the soil unavailable to plants. One solution is to change the pH. It's easy and inexpensive to add dolomitic lime to soil to make it less acidic. Fall is the best time of year to do so, because it takes several months for the lime to take effect. Addition of sulfur helps acidify alkaline soils. The amounts to use probably came with your soil test results. If not, consult your local extension service for recommendations.

WATER

Although our area usually receives ample rainfall (see the charts on page 227 for the average rainfall in your county), that rain doesn't necessarily fall right on schedule when your plants need it. That means that homeowners often have to water the plants in their yard.

So you need to know a few things about water: when to water, how much to use, and how to apply it. The rule of thumb is that plants need 1 inch of rainfall each week. You might think that means you're going to have to pull out the hose and sprinkler every week when it doesn't rain that much. But it's not quite that simple. Some plants need watering more often than others.

Plants that have been set out in the past six months (and especially those planted within the past week or two) are going to need more moisture. That's because their root systems are still small.

Many established plants—large trees, for example—may never need supplemental watering except during drought. (See the section on coping with a drought, beginning on pages 151–155.)

Plants growing in shade or in clay soil need less frequent watering than those in full sun or sandy soil. The hotter the weather and the harder winds blow, the more moisture plants may need.

If you know your plants well, you will see signs that they need watering: droopy or dull leaves, fewer or smaller flowers or fruits, and leaves that drop off the plant prematurely. Grass will look grayish instead of bright green.

But mostly you have to measure to see how much moisture is in the soil. Carefully insert a thin bamboo stake into the soil near a plant (but not so close that it harms the plant's root system) and then pull it out. See whether any part of the stake is damp. That shows how deep the moisture is in the soil. For larger plants, such as trees, the soil should be moist at least 12 inches deep; water when the soil is dry about 6 inches down. For more shallow-rooted plants, water when the soil is dry about 4 inches deep—and water enough to wet the soil to about 8 inches deep.

How much water do you have to apply to moisten the soil 8 inches deep? It depends on how you apply the water and what kind of soil you have. How long it takes for the water to penetrate depends very much on the type of soil and somewhat on technique.

If you use a sprinkler, put small tuna cans around to measure the amount of water delivered. For other methods, measure the soil moisture twenty-four hours after watering to see how deeply the water penetrated.

The most common method of watering is by HOSE.

- **Advantages:** It's cheap and easy. The gardener controls where the water is applied. Less water is wasted because someone is paying attention to how much water is each plant receives.

- **Disadvantages:** It's easy to use too much force, which can damage plants and cause runoff. Also, it's very easy to water inadequately when using a hose because it's tiring to stand there holding the hose.

SOAKER HOSES, often made from recycled materials, are generally black and have small holes or pores through which water seeps.

- **Advantages:** Soaker hoses are inexpensive and easy to use. They are flexible, so they can be woven in and around plants. Because the water is delivered at a slow rate, there's reduced runoff. The gardener need not stand there while the hose delivers the water.

- **Disadvantages:** The pressure of the water decreases as the length of the hose increases. And the hoses don't always last long.

OSCILLATING SPRINKLERS deliver water in a back-and-forth motion.

- **Advantages:** Oscillating sprinklers allow slow penetration of water into the soil. They are useful for large, even areas, such as lawns.

- **Disadvantages:** Water can be blown about by the wind. It's also likely to evaporate more than with other methods of watering. Water at the edge of the pattern may run into the street, driveway, or sidewalk, wasting water—and money.

FAN SPRINKLERS deliver a fine spray of water in a semicircle pattern.

- **Advantages:** The more delicate spray is useful for ground covers and is more accurate than oscillating sprinklers.

- **Disadvantages:** A fan sprinkler doesn't cover as much ground as an oscillating sprinkler, plus runoff and evaporation may occur.

DRIP IRRIGATION resembles soaker hoses somewhat, but the tubes are smaller and are embedded with emitters that can be spaced according to need.

- **Advantages:** Drip irrigation delivers water slowly, so there's little runoff or evaporation, and it can be tailored for plants needing special attention.

- **Disadvantages:** If the drip irrigation system is under mulch, it's hard to tell whether all the emitters are working. And the system takes time to install, since a pressure reducer and filters must be attached. It's also hard for gardeners to get used to how slowly water is applied by drip irrigation, and they're apt to turn the system off before it has delivered enough moisture.

IN-GROUND IRRIGATION SYSTEMS may be just what's required for a large property or for homeowners who are very busy or away a great deal.

- **Advantages:** They can have a positive effect if your soil is rocky or otherwise doesn't hold water well. Collect and read brochures, and then talk to several dealers before you decide whether to install an irrigation system and what type to install. It also helps to talk with homeowners who have different systems to find out what they like and don't like about them.

- **Disadvantages:** They are permanent and costly.

FERTILIZER

Plants need at least sixteen nutrients for growth. They obtain three of these nutrients from air and water. The rest they take up from the soil (one important reason to improve your soil with organic matter). A soil test tells you which nutrients your soil lacks and the type and amount of fertilizer you need to apply to correct the deficiency.

Fertilizers may be chemical or organic. In the past, organic fertilizers weren't always readily available to homeowners, but that has changed. Instead of looking for cottonseed meal, blood meal, fish emulsion, kelp, or composted manure—which are fine to use but may not always be easy to find—gardeners can now find boxes and bags of balanced organic fertilizers at almost every garden center and nursery.

Every fertilizer container has three numbers listed prominently on it. They may be something like 10-10-10 or 6-12-12. The numbers indicate the percentages by weight of the three major elements:

- The first number indicates nitrogen (N), which promotes rapid growth and greening of stems and leaves.

- The second number is for phosphorus (P), which encourages root growth, stimulates flowers, and aids seed formation.

- The third number represents potassium (K), which increases disease and drought resistance.

TERMINOLOGY

- A fertilizer that contains all three of those components is called a **complete fertilizer**.

- A **balanced fertilizer** is one for which all three numbers are the same (5-5-5, for example); the product contains equal amounts of the major elements.

- An **acidic fertilizer** (sometimes called azalea-camellia fertilizer or blueberry fertilizer) contains an acidifying ingredient and is used around acid-loving plants, especially if the pH of the soil is higher than desired.

- **Water-soluble fertilizers** come as powders or crystals that are mixed with water and applied when watering. These may also be applied to the foliage of a plant for quick absorption. (This technique is called foliar feeding.) Although the effects of water-soluble fertilizers are fast, they are not long-lasting, so these fertilizers must be re-applied more frequently.

- **Slow-release fertilizers** provide a long, steady supply of nutrients to plants. This can be beneficial because repeated applications aren't necessary and the nutrients are available when the plants need them.

Organic fertilizers are generally slow-release. They are either derived from the remains of once-living organisms or are animal manures. They improve the soil's condition as they feed it.

Usually, organic fertilizers contain small amounts of nitrogen, phosphorus, and potassium. Many gardeners see this as an advantage, as it leads to slow but steady growth—which is good for plants.

Avoid fertilizers that contain weedkillers. If you need a weedkiller, apply it where needed, not over a wide area of your garden or lawn, as you fertilize.

LANDSCAPING

There's more to a yard than simply putting plants about and then taking care of them. A good-looking yard—one that you'll be proud of—is the result of planning. It comes from putting all the basics together into one beautiful picture.

First, look at what you have. Find the property survey that was done when you bought the house. If you can't locate the survey, sometimes the mortgage company has a copy it can send you. The alternative is to draw an approximate map of your land, noting on it any structures (including their measurements), existing trees, shrubs, flower beds, vegetable or water gardens, fences, walls, driveway, walks, playhouses, storage sheds, decks, and patios. It's also a good idea to note drainage ditches (or drainage problems), slopes, and berms. This is called your base map. You may want to make several copies.

Next, be critical. Have the foundation shrubs grown halfway up the living room windows? Does the hedge have bare spots? Are junipers blocking

■ *The plants in a perennial border—daylilies and callas, for example—are planted once and then bloom each summer from then on, whereas annuals must be replanted every spring in order to put on a show in your yard.*

your view of the street when you back out of the driveway? Also note plants that you simply don't like.

If a plant has been neglected, it may respond to pruning, fertilizing, and other regular care. If you like the plant where it is, it's worth trying to keep it. But some plants are probably best removed and replaced. You can put a big X over those on your landscape plan.

Now, think about what you want your landscape to do for you. I'll bet you never thought of your yard in that way before. Very likely, you've thought mostly about how your yard looks, not how it works. But just as your home is laid out so it's useful, a landscape should also meet your needs. To help you decide what those are, ask yourself:

- How much outdoor entertaining do I do? What type, and how many people at a time?

- Do I need a play area for children?

- What about dogs?

- Does the yard need more privacy?

- How much time can I devote to maintenance?

- Do I have favorite plants or a favorite style that I want to include?

- Am I interested in growing vegetables or fruits?

- Would I like a water garden?

- Are the driveway and off-street parking adequate?

- Do I need paths?

Dream big when you're planning a landscape, but don't get carried away. If you have three young preschoolers, or your backyard is the impromptu football field for a group of middle-schoolers, an elegant plant-filled landscape may not be in the cards for a few years. But no one says you have to

do everything at once. In fact, it's often a good idea to accomplish your landscaping goals over time, not just to ease the budget (which it does), but because once we get started, sometimes we change our minds or modify our opinions.

Landscape architects and landscape designers can create a landscape plan for you, if you don't feel comfortable doing it on your own. They can also supervise the installation of the project. Ask for references and take time to check them out carefully.

Whether you'll be working with a professional or doing it yourself, collect photos of yards and plants that you like. You'll also get landscaping ideas by driving through neighborhoods (especially established upscale communities), talking with good gardeners and personnel at top-notch nurseries, and reading *Tennessee & Kentucky Garden Guide*.

In a landscape around a new home, consider first trees, then shrubs. These need to start growing first, and they set the tone for what's to come. When renovating an older property, make a list of priorities: ground covers to replace too much lawn this year, maybe a small water garden next year, and a larger deck two years down the road.

Consider plant textures and color combinations, especially in connection with your house; different shades of brick can clash with red flowers that might be planted against it. Strongly variegated plants, while showy and wonderful, may also have to be carefully positioned to harmonize with their surroundings.

Draw some of your ideas on a piece of tracing paper placed over your base map. (Or if you have plenty of copies of the base map, draw your ideas right on the map.) Then take the map out into the yard and envision what you have drawn. You may even want to go so far as to drag a hose into the shape of a flower bed or pond to see whether the proportions are right.

MULTISEASON PLANTS
Your landscape will be more attractive and versatile if you ask one question: How does this plant look

■ *Measure the position of all the features of your yard, relative to the property lines.*

■ *Use the survey measurements to create a rough drawing of your yard.*

in fall or winter? So often, our favorite plants are the ones that are at their peak in spring, such as daffodils, redbud trees, and creeping phlox (thrift). And there's nothing wrong with that. But you get more impact from multiseason plants, those that look good during more than one season of the year. Dogwood trees with flowers, berries, and bright red leaves are a familiar example. But here are some others.

- Japanese maple: attractive foliage in spring and summer, fall color, interesting shape in winter

- Red maple: red flowers very early in the season, shade in summer, good fall color

- Sourwood: tassled flowers in summer, fruits and neon-red fall leaf color

- Yellowwood: white flowers in summer, good fall color, interesting bark in winter

You'll also be able to find shrubs that shine in several seasons. Kerria, for example, flowers in spring and has green stems in winter. Azaleas and

rhododendrons flower in spring and retain their leaves during winter. And many shrubs produce berries, which add an extra dimension to the landscape (and often feed migrating birds).

As you're planning, see what's available at local nurseries. Then decide on one area that you want to focus on first—maybe the entrance to your house or the area beside the deck. When you've finished your first project and you see how much better the area looks (be sure to take before and after photos), you'll have a wonderful feeling of accomplishment—and you just may be ready to tackle something bigger.

Don't think of gardening as a chore. Think of it as exercise or as a way of beautifying your surroundings. Make it fun and relaxing. As you work through the monthly lists of things to be done in the yard, don't get so busy that you forget to take time to enjoy the pleasures of your landscape— from a tiny fern frond unfurling in spring to the majesty of an oak that's been providing shade to several generations and will continue for several more. Your yard is a living work of art, and you're the artist.

January

In one way, January is the most enjoyable time of the year for gardening. No, you can't get outside and do much, but you can dream and plan. Where in your yard would you put a couple of cannas that are sporting gold-and-maroon-striped foliage? Is this the year you order all those lilies you've been admiring? Wouldn't you love to be eating striped, orange, and purple heirloom tomatoes from Independence Day until frost? What about redoing your patio to make it more enjoyable for casual entertaining? Anything's possible in January. You're limited only by your imagination.

So this is the month to dream big and investigate how to make those dreams come true. The key to having a great-looking yard isn't having a green thumb, but discovering what needs to be done and planning how to get there.

Now's the time to pull out those magazine clippings that show glorious gardens, pore over the catalogs that have arrived, and search the Internet for design ideas and tips. As you drool over the photographs, also read the articles carefully to see whether these plans and plants are right for your landscape. Do they require more sun than is available in your shady yard? Are they too formal to have the right look around a casual lakefront cabin? Are they ideal for California but maybe not for Kentucky and Tennessee? (If you have questions about which plants do best in this region, consult *Tennessee & Kentucky Garden Guide.*)

If your plans are relatively simple—a new vegetable garden or a bed of colorful annuals near the front door to welcome guests—consider drawing them up this month, because a planned bed is always going to be more successful than a group of plants set out haphazardly. And if you wait until planting time, April or May, to draw a plan, you may be much too busy with other spring activities to get around to it, to arrange to obtain soil amendments, or to have the soil tilled. The first month of a new year is an ideal time not only to dream about a wonderful new garden but also to take the first steps toward making it a reality.

PLAN

ALL

If you don't have a garden notebook, January is the ideal time to start one. It can be as simple as a spiral notebook, or anything that will keep all your notes together in one place so you can refer to them in future years. Start by recording this month's temperature ups and downs, which can be considerable, and the amount of precipitation. Once you've formed the habit of writing down the day-to-day details of the garden—the weather, the plants, what blooms when, what you hope to accomplish in the future—and added a note or two about plants you'd love to own—you'll wonder how you ever managed to do without a garden notebook.

If you already have a garden notebook, sit down beside the fireplace or some other cozy spot, put your feet up, and read back over your entries for last year. That will remind you what went well last season and what didn't, what you'd like to duplicate this year and what you want to avoid.

As you look over those garden catalogs that are so enticing at this time of year, look for these important words: *disease-resistant* and *insect-resistant*. Homeowners often insist that they want a low-maintenance landscape. Well, one key to having that is to avoid plants that are highly attractive to insects or that are subject to certain diseases. Why buy trouble?

Have you had your garden soil tested within the past three years? Have you added large quantities of wood ash or other amendments to the garden since the soil was last tested? If you answered no to the first question or yes to the second, it's time to take samples of the soil and send them off for testing. Your county Extension office will have all the details.

Will you need any new gardening tools this year? Maybe you've been thinking about buying a new pair of pruners, a backpack sprayer, or other equipment. Pruners and many other hand tools are now being ergonomically designed and require less brute strength than previously. If you haven't looked over the tool selection in the past few years, you may be pleasantly surprised.

EDIBLES

Is one of your garden plans this year to raise fresh vegetables and herbs in your own backyard? But would your hard clay soil or poor drainage interfere with enjoying homegrown tomatoes and basil? The easy answer is raised beds. Use long-lasting

■ *Keeping good records of previous gardening seasons—how much it rained, if temperatures were a great deal above or below normal, which plants performed well and which didn't—helps you be successful in future seasons.*

Gardening Notes.

HOW TO BUILD A RAISED BED

■ *Raised bed gardens are ideal for beginners, those with poor soil and those who find it difficult to bend over.*

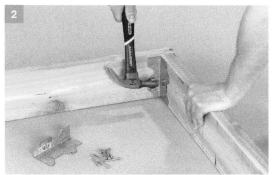

1. Cut the wood and assemble the frame upside down on a flat surface. Drive deck screws through pilot holes at the corners.

2. Reinforce the corners by nailing metal corner brace hardware. Use galvanized joist hanger nails to fasten the braces.

3. Position the bed frame in your garden location. Bury the bottom at least 2 inches below grade.

4. Fill the bed with a suitable planting soil and rake smooth. The surface of the soil should be at least an inch or two below the top edges of the frame.

wood to build a frame at least 2 feet high. Be sure to attach the corners securely. Fill it with high-quality, weed-free topsoil, and you are ready to plant. Raised bed frames can be put together on nice days between now and March, so that you can plant when the mood strikes and the weather cooperates. You may also want to use these dreary winter days to track down a good source of topsoil for your raised beds.

Many vegetables and herbs are easily grown from seed, so make a list of the seeds you need and order them or buy them from local seed racks. Herbs that are easily seed-grown include basil, chervil, cilantro, dill, fennel, hyssop, lovage, marjoram, parsley, sage, summer savory, and thyme. With a few exceptions (see the Plant section), most seeds should be started in February or March, but you'll want to take time now to round up the equipment you'll need—containers, commercial potting mix, maybe even grow lights.

The January issue of many garden magazines often reports on new vegetables and other plants and how they perform. Spend some chilly evenings carefully reading garden catalogs. Even when you buy mostly locally—always a good idea—you can learn a great deal from catalogs. They include charts and general growing information, as well as descriptions and length of time to harvest. Planting so that you spread out the dates to maturity is important for at least two reasons—most gardeners want to begin harvesting as soon as possible, and they want to keep the harvest going for as long as possible.

HOUSEPLANTS

Now that the holidays are past, you may be in the mood for some splashes of color around the house. That means new houseplants. Make a list of spots where a plant would be welcome—near an east-facing window, in the master bathroom, in the family room, or in the kitchen. Note the light in each spot (using the test on page 28). Take your list to the store where you usually buy houseplants. Look first for plants that match the light conditions in your home, then opt for color—plants with variegated leaves and flowering plants. For example, moth orchids look elegant, but aren't difficult to grow.

■ *Flowering houseplants, such as this moth, or Phalaenopsis, orchid, add color and interest to living areas in the duller days of January.*

LAWNS

Is this the year you buy a new lawn mower? Start the year off right by spending some time talking to dealers, collecting brochures, comparing features and prices, and figuring out the right model for your yard. Chat with friends to find out what they like, or don't like, about the mowers they own. And ask the person who runs your favorite lawn mower repair shop for his or her experienced opinion.

ROSES

Anyone who wants to grow roses should start the year off right and purchase a pair of thorn-proof gloves. These are available at garden centers, at home stores, and by mail order. They'll make your rose-growing experience much rosier.

If you plan to add new roses to your garden this year, January's the time to decide what they will be and to get them ordered, if you haven't already. Send off for catalogs as soon as possible. If you're new to roses, see the American Rose Society's Website (http://www.ars.org) or ask someone at your local rose society to recommend mail-order suppliers. The advantage of mail order is that you can usually find a much larger and more varied supply. But locally you'll be able to look over the bushes and see exactly what you're getting.

You will be warmly welcomed at a meeting of your local rose society this month—or anytime. It's a great place to learn the local ins and outs of rose growing.

PLANT

BULBS

Is it too late? If for one reason or another, you never got around to planting your tulips, daffodils, and other spring-flowering bulbs, you can still plant them—as long as the soil isn't frozen. Check them over to make sure they're still okay (they aren't soft, don't have any damaged spots, and don't have an odd odor), then get them in the ground. (See instructions on pages 178–179.) January-planted bulbs will probably bloom later than those planted last fall or in previous years, but most should flower. Tulips that were not kept in a refrigerator are the most iffy, since they need three full months of cool temperatures in order to bloom. But even they should bloom next year.

EASY VEGETABLES TO GROW FROM SEED

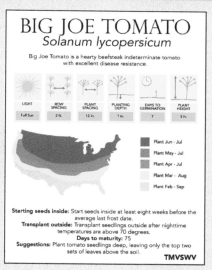

If you're new to vegetable gardening, these are the easiest veggies to grow. Because all are grown from seeds, they are also inexpensive.

- Beans
- Beets
- Cucumbers
- English peas
- Leaf lettuce
- Radishes
- Summer squash
- Spinach

Indoors, keep an oscillating fan running in the room where you have started seeds. Good air circulation helps prevent fungal problems.

Amaryllis bulbs (*Hippeastrum*), sometimes already potted, are often on sale in January. Pick up a couple in different colors. Choose named varieties if they're available. They'll be of higher quality than those identified only by flower color (red, white, pink, and so on).

- If the bulb is already potted, wet the potting mix thoroughly with tepid water and place the bulb in a warm spot (at least 70 degrees Fahrenheit) that does not receive direct sunlight. Don't water again until you see green shoots emerging from the bulb. Then move the plant into bright light and keep it warm. Amaryllis prefers moist soil.

- For amaryllis bulbs that need to be potted up after you get them home, see page 197 for directions.

Pot up some paper-white narcissi for indoor growing, if you can find the bulbs. They really brighten the dreary days typical of January. (See pages 209–210 for directions.)

EDIBLES

Sow seeds of parsley indoors this month. The seeds are hard, so to speed up germination, soak them in warm water for twenty-four hours before planting or nick them (or do both). (Nicking a seed is to breech the seed coat, using a file, a knife point, or sometimes sandpaper.)

Several cool-season vegetables may also be started indoors during January: broccoli and cauliflower (which need a five- to seven-week head start before going outdoors), cabbage (which takes four to six weeks to reach transplant size), Brussels sprouts (which need eight weeks), and onion (which goes outdoors in February). See page 38 for directions on sowing seeds.

TREES

You may transplant small trees from one part of your yard to another this month if the cold ground will cooperate.

PLANTS FOR DEEP SHADE

Many perennials grow well in light or dappled shade, but deep shade—such as beneath evergreen trees whose branches start lower than 10 feet off the ground—is often difficult for perennials. The following perennials (and one grasslike plant) generally grow well in such situations:

- Many ferns
- Liriope
- Hardy begonia
- Lungwort
- Hosta
- Trillium
- Lenten rose

CARE

BULBS AND PERENNIALS

Is that a bulb you see? Sometimes a cycle of warm days followed by below-freezing temperatures heaves bulbs out of the ground. If that happens, gently put them back into the hole, being careful to pack the soil around them (so there are no holes in the soil for cold air to get into). Then add to or replace the mulch on top. Mulch moderates soil temperatures to help prevent effects from freezing and thawing.

Check the mulch over and around your bulbs and perennial plants to make sure it's still 3 inches deep. Discarded Christmas trees make excellent mulch for bulb beds—you can prune off limbs and place them over beds or just cut off needles.

If your amaryllis is blooming, give it about four hours of sun daily, but avoid the noonday sun, which can burn the foliage and cause the blooms to wilt prematurely. The plant likes daytime temperatures about 70 degrees Fahrenheit and in the 60s at night. If you have the plant on a windowsill, be sure the straplike leaves don't touch the glass when outdoor temperatures are below freezing.

Remove the entire flower stalk after your amaryllis plant finishes blooming. Pinch off spent

■ *Keep the leaves of houseplants clean by lightly hosing them about once a month. That will help the leaves absorb more light and can help deter pests such as spider mites.*

flowers from paper-whites and potted bulbs from the florist.

EDIBLES

If you're growing herbs on sunny windowsills over the winter, pinch them back regularly to keep them from getting leggy. Use the cuttings of culinary herbs to add some zip to winter salads.

HOUSEPLANTS

When you bring a new houseplant home, isolate it from other plants for about a month. That way, if it has some hidden insect or disease problem that wasn't noticed at the time of purchase, it won't spread to your other plants.

If you acquired an ivy topiary over the holidays, it's important to keep the humidity high around it. Spider mites may severely damage ivy if the air is too dry. (You'll first notice their presence when leaves begin to look dull and less green.)

Each time you water your houseplants, groom them by cutting off yellowing leaves and removing dead or dying foliage. Are the leaves dusty? Dust prevents plants from absorbing as much light as they should. Move plants with smooth foliage to a sink or shower (depending on their size) and gently shower them clean. See page 203 to learn how to clean plants with hairy leaves.

LAWNS

Watch where you walk. If possible, avoid walking on the lawn when it's wet or frozen—that compacts the soil.

SHRUBS

If temperatures are predicted to fall into the low 20 degrees Fahrenheit range or below, move shrubs growing outdoors in containers into the garage overnight for protection. They shouldn't be placed in a heated area (this could cause them to break dormancy, which could be fatal when they are moved back outside). But place them near windows if you expect to keep them in the garage or basement for day or two, during a prolonged cold spell.

Some camellias will bloom during warm spells this month. Check the weather forecast each morning and evening so you can cut the blooms and bring them indoors to vases when cold is predicted. If the predicted cold is just overnight and the next day is expected to warm up above freezing, you may be able to protect the flowers by covering the bush with a heavy quilt or blanket. (Don't use plastic; when the sun shines on it the next day, it burns the leaves of the camellia.) Temperatures in the 20s don't harm camellia buds that haven't opened—just the opened flowers.

When the ground freezes, evergreen shrubs can't take up water from the soil to replace that lost through respiration. Then, when morning sun hits the frozen leaves, they "burn"—dry out and turn brown. (This can also happen when shrubs are buffeted by drying winds.) Some gardeners spray susceptible evergreen shrubs with an antidessicant spray, such as Wilt-Pruf, to prevent this. Not everyone agrees that this helps, but you may want to treat a few shrubs that have had this problem in the past and leave one or two untreated to see what you think.

Anytime a shrub has dead or damaged branches, cut dead branches back to the main branch or to the ground. Prune damaged branches to live wood and just above a bud. In winter, how do you know whether a branch is dead or alive? The fingernail test will tell you: Scrape a tiny bit of the surface with your fingernail. If you see green underneath, that's live wood. If it's brown and dull, it's dead.

TREES

If you or a next-door neighbor have quite a few trees, you'll find stray leaves blowing onto your lawn all winter. On a nice day during the January thaw, get your exercise close to home by raking leaves instead of heading for the gym and working out. Or haul out the lawn mower—if it wasn't winterized and if the lawn is dry enough—mow over the leaves until they're finely chopped. Let the shredded leaves (if not excessive) remain on the lawn as topdressing. This helps reduce problems with thatch (a layer of undecayed material between the soil and the grass that lessens water penetration into the soil).

If you had a tree professionally installed last year, and it was staked, the apparatus should be removed within twelve months. Often it can be removed sooner. Until then, be sure that the guying material (which fastens around the tree) is not cutting into the bark and that the wooden stakes have not come out of the soil. Winter is the time to prune deciduous trees that need it—as long as they are not ones that flower in winter or spring.

VINES

On a day when you'd like to get a breath of fresh air, check perennial vines to make sure they're attached to their supports. Take some soft twine or vinyl-coated twist ties with you so you'll be prepared to tie up any vines that have come loose.

If you got busy and didn't take down the frost-killed foliage of annual vines in fall, do that on a pleasant January weekend. The garden will look neater and be ready for spring.

WATER GARDENS

If you have a pond that's at least 24 inches deep, your fish should be fine for a week or a bit more when the surface of the water is a solid sheet of ice. But if the ice lasts ten days, you'll want to make a hole in it to release trapped methane gas. The wrong way to do this is with a hammer, which creates shock waves that can kill the fish. The right way is to pour boiling water at a spot along the edge of the ice to melt enough so the gas will escape. Or you can buy a pool heater that will keep a small section of the surface thawed. A submersible pump with a bubbler will do the job too.

If you keep a pump on all winter in your water garden, check it anytime the power goes out for more than a few hours in cold weather. Sometimes when the power goes out, the discharge pipe becomes covered with ice.

WATER

Use tepid water on flats of seeds or seedlings indoors. Cold water straight from the tap can shock the plants. The best method is to fill a clean milk jug with water and let it stand at room temperature at least overnight before using it. Keep seeds moist, but not wet, till they germinate. Once seeds have become young plants, let the soil's surface dry slightly before watering. Soggy soil—especially if the temperature is chilly—can cause seeds or young plants to rot.

BULBS

Don't let paper-whites dry out. Keep the soil around amaryllis moist but not soggy. Check bulbs that are being forced to make sure the soil stays moist.

HOUSEPLANTS

Because of lower temperatures and less light, indoor plants need watering less frequently in winter. Always check the soil before watering. Overwatering, combined with cool temperatures, can lead to root rot.

FERTILIZE

BULBS

About every six weeks, fertilize indoor amaryllis plants that have finished blooming; use a regular houseplant fertilizer. Pots of spring-flowering bulbs

HERE'S HOW

TO START AN AVOCADO FROM SEED

Starting an avocado from seed is fun, and you get a free houseplant for your efforts. Florida avocados (with dark, rough skin) germinate faster and grow more quickly than those from California (with smooth skins). Here's how:

1. Carefully remove the pit from the avocado. If it has already sprouted, skip the next two steps and go directly to step 4. Rinse it off in tepid water, and dry it with a paper towel.

2. Place the pit somewhere warm for twenty-four hours.

3. Peel the parchmentlike coating from the big seed.

4. Fill a 6-inch flowerpot three-quarters full with dampened potting mix.

5. Place the pit on the soil with the base—the flatter, larger, indented end—down.

6. Add more soil, but make sure the tip is exposed.

7. Water the planted pit.

8. Put the pot in a spot that has warmth and good light.

9. Keep the soil moist until the pit germinates (usually within a month, but sometimes as long as three months).

10. Once new growth is 4 to 5 inches high, cover the tip of the pit with soil.

11. Avocados like bright light and moist soil.

12. Begin pinching stems back when they reach 6 to 8 inches tall, to cause them to branch.

You may also germinate an avocado seed over water, but eventually you'll have to pot it in soil. Wash the pit and pat it dry with a paper towel. Insert three toothpicks around the middle of the pit and suspend it over a glass of water so that the rounded end is partially submerged in the water. Put the glass in a warm spot with bright light, but no sun. Replace the water twice a week so it stays fresh and the pit remains wet. Pot the plant in soil when you think the avocado has developed enough leaves to live on its own.

WHEN TO CUT CAMELLIAS

The best time to cut a camellia bloom to bring it indoors is when the bud is just beginning to show color. It should last in a vase for up to a week, especially if kept in a cool room.

purchased in bloom don't need plant food. Neither do paper-whites or bulbs that are being forced.

Outdoors, if you did not use a slow-release fertilizer on your spring-flowering bulbs last fall, keep an eye out for the first signs that the bulbs are coming up. When they're 1 inch above the ground, fertilize with 1 tablespoon of 8-8-8 fertilizer per 100 square feet of bed. If the ground isn't frozen, water in the fertilizer gently.

HOUSEPLANTS

The only houseplants that need feeding in January are those that are actively growing or blooming. Feed those monthly with a water-soluble fertilizer, using the amount listed on the label. You can use a balanced fertilizer such as 20-20-20 on both types of plants, but if you have a number of flowering plants, you may want to buy a fertilizer for African violets or flowering plants—and use it when buds are forming and flowers are blooming. Some gardeners like to alternate using all-purpose and flowering formulas.

Don't fertilize cacti, succulents, or nongrowing foliage plants this month or next. They're resting.

TREES

Fertilize young trees once yearly. It may be anytime between late November and the end of February, or it can be done in March or April. See pages 84–85 for directions.

PROBLEM-SOLVE

BULBS

What happened to my bulbs? The coldest part of winter is usually when mice and other wildlife begin to hunger after your bulbs. Keep an eye out this month and next for any signs that bulbs are

being dug up. These temporary steps may help prevent further damage.

- Place chicken wire on top of the ground over bulbs to keep the squirrels or deer from digging into the area.

- If temperatures are above freezing and will remain that way for forty-eight hours, and no precipitation is predicted, spray the ground and any shoots with Bulb Guard®, Ro-Pel®, or another wildlife deterrent.

If you've bought pots of tulips or other plants at the grocery store or florist and all of a sudden you see tiny insects on the tips of the leaves or on the flowers, they are most likely aphids. Place the pot in the kitchen sink and use the sprayer to dislodge as many as possible. After the plant dries off, spray any remaining aphids with insecticidal soap. You may need to do it several times, a few days apart.

HOUSEPLANTS

Too little light? It's a big problem in January. Symptoms include:

- Leaves cupping upward

- Plant growing toward the light

- New leaves that are smaller than old leaves and pale green

- No flowers

- Leaves falling off the plant

What can you do about it?

1. If plants are growing on a windowsill, move them to the next brightest window until mid-March. That is, if a plant is growing on a north-facing sill, move it to an east-facing one. If it's growing on a sill with an eastern exposure, move it to one that faces west.

2. Move plants that are not on windowsills or in front of windows closer to the light.

3. Give plants extra hours of light from ordinary lamps or from a portable lamp or spotlight. If a houseplant shares an end table with a lamp, turn the lamp on in the evening as soon as natural light has gone and leave it on till you go to bed. Those extra hours can make quite a bit of difference. Consider doing the same with a portable light clipped to the edge of the pot of a large plant.

Does it look as if there's cotton on your plant? It's mealybugs. Dip a cotton swab in rubbing alcohol and lightly rub the cottony masses. Be sure to check under leaves and where stems and leaves join. After twenty-four hours, pick off as many of the masses as you can. Then spray with insecticidal soap twice a week until the problem seems to abate. Often the mealybugs return and must be treated again.

LAWNS

If the soil beneath your lawn hasn't been tested in the past five years, have it tested now. If your lawn needs it, liming should be done before spring since it takes some time for the lime to become effective. But lime and nitrogen fertilizer should not be applied together.

ROSES

Apply a lime sulfur spray to rosebushes and to the surrounding soil if you didn't last month. This helps kill overwintering diseases and insect eggs. Read the label carefully and follow instructions regarding weather and temperatures.

Spider mites are often a problem on miniature roses grown indoors. When spider mites are present, leaves will appear dull and then mottled. They may seem to be dusty underneath. Eventually the foliage will curl up and fall off. To prevent spider mites, raise the humidity level around the plants and spray water on the foliage (both the tops and the undersides of the leaves) each week.

SHRUBS AND TREES

Keep an eye out for deer or rodent damage, if that's been a problem for you in the past. On warmish

■ *Spider mites can be a problem on indoor plants.*

days, you can spray repellents or pepper sprays on your shrubs to keep animals from doing too much damage. If tree trunks are being damaged by wildlife, loosely circle the shrub with a cylinder of chicken wire.

Where deer and rodents are big problems, reapply repellents this month. Some home remedies (spreading human hair about, hanging cakes of Irish Spring soap, and so on) work for a short time, but most are not long-term solutions. One advantage of commercial products such as Deer Off is that they don't have to be reapplied after every rain. The only real solution for deer is an 8-foot fence, but until you get desperate enough to build one, try alternating several remedies instead of depending on just one.

WATER GARDENS

The off-season is the best time to find solutions for problems that affected your water garden last summer—including algae, predators, insects, runoff, and plants not blooming as much as you'd hoped. During January, talk with an expert or a fellow water-gardening enthusiast, read a book, or call your local Extension office.

■ *In areas where destructive deer or rodents are prevalent, loosely circle the base of young trees with hardware cloth, chicken wire, or a similar product in order to protect them, especially during winter.*

TO CHOOSE A ROSEBUSH

Most of us choose a rose because we like how it looks. There's nothing wrong with wanting to grow roses that we love—but all roses aren't equal. Some roses perform better than others. They grow better, they have bigger blooms and more of them, they're less disease-prone, and they're not as likely to be killed during a cold winter.

That's not to say that you will have to settle for ugly roses—if there is such a thing as an ugly rose. Instead, if your aim is relatively carefree rose growing, you'll have to find out which roses are the absolute best and grow them instead of choosing casually from a catalog picture or picking out a potted rose at the garden center without knowing anything about it.

So how do you discover which roses are going to perform best? There are several ways. On its website (http://www.ars.org), the American Rose Society has a list of those rated 8.0 and above. This numeric rating system ranges from 5.9 (and lower) up to 10 (which is considered perfect). These are the ones that you want to grow. The organization also publishes an annual booklet called *Handbook for Selecting Roses*, which is a handy size to carry with you when you go rose shopping. Instead of listing just the top-rated roses, it lists and ranks most of the roses sold at garden centers. (Exceptions are roses introduced in the past year or two, which are too new to be ranked.)

There are a number of rose societies in Kentucky and Tennessee that are associated with the American Rose Society, and most of them have lists of the top roses recommended by their members. These are the ones that have done best in the yards of Memphis, Louisville, Nashville, Lexington, and Chattanooga. Contact information for the clubs that are part of the Tenarky District (Tennessee, Arkansas, and Kentucky) is available on the ARS website. Also included are links to the societies' websites, which contain lots of helpful information on choosing and growing roses. If you're not able to locate this information, write the ARS (P.O. Box 30000, Shreveport, LA, 71130) or call the Extension service in your county and ask whom to contact about the nearest rose society.

Each society has at least one and often more consulting rosarians. These are experienced rose growers who are available to give free advice on selecting roses and just about anything else you'll need to know to make roses happy in your yard.

Roses that have won the All-America Rose Selections (AARS) award (see http://www.rose.org) are also excellent roses. These roses have been tested in many different parts of the country, and while there may be an occasional less-than-stellar performer in our hot, humid climate, you can usually buy AARS winners with confidence. This is especially true of those that have won in the past ten years. They are particularly disease-resistant, which is important for the home rose grower.

February

January is supposed to be the time that we look forward and backward at the same time, but I think that gardeners in Kentucky and Tennessee do that most in February. It's often one of the worst months of the year for winter weather, but there are often several days of warmth to remind us that spring is just around the corner. So we buy flowering houseplants to give our spirits a lift indoors, and we burrow down by the fireplace, dreaming—often with the help of garden books (some new, some tried-and-true friends from years past)—of fruitful months to come.

On days when the weather is nice outdoors and temperatures are moderate, some of us will get outside and walk around the yard, pruning roses so they'll be glorious in May and for months afterward. Most will just observe and plan. Maybe this is the year you redo the back yard so it's just right for entertaining a larger group of friends?

During February, we gather flats, fill them with potting or seed-starting mix and sow the seeds that will become ripe, red tomatoes in July—oh, how we long for that unmatched taste!—and pretty pink cosmos, which is often hard to find in garden centers. That's the joy of starting from seed—you grow exactly what you want to without worrying if you'll be able to find it for sale come spring. I can't imagine gardening without a particular variety of bell pepper and a wonderful little cultivar of cherry tomato that, for me, outperforms all others. But I can't find either in local nurseries or greenhouses, so I have to grow them myself.

That's not a chore, though. In February, it connects me to the garden in a way nothing else can. And it gives me hope. Admittedly, our winters aren't severe or even very long compared to those in, say, New England or Minnesota. But by the end of February, after the glow of Valentine's Day is past, we're tired of winter. We're ready to move on past February and start growing. So we start seeds and root cuttings of annuals brought indoors in fall, we maybe prune roses, and we have faith that this year is going be our best gardening year ever.

PLAN

ALL

During winter months when there's little going on in the garden, attend a gardening class, visit a flower show, or take a plant-related workshop. Enjoy yourself and find an idea you can look forward to putting to use.

Record low temperatures and amounts of snowfall in your garden notebook.

Get answers to your questions now. It never fails: the first warm weekend in April brings everyone out to garden centers, and the phone rings off the hook at your county's Extension office. If you have gardening questions, now's the time to ask. The pros will have more time to talk with you.

Use the catalogs you've been collecting to come up with a list of plants you want to grow this year. Stop by your favorite nursery or garden center to see what sorts of seed packets they have and what plants they're expecting to offer in the spring. Some years ago, gardeners considered the seeds sold by local garden centers rather dull. But many now offer seeds from big mail-order nurseries and lines of specialty seeds. You may be pleasantly surprised by what you find.

Consider growing plants that receive awards (from All-America Selections or state Extension office, for instance). They are often superior plants.

Did you get the soil test recommended in January? If so, read it over and call your county's Extension office if you have any questions. If you have procrastinated, take samples of your soil and get them in to be tested now. It could save you quite a bit of money if you learn that you don't need to apply all the nutrients you usually do.

ANNUALS, EDIBLES, AND PERENNIALS

Are those vegetable and flower seeds that you saved from previous years still good? To determine

■ *Wrap 10 seeds in dampened paper towels placed inside a plastic bag and put them in a warm spot. Beginning in three or four days, check to see how many have germinated. This will tell you whether seeds from previous years are still good.*

■ *Flowers in winter? Yes, if you plant Lenten roses, lovely perennials that are easy to grow. Many new Lenten roses are being introduced each year so check catalogs and online to find flower colors and shapes you like.*

whether you can use them this season or if you should buy new seeds, test them.

1. Wet a paper towel and sprinkle it with ten seeds, evenly spaced.

2. Roll up the towel with the seeds inside, place it in a plastic bag, and seal it. Place the bag in a warm spot (on top of a water heater or refrigerator works fine).

3. Begin checking in three days to see whether any seeds have sprouted.

4. The number of seeds that germinate within fifteen days gives you the germination percentage. (For example, eight sprouted seeds out of ten equals an 80 percent germination rate.) If the rate is 50 to 70 percent, you'll know to sow the seeds more thickly than usual. When the germination rate is less than 50 percent, buy fresh seeds.

BULBS

As the earliest bulbs—snowdrops, crocuses, and some miniature daffodils—open their little flowers, think about how welcome these harbingers of spring are and how happy they make us feel when we see them blooming, no matter how cold the weather is. But also think about your plantings of early bulbs a bit more critically: Are you happy with the number you have? The color combinations? The locations? On the September page in your garden journal, note what improvements you'd like to make. Let that serve as a reminder for your fall bulb purchases. Enjoy their blooming this spring, then mark the spot for some that you'll move at a later date.

PERENNIALS

If you're planning a new perennial bed this year, have its soil tested right away. That way you'll know which plants do well in your soil's pH, whether you need to apply lime, and how much and what type of fertilizer is recommended.

When you're choosing perennials and ornamental grasses, check their USDA plant hardiness zone rating to be sure they'll make it through the winter in your part of the region. When you're dealing with mail order or a plant or group of plants that's unfamiliar to you, you might also check the hardiness and heat zones in a garden reference book. A catalog may say that a certain plant is rated for hardiness zones 5 to 9, but it still might not stand up to the summer heat and humidity common in our part of the country.

If you plan to buy perennials or grasses by mail, place your orders soon. Popular plants, especially new introductions, often sell out quickly. Getting your order in early doesn't mean you will receive plants right away; you can have them delivered near the frost-free date for your area or just ask that the plants be sent at the proper planting time.

There are advantages to buying perennials and grasses from a local nursery:

- You can see the quality of the plants and make sure they're disease- and insect-free.

- You can get larger plants than are available by mail order.

- The price is generally lower.

The main advantage of mail order or online purchases is locating rare or unusual plants that aren't yet available locally. It may also be more convenient to order at night in your own home instead of going to a nursery on a cold day—although many gardeners enjoy visiting garden centers to see what's available.

BEWARE BONEMEAL

Don't use bonemeal with bulbs. Why? Bonemeal isn't made the way it was in the past and no longer contains all the nutrients that bulbs need. It may also cause dogs and other animals to dig in the area where it's applied. Instead, apply a slow-release fertilizer made for bulbs. There are organic brands available.

Lenten roses may be blooming in some areas this month. It's delightful to have such fascinating flowers to enjoy in late winter. If you don't have any, consider buying and planting some in spring. If you have a grouping but it's not in a spot you walk by every day in winter, start another bed. The flowers are quite variable in color and markings, so try to choose them when they're in bloom. Since Lenten roses spread and also reseed, see if a neighbor has plants of this wonderful evergreen perennial to share when warm weather returns.

SHRUBS

Look at your yard, paying particular attention to your shrubs. What do you see? Are the shrubs in your landscape providing color this time of year, or do they mostly fade into the background? If you'd like a more lively winter landscape, consider the following deciduous shrubs. Their colorful or interesting bark, stems, twigs, or buds are visually appealing in a season when everything else seems to be brown.

- Crapemyrtle (*Lagerstroemia* spp.)—many have beautiful bark

- Deciduous holly (*Ilex* spp.)—berries that persist into winter

- Harry Lauder's walking stick (*Corylus avellana* 'Contorta')—twisted stems, leaves, and twigs

- Kerria (*Kerria japonica*)—bright green stems

- Witch hazel (*Hamamelis* spp.)—red, orange, or yellow flowers in winter

TREES

If winter has been colder and snowier than usual, about the first of February you may be longing for trees to turn green. It's not necessary to wait until spring if you have evergreens. They're always green.

Needled evergreen trees you may want to have in your landscape include:

- Canadian hemlock (*Tsuga canadensis*)

- Many *Chamaecyparis* species and hybrids that grow 20 feet high and taller

- Japanese cedar (*Cryptomeria japonica*)

- Norway spruce (*Picea abies*) in the cooler parts of the region

Broadleaf evergreens that are useful in Tennessee and Kentucky yards:

- American and hybrid hollies (*Ilex* spp.)

- Southern magnolia (*Magnolia grandiflora*)

- Sweet bay 'Henry Hicks' magnolia (*Magnolia virginiana*)

- Cherry laurel (*Prunus laurocerasus*) cultivar

Also consider whether a few dwarf fruit trees might fit into your landscape plan, especially near the vegetable garden. It's wonderful to have fresh fruit from your own trees, but remember that these are high-maintenance. They need yearly pruning and regular spraying.

Do you have any spots in your lawn where grass simply won't grow? If the lack of grass growth is due to excessive shade, maybe this is the year you give up on the grass and plant a shade-loving ground cover instead. Once it gets established, it requires much less maintenance than trying to grow grass in a spot that's no longer suitable for it.

PLANT

ANNUALS

If you brought plants or cuttings of some annuals into the house last fall—coleus, geraniums, scaevola, and wax begonias, for instance—this is a good time to take cuttings of them.

- Stems of begonias and coleus root easily in a glass or jar of water. Keep the water clean, and transplant the cuttings as soon as they've developed a small mass of roots. (If you leave cuttings in water too long, they may rot or have problems adjusting to growing in soil.)

■ *Want free annuals in your garden this year? Take cuttings from the plants you brought indoors in fall and have grown over the winter.*

- Or, even better, root stem cuttings of annuals in a pot or flat of a sterile medium such as half perlite and half peat moss or equal parts peat moss, sharp sand, and vermiculite. Fill the container to within one-half inch of the rim with moistened rooting medium. Take the cuttings and dip the ends in a rooting hormone such as Rootone®. Insert a pencil in the rooting mix to make a hole for the cutting. Once you have all the cuttings in place, place the pot in a clear plastic bag, or cover larger containers with plastic. Don't let the cuttings and plastic come into contact with each other. Put the container in a warm spot that receives indirect light. Make sure the soil stays moist, but not wet. If the plastic collects too much moisture, open the bag or vent the plastic to let the cuttings dry out a bit. When new growth appears, carefully remove the cuttings from the rooting medium and transplant into small flowerpots.

HOW TO START SEEDS

fungi in it that kills emerging seedlings. Use a pencil to poke holes for the seeds in each section of the tray in which you'll plant the seeds

2. Plant one or two seeds per section of the seed starting tray. Then water the soil until it is as moist as a wrung-out sponge. Depending upon the size of the sections in the seed starting tray, you might or might not have to transplant plants into larger containers to grow before planting outside.

3. Cover the seed starting tray with the plastic lid or with clear plastic cling wrap. This will keep the seeds moist. The top of the lid may become moist with condensation as the seeds begin to sprout. The condensation is a good thing, because it means you'll have to water the seeds less.

4. Check on the seeds as they're sprouting. If the top of the soil is dry, mist them with a spray bottle or very lightly water them. (Misting is better than watering because it is less likely to wash the delicate seedlings out of their spots in the trays.) Don't ever let seeds dry out while they're sprouting, or they'll die.

5. When seeds have two or more sets of "true leaves," you can transplant them into larger containers. Moving them up to four-inch pots gives them room to grow and get larger and stronger before planting outside.

1. You can buy seed starting tray kits at garden centers or home-improvement stores. Usually you have to buy special seed starting mix separately. This is a lightweight soilless mix made especially for starting seeds. Never use regular garden soil, as this soil can have

EDIBLES

If you plan to start seeds indoors, check the seed packets for the recommended length of time between sowing and setting the plants outdoors. Use that figure to count back from your area's average last-frost date (see page 228 for an approximation), and you'll know when to sow the seeds. There's little point in starting too soon—the plants will grow leggy while waiting to go outdoors.

Herbs that need to be started six to eight weeks before setting them outdoors include chervil, cilantro, dill, hyssop, lovage, marjoram, sage, and thyme. If you didn't start parsley last month, do it now (see opposite page).

About the only way gardeners in this region can consistently grow iceberg or other head lettuce is to plant it in a cold frame in February. Start the seeds indoors and transplant them into the cold frame early in the month or sow them directly in six-packs or in a bed of rich soil in the bottom of the cold frame.

Some gardeners like to get a jump on the season by planting onion sets and English peas (especially 'Alaska') this month. In zones 6, 7, and 8, mid-to late February is the time for a first sowing of spinach and Irish potatoes, if the soil isn't too wet to work (or if it was prepared in the fall). It's fine to wait till early March, though, since sometimes too-cold and too-wet soil causes seeds planted early to rot. Work about 1 to 1½ pounds of 6-12-12 or 10-10-10 fertilizer into 100 square feet of soil before planting. You may want to buy row cover fabric to keep handy to toss over plants if temperatures threaten to fall much below freezing.

HOUSEPLANTS

Because of their heart-shaped leaves and red flowers (other colors are available, too), anthuriums are widely available in February. They're a good choice to brighten up the house, so look for them as you shop this month. They need warm temperatures (60 degrees Fahrenheit is the minimum), bright light but no direct sun, and evenly moist soil while they're in bloom. Feed them twice a month as long as they are in flower.

Stores also offer miniature roses in February. Don't fall for them unless you have a spot in full sun and are willing to give them a fair amount of attention

HERE'S HOW

TO REPOT AN OVERGROWN ORCHID

1. Buy a prepared orchid potting mix.
2. Choose a pot that's 2 inches wider in diameter than the current container. Clay is the best choice unless you know you won't overwater the plant.
3. Remove the orchid from its pot.
4. Tease the bark chips and other material from the roots, or wash them away.
5. Trim back any black or mushy roots.
6. Moisten the potting mix.
7. Add a layer of potting mix to the pot.
8. Place the orchid on the mix at the same depth it grew before.
9. Add more mix, pushing the bark pieces through the roots.
10. Water the plant thoroughly.
11. Return it to bright light. New growth should start in spring, if not sooner.

until you can plant them outdoors. Or, since they're inexpensive, you can treat them as temporary plants, tossing them out when they begin to fade as you would with cut flowers. In either case, give them sun and moist soil. If you plan to keep the plant, fertilize twice monthly as long as it's in flower. Watch out for spider mites.

SHRUBS AND TREES

Toward the end of the month, you may also begin planting container-grown trees or trees that are balled and burlapped that were purchased at a local nursery.

CARE

ALL

Once seeds grown indoors have sprouted, give them ample light. Fluorescent shop lights are an inexpensive way to supplement February's sometimes missing sunshine.

Warmth is needed for seeds to germinate. But once the plants are up and growing, the room where they are can be cooler (65 to 68 degrees Fahrenheit in the daytime, down to 60 degrees at night).

BULBS

If tulips, hyacinths, and daffodils have come up several inches and unusually cold weather threatens, cover them with pine straw.

Check summer-flowering corms and rhizomes stored in the basement or garage. Remove any that are beginning to rot or have rotted and any that appear to be diseased. If the bulbs start to shrivel, sprinkle them very lightly with water. When temperatures plunge outdoors, make sure that the area in which the bulbs are stored doesn't freeze; ideal temperatures should be in the range of 40 degrees Fahrenheit. One exception is for caladiums, which must have warmth; when winter storage temperatures are much below 65 degrees Fahrenheit, the bulbs probably won't survive.

When amaryllis finishes flowering, make sure the plant receives enough light. It should be placed so it's in sun either all morning or all afternoon (but not at midday). If the leaves aren't a nice medium green, the plant may not be receiving enough light.

EDIBLES

At the end of the month, pull the mulch back from part of your asparagus bed. That portion will warm up and bear soonest, extending the harvest.

If you're growing herbs on sunny windowsills over the winter, pinch them back regularly to keep them from getting leggy. Use the cuttings of culinary herbs to add some zip to winter salads.

HOUSEPLANTS

During the usual February thaw, you may be tempted to take your large houseplants outdoors so they can enjoy the sunny and warm days. Bad idea. What feels, to a person, like a warm day in winter is often much too chilly for a tropical houseplant. Also, after months of living in low light, plants are suddenly asked to cope with six hours of sun. That means the same thing for plants as it does for people—possible sunburn. So resist the temptation to take your houseplants outside until May, and even then, move them into sun gradually.

Give all houseplants a one-quarter turn each time you water so that they grow evenly. If the foliage of variegated plants is becoming all green, light levels are too low. Move the plants so they will receive more light.

At night, move *Cattleya, Paphiopedilum*, and *Phalaenopsis* orchids to a cooler part of the house. These orchids should be kept about 10 degrees Fahrenheit cooler at night than during the daytime.

COLD FRAMES

Cold frames are available in many garden catalogs and from some garden centers. Gardeners can also make their own from old storm windows and scrap lumber. Unless you're home all day, buy an automatic opening device that will crack the lid when temperatures inside the frame reach a certain level. Otherwise, on sunny days, plants can get much too warm. Cold frames are also useful for hardening off (acclimating) cabbage, broccoli, and Brussels sprouts seedlings before placing them in the garden.

LAWN MOWER MAINTENANCE TIPS

■ *Filling The Mower with Gasoline* Always fill the gas tank of the mower while the mower is still sitting on the sidewalk or driveway (never in a closed room). That way, if you spill gasoline, you won't kill the grass and damage the soil. Fill the gas tank only 75 percent full so that there's room for the gas to expand.

■ *Checking the Air Filter* You should replace the air filter at the beginning of every season. It is a good idea to check the air filter once a month or so to make sure it looks clean and doesn't need to be replaced midseason. You can remove the air filter and tap it on the ground to dislodge some of the dust to extend its life.

■ *Checking the Oil* Most lawn mowers have a dipstick as part of the oil cap. Remove the dipstick and look at the oil on the end, which should be clear to light brown. If it is any darker, you'll need to change the oil. Consult your owner's manual about how to change the oil, and recycle the old oil by taking it to a local mower or engine repair shop.

Refill the oil by using the right weight and type of oil for your mower. Your owner's manual will have information about whether to add two stroke or four stroke oil.

■ *Cleaning Out the Bag and Undercarriage* Always empty the mower bag after you're finished mowing. (If you have a mulching mower, there's no bag to worry about.) Grass clippings make great mulch for your vegetable garden or are perfect additions to the compost pile. In the fall, use your mower and bag to chop up and vacuum leaves from the lawn.

Use a broom or leaf blower to clean off the top of the mower. Never hose off the mower, or you'll cause it to rust.

■ *End-of-Year Maintenance* You can stop mowing when the grass stops growing for the year, which will be sometime between late October and December for most gardeners. Run the mower until the gas tank is empty. Move the mower to a hard surface in a well-ventilated area, and drain the oil. Disconnect the spark plugs, and use a hard-bristle brush, an old rag, and a bucket of soapy water to clean off the underside and top of the mower. Add a fresh quart of oil to the oil tank and engine stabilizer to the gas tank. Never run water through the gas or oil tank to clean it.

Regularly remove fading flowers from African violets. When an occasional houseplant leaf turns yellow, cut it off. Yellow attracts some insects.

LAWNS

If your lawn's soil test indicates a need for lime (that is, the pH is below 6.0), use a drop or gravity spreader for the most even application. Many gardeners believe that lime pellets are less messy to work with than ground limestone.

Before you know it, lawn mowing time will be here. Is your mower ready for the eight or nine months of work ahead? February is a good time to get your mower into the shop for a tune-up—especially to have the blade sharpened. Avoid the inevitable crowds by getting your mower in now. If you'd like to do the job yourself, here's what's involved for a walk-behind mower:

- Change the spark plug.

- Clean the fans.

- Change the engine oil. Check the manufacturer's directions for the right type of oil to use.

- Install a new air filter.

- Sharpen the blade.

- Remove all those caked-on grass clippings from beneath the mower's deck.

- Check to see whether the wheels need lubricating.

ROSES

In most parts of our region, gardeners may prune all roses—*except* climbers and old garden roses—when forsythia blooms. That's typically about the middle of this month in zone 8. Because of widely variable temperatures this month, some growers in zone 7 wait to prune until about March 1. Gardeners in other, colder parts of the region prune roses at different times, due to variations in weather. But use

■ *These deciduous shrubs are having no problems after a heavy snowfall, but sometimes the limbs of evergreen shrubs can bow over or break under a load of snow. See if they might need you to gently brush snow off or carefully lift the limbs from beneath with a broom.*

the flowering of forsythia in your location as your guide.

Make sure your cutting tools are sharp. Use hand pruners for canes up to ¾ inch in diameter, loppers for stems ups to 1¾ inches around, and saws for anything larger. The folding type saws can be handy when you're working in tight quarters and for climbing roses.

SHRUBS AND TREES

In most parts of our region, snow does not last too long because temperatures warm up in a day or two and melt it. But occasionally we get a heavy snow that hangs around a few days. These can sometimes make shrubs bow over. Most deciduous shrubs are flexible enough to shrug off snow, but the leaves and needles of evergreens can catch and hold the snow. If you think the weight of the snow may cause damage, try to carefully brush the snow off yews or, on other shrubs, lift the branches up from beneath using a broom. Don't do anything if shrubs are covered with ice; you're more likely to cause harm than to help.

On trees, let the ice melt naturally off the leaves and needles, and take care of any damage later. If smaller evergreens (especially Canadian hemlocks) are uprooted by a heavy load of ice or snow, reset them as soon as you're able to get out in the yard. Give them support, if needed, to stand upright, mulch, and then water regularly and fertilize lightly during the next year if growth is evident. Often these trees recover without a hitch.

Toward the end of the month, if the weather is mild, you may want to start pruning overgrown deciduous shrubs that produce berries or that flower during the summer. These include beautyberry, burning bush, deciduous holly, rose of Sharon, and summersweet. Prune butterfly bush and smooth hydrangea (*Hydrangea arborescens*) to about 1 foot tall. Wait to prune other hydrangeas. Do not prune any spring-flowering shrubs now. Wait until they've finished blooming.

Although February is an excellent month to prune most trees, there are certain trees that you may not want to prune in winter because they "bleed"; that is, their sap runs freely when they're pruned

CLEMATIS BLOOM TIMES

Whenever you buy clematis, save its tag; it will come in handy when you're trying to figure out when you need to prune. Or observe when and how the vine blooms:

1. If the clematis blooms on old wood (stem growth from last year) in late spring, little pruning is needed except to keep the vine in shape. Examples include *Clematis armandii*, *C. montana*, *C. macropetala*, *C. indivisa*, and *C. alpina*.

2. If a clematis vine blooms twice—in early summer on old growth and in late summer on new growth—then undertake mostly light pruning, or you may remove flowers inadvertently. Remove weak or dead stems this month. Prune back flower shoots after blooms fade. Clematis in this group are 'Nelly Moser', 'Barbara Jackman', 'Belle of Woking', 'Hagley Hybrid', and double-flowered varieties.

3. Clematis that bloom on new wood are pruned hard in early spring. This month or in early March, cut back to one pair of buds 12 inches from ground level. This group includes *C.* × *jackmanii*, *C. flammula*, *C. integrifolia*, *C. orientalis*, and *C. viticella*.

in cold weather. Bleeding won't kill a tree, but it's unsightly. Wait until after May 1 to prune dogwood, elm, maple, river birch, walnut, and yellowwood trees.

VINES

In early spring, just before new growth starts, prune vines that flower on the current year's stems. In some years and in the warmest parts of the region, that may mean late February. In other areas and years, this pruning is done in March. However, wait to prune these vines: Carolina jessamine, climbing rose, goldflame honeysuckle, and trumpet honeysuckle. They're pruned after they finish flowering.

VINES THAT GROW WELL FROM SEEDS

If you enjoy growing plants from seed, some of the most colorful flowering vines are quite easy to start from seed. Look for seed packets this month so you can plant in late February or early March. Readily available vine seeds that grow well in this region include:

- Black-eyed Susan vine (*Thunbergia alata*)
- Cardinal climber (*Ipomoea × sloteri*)
- Cup-and-saucer vine (*Cobaea scandens*)
- Cypress vine (*Ipomoea quamoclit*)
- Gourds (*Cucurbita* spp.)
- Hyacinth bean (*Dolichos lablab*)
- Moonflower (*Ipomoea alba*)
- Purple bell vine (*Rhodochiton atrosanguineus*)
- Spanish flag (*Mina lobatas*)

How to prune vines:

- Trim back damaged shoots and those that have grown out of bounds.

- To thin crowded vines, cut some side stems back to the main stem.

- If a vine is lanky, cause it to branch out by cutting or pinching a few inches off the ends of the stems. Doing that encourages the vine to branch and fill out.

- In late winter or early spring, cut back to 12 inches high those vines that flower on the current season's growth.

- Rejuvenate a severely overgrown vine by cutting it back to 12 inches high, or cut it back to one or two young stems at the base, leaving several vigorous side shoots. Pinch the tips of the new stems lightly when they're 6 inches long so the new growth will be full.

WATER GARDENS

On warmer days as you're out in the yard, you may see some movement from the fish that live in your water garden. Does that mean you should feed them? No. The rule on feeding fish is to do it only when *water* temperature (not air temperature) is above 50 degrees Fahrenheit and seems likely to remain there.

On a nice day, remove fallen leaves or twigs that have accumulated on the pond's surface or bottom, to reduce algae growth. (Small pools aren't able to cope with excess debris as readily as larger ones are.) After you've finished, make a note to put up a net over your water garden next fall to catch falling debris.

WATER

ALL

Keep soil moist but not soggy for cuttings that you're rooting indoors and seeds that you've started. It's a skill that you usually learn by observing results. Letting the soil dry out reduces the number of seeds that germinate and puts stress on young plants that have sprouted, but roots will rot in soil that's kept overly wet. So how do you manage to hit this desirable middle ground? Water the soil thoroughly each time, and then let the soil surface dry slightly before watering again. (Test the soil by touching it with your fingertip to see whether it feels wet or dry.)

HOUSEPLANTS

Keep the soil of amaryllis plants moist, whether the plant is in flower or not. When growing paperwhites in trays of water, check the water level daily to make sure it stays just at the bottom of the bulbs.

When temperatures and sunlight levels are low, it's easy to overwater houseplants, causing their roots to rot. Don't water until plants need it, and never let plants stand in water.

SHRUBS

If precipitation has been less than usual, container-grown shrubs may need watering whenever the soil isn't frozen.

FERTILIZE

BULBS

If you didn't fertilize tulips, daffodils, and other spring-flowering bulbs last fall, or you did not use a slow-release fertilizer made for bulbs, fertilize spring-flowering bulbs as soon as you can see 1 inch of green shoot. The recommended rate is 1 tablespoon of 8-8-8 granular fertilizer per 100 square feet of soil surface.

HOUSEPLANTS

This month, feed African violets, amaryllis, bromeliads, poinsettias, miniature roses grown indoors, and orchids with a water-soluble fertilizer made for flowering plants. Wait until next month to fertilize all other indoor plants.

ROSES

When to fertilize rosebushes? Some rose growers like to fertilize right after pruning. Others prefer to spread the season's first fertilizer two weeks after pruning. And there are those who wait to fertilize when new growth appears. If you live in zone 7 or 8, this is a decision you'll be making this month.

PROBLEM-SOLVE

ALL

If a seedling suddenly begins to wilt, that's a sign of damping-off (a disease that kills seeds or seedlings) Remove the plant from the seed-starting container right away to avoid having the problem spread. Also keep an eye out for insects. Aphids and whiteflies are the most common.

BULBS

It's a sad fact of gardening life that deer, chipmunks, and other rodents may treat your bulb beds as banquet tables. You have several options:

- Plant daffodils, which aren't bothered by wildlife since the bulbs are poisonous to them. Other bulbs that usually aren't bothered include crown imperial, grape hyacinths, hyacinths, snowdrops, Spanish bluebells, and spring snowflakes. (Please note the word "usually" in the previous sentence.

It often depends both on how hungry the animals are and on location—deer in one part of the area will completely avoid a particular plant that's a favorite of deer in another location.)

- Spray or soak your bulbs with a wildlife repellent before planting. Spray again after leaves appear.

- Wrap chicken wire around or over the bulbs.

- Plant bulbs and hostas with sharp clays such as Permatil® or Turface® to prevent vole damage.

HOUSEPLANTS

It's easy to recognize whiteflies—they are small white flying insects. They suck sap from leaves, which causes the foliage to turn yellow. They may also leave the foliage—especially the undersides of the leaves—sticky. Treat the plant in the evening when the whiteflies are less likely to fly away:

1. Vacuum as many as possible using a portable hand vac. (Enclose the vac in a large plastic bag, seal, and open outdoors—away from plants—the next day.)

2. Then spray with insecticidal soap, making sure you treat the undersides of the leaves.

3. Get a yellow sticky trap at the garden center and insert it in the pot. Whiteflies are attracted to the color and then get stuck in the glue.

You may need to repeat steps 1 and 2. Remove the sticky trap from the pot when you spray and then put it back afterwards. When half of the trap's surface is covered by whiteflies, replace it.

LAWNS

If wild onions and wild garlic are in your lawn, they're highly visible this time of year. Wait till rain has moistened the soil, then pull or dig them out by hand. Do not compost these weeds.

PERENNIALS

If February is rainy, try to walk by your perennial beds after a day or two of rain. Look at the soil: Is it soggy? Is there standing water in places? Poor drainage during winter months kills perennial plants faster than anything else. Plan to improve the drainage in the spring.

ROSES

Borers can be a real problem with roses, even going so far as to kill most of the canes. Since they enter the bush through the soft ends of canes that have been pruned, there is a simple way to prevent borers from causing damage. When you prune, immediately seal the cut tips of the cane with nontoxic glue (white glue, such as Elmer's), shellac, or a rose-pruning sealant or wax.

SHRUBS

Keep deicing salt away from the roots of shrubs; it can damage them. If large or valuable shrubs are right next to the front walkway or your driveway, consider using the more environmentally friendly magnesium chloride or calcium acetate.

If scale or lace bugs have been a problem on shrubs over the past year, a warm February day is a good time to apply a coat of horticultural oil, sometimes called dormant oil. This organic treatment smothers the scales and other insects. Make sure temperatures will remain above 45 degrees Fahrenheit for twenty-four hours after application and that no precipitation is in the forecast.

HERE'S HOW

TO PRUNE ROSES

- Remove diseased or damaged canes or stems, canes that are rubbing against one another, and canes that are growing toward the middle of the bush instead of toward the outside.
- On grafted roses, dig up suckers that grow from ground level. Also, remove all growth that comes from on or below the bud union. This growth will not be the same rose as the variety you bought, and since it's overly vigorous, it will take over, giving you inferior red roses.
- Make all cuts at a 45-degree angle so water will run off the tips of the canes, decreasing the chance of decay. Cut ¼ inch above an outward-facing bud.
- If a cane is discolored, cut back until you reach green wood.
- Remove canes that are the diameter of a pencil or less.
- Clean up all debris and remove it from the rose garden.

SPECIFIC PRUNING ADVICE BY TYPE

- Hybrid teas: You want to end up with three to six healthy canes that are from 12 to 18 inches tall.
- Floribundas and polyanthas: You should leave six to eight healthy canes (remove the oldest ones) about 20 to 28 inches high.
- Grandifloras: After pruning, there should be four to five large healthy canes about 36 inches high.
- Climbers, ramblers, and old garden roses: These are pruned after blooming since they often bloom on the previous year's wood (unlike the roses listed above, which produce flowers on canes that grow this year).
- Miniatures: If you have just a few miniatures, prune them like hybrid teas to 10 to 16 inches high. If you have many, just clip them back with hedge trimmers.

HERE'S HOW

TO FORCE A FLOWERING SHRUB BRANCH INTO BLOOM

Branches of flowering shrubs may be forced into bloom in the house a month or two before they would bloom outdoors. Some good choices are forsythia, flowering quince, kerria, and spicebush (*Lindera benzoin*). Here's how to do it:

1. Cut 12- to 18-inch stems with the biggest buds on them. Do this on a day when the temperature is above freezing.

2. Slit and scrape the ends of the branches about 3 inches up. (Some gardeners hit the ends of the stems with a hammer to slit them.)

3. Place the branches in a bucket or large vase of warm water for twenty-four hours.

4. Pour out the water from the bucket or large vase and fill it with cool water mixed with floral preservative (from a florist or craft supply store).

5. Place the container in a relatively dark spot, such as a basement, where the temperature is kept between 60 and 65 degrees Fahrenheit.

6. When the buds show color, move the container into average household temperatures and where the branches can get light but no sun (a north-facing windowsill or back a bit from an east window).

7. Add water to the vase as necessary, or replace the water if it isn't clean. Add more floral preservative.

8. When flowers begin to open, move the vase into full sun.

March

March is a month of hope. You should have daffodils blooming, as well as forsythia and a few other early shrubs. They lift your spirits by letting you know that winter and cold weather are on their way out—although obviously, they haven't left yet—and that azaleas, dogwoods, irises, and all the wonderful woodland wildflowers are almost here, if some haven't already popped up.

This is also a month that calls for gardeners to be patient. Typically rainy, March is a time when you may need to stay indoors more than you want, looking longingly out the windows at the garden, where there's so much to be accomplished before the yard looks the way you want.

This is a month that calls for flexibility too. Although you're eager to plant vegetables, cold weather may deter you, so you dig holes and set out new roses instead. You'll be thrilled in May, when the tomatoes you set out in April will be growing sturdily *and* you have gorgeous pink, red, white, or bicolored blooms in your garden just in time to cut some of the fragrant flowers for Mother's Day.

But that's in the future. Right now you're tending seedlings started from seed that will be set out next month, planning new flower beds, eagerly awaiting the arrival of the first tulip blooms and maybe mowing the grass for the first time since last fall.

I always buy and plant a six-pack of snapdragons in March. I know that they won't do much in midsummer—they prefer the cooler weather of spring and fall —but that's good enough for me. I have a real fondness for these old-fashioned flowers. I enjoy showing children how to make the flowers snap shut like dragons' jaws. It's something I've never forgotten since childhood, and I hope the idea of yellow and red "dragons" snapping on my porch is something they will remember a long time too. That sort of thing is one of the joys of gardening, I think. It encourages kids to want to grow plants, and to stick with it when they become adults.

March shows us that gardening isn't just a list of chores, but can also be fun. Some days, we're sitting and anticipating the beauty to come. Some days, we're actively working outside. And all the time, the fun and memories are right there.

PLAN

ANNUALS

Where are you going to plant annuals this year? Now's the time to plan the locations of any new flower beds or to enlarge existing beds. Here are a few ideas:

- Island beds, in lawns or among trees and shrubs, allow the flowers to be seen from all sides.

- Borders can go beside sidewalks, drive-ways, paths, walls, the house, or along the street. They create ribbons of color in your landscape.

- Flower beds and borders may be formal (marked by straight lines such as squares and oblongs) or informal (characterized by flowing lines). Informal looks more natural, but take into account the architecture of your house and the style of your neighborhood when deciding.

It's fine to dig new flower beds anytime this month if the ground isn't frozen or soggy from lots of rain. See directions on page 74. Cover newly dug beds with an airy mulch such as pine straw so they'll stay in good shape until you're ready to plant.

Think about creating a special bed for flowers you can cut and take indoors. The best spot is a bit hidden, so it doesn't matter how it looks when you remove the flowers just as they reach their peak. Good choices include a raised bed in an out-of-the-way spot or a section of the vegetable garden

■ *Choose various varieties of daffodils—one of the easiest bulbs to grow—and you can have them in bloom from February through April.*

■ *Acclimate, or harden off, annuals, such as snapdragons, that are cold-tolerant to outdoor conditions before planting them in the yard. It's fun to have annuals blooming in March!*

that you're not using anymore. (See page xx for a list of annuals that make good cut flowers. But don't buy annual bedding plants before it's warm enough for them in your area.)

ANNUALS, EDIBLES, AND PERENNIALS

If you plan to build raised beds, purchase the materials—wood or other framing, nails, and high-quality topsoil—sometime this month. (See page 21 for instructions.)

BULBS

Why did some daffodils bloom one week and others the week before or after? There are many different members of the *Narcissus* family. They vary in size, appearance, and blooming time. If you're used to daffodils that are all yellow and have large cups, you may be surprised to find that some are all white, some have small orange cups, some produce a number of flowers on each stem, some have double flowers—the choices are endless. With

a little planning, you can have one daffodil or another in flower from February until the end of April (or even the first of May in some sections of the region).

EDIBLES

If you want to grow vegetables or herbs in containers, begin shopping for pots now. Clay and terra cotta are often the most attractive, but they don't hold moisture in as well as plastic pots do—and you need a place indoors to store them over winter (they can crack in below-freezing temperatures). Wood can be attractive but is heavy and difficult to move. Check out the newer containers that mimic the look of terra cotta, but are lightweight and impervious to the weather. Whichever type you choose, be sure the pots are large enough and have ample drainage holes in the bottom.

LAWNS

March is the beginning of the active lawn care season in many parts of the region. But that doesn't mean you don't have some planning to do for later in the year. If your lawn isn't in good shape—lots of weeds, bare spots here and there—you may be getting all geared up to tackle this renovation on the first warm, sunny weekend. Wait. Spring is not the time to renovate cool-season lawns in this part of the country. Fall is the ideal time if you really want to ensure success. Summer's heat stresses cool-season grasses, and a lawn that's had only a couple of months to get established before high temperatures arrive isn't going to fare well. But when renovation takes place in September, the grass has a long time to establish deep roots that will let it sail through the next summer with ease.

If you've been dreaming of transforming your plot of Kentucky 31 fescue into a carpet of zoysia or bermudagrass, you have at least two months before you need to start, and that's plenty of time to do research on what's best for your lawn and what's available.

PLANT

ANNUALS

If the plants have been hardened off (been grad-ually exposed to outdoor temperatures) at the nursery, you may plant pansies, English daisies, calendula, and snapdragons anytime this month if you find them in garden centers and the ground

isn't frozen. All tolerate chilly weather. Mulch them well. If temperatures fall below 20 degrees Fahrenheit, cover the plants with pine straw or several layers of newspapers (anchored with rocks so they won't blow away) to protect them from cold.

Once the cuttings you took from last year's annuals have developed roots, and the young seeds have sprouted and have grown two sets of true leaves (that is, three total sets of leaves), transplant them into larger containers—either spaced farther apart in new flats or in individual containers. Here are some transplanting tips:

- Use new or carefully cleaned containers and fill them a little more than half-full with a packaged potting soil that's been thoroughly moistened.

- Tiny seedlings are very fragile; handle them carefully and never pick them up by the stems.

- Use a plastic spoon or a tongue depressor to lift individual seedlings out of the soil. Disturb the roots as little as possible, and try to keep as much of the growing medium around the roots as you can.

- Place the plant in the new container at the same depth it grew before. (If you're trans-planting to another flat, space the little plants

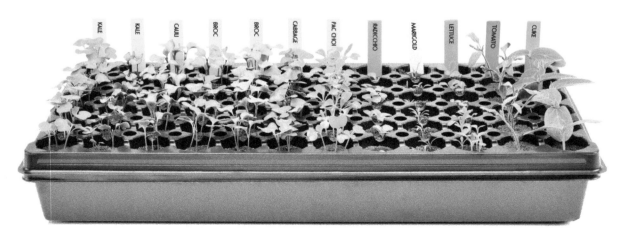

■ *When cuttings you took have rooted and the flower and vegetable seedlings have developed two sets of true leaves, they need repotting to give them more room.*

2 to 3 inches apart.) Lightly firm the soil around the stem.

- Water the plants well.

- Give them slightly lower light levels for three or four days before moving them to a brighter location.

This month, gardeners in warmer parts of the region can sow seeds of plants that need to be started four to six weeks before the last-frost date. These include cosmos, marigold, and zinnia. See page 38 for seed-starting basics.

Cut back geraniums that you brought indoors last fall and repot them into larger containers if roots are growing out the drainage hole or if the roots are growing around and around the ball of soil. Water the geraniums well and place them in a warm spot that receives bright indirect light. They will start growing soon and be ready to go outdoors when the weather warms.

ANNUALS, EDIBLES, AND PERENNIALS

About the end of the month, gardeners in zone 8 can begin hardening off seedlings that were planted earlier and are ready to be planted outdoors. Take them outside and expose them—gradually over a period of seven to ten days—to sun, wind, and cooler temperatures. (For more information, see page 70.) Avoid leaving the seedlings outdoors on nights when frost is expected.

BULBS

Start dahlia tubers indoors late this month or outdoors anytime between the end of April and the first of July. For indoor growth:

- Buy deep pots or trays for starting dahlias indoors, since the tubers are large.

- Fill with commercial potting mix that has been thoroughly moistened and mixed with a timed-release fertilizer such as Osmocote.

- If the tuber was divided last fall when it was dug, make sure each piece of tuber has an eye or bud.

- Place the tuber on top of the soil and press it slightly down into the soil. Water again.

- Apply bottom heat, either with a heating mat or by placing the container on top of your home's water heater.

- Shoots should appear in two weeks. Provide bright light.

- If the tuber wasn't divided in the fall, divide it when new growth is 1 inch tall and replant in pots or flats.

- Give the plants sunshine, moist soil, and warm temperatures as they grow.

- Plant outdoors when all chance of frost has past.

EDIBLES

Prepare the soil anytime this month when the soil isn't too wet. (See page 94.) Then you may plant seeds of carrots, peas (English or snap), radishes, spinach, and turnips. (See pages 113 and 114.) You don't necessarily have to plant in narrow rows. Alternatives include broadcasting vegetable seeds in wide rows (16 to 20 inches apart) or in squares (typically 1 to 2 feet square, depending on the size of the plant—squash, for instance, requires more room). These techniques produce more vegetables in the same amount of space than evenly spaced rows do. But broadcasting requires the gardener to know the difference between a weed and a veggie, and it precludes the use of a tiller or even a hoe for weeding.

Once soil has been prepared, set out transplants of broccoli, cabbage, cauliflower, and onions (also onion sets) anytime this month.

Plant two-year-old asparagus roots by digging a hole 8 to 12 inches deep and 18 inches wide. In the bottom of the hole, make a mound of soil that's been mixed with compost and other organic matter. Drape the roots of the asparagus plant over the mound, leaving the crown (top) about 3 inches below the soil level. Fill the hole with amended soil, firming it around the roots. Water well. Space the plants about a foot apart.

HOW TO SEED A BARE SPOT IN YOUR LAWN

1. Start by using a hard rake to spread compost, topsoil, or garden soil in a one-half-inch layer covering the bald spot. While you can sow seeds directly in the bare spots, the grass will sprout more quickly and won't dry out as easily if it can start growing in loose, fresh soil.

2. Use a hand spreader to spread grass seed thickly and evenly over the entire area, slightly overlapping the edges of the grass that isn't covered with soil. When you're done seeding, the ground should look like it snowed lightly.

3. Sprinkle wheat straw, which you can get at garden centers and home-improvement stores, over the newly seeded area. This will help the seeds stay moist until they sprout. It's easy to grow new grass seed as long as you keep it moist. The biggest problem that people have when overseeding or replanting lawns is that they don't keep the grass seed moist while sprouting. The straw mulch helps eliminate that problem.

4. Grass seed must stay moist until it sprouts. Watering once a day for a couple of minutes isn't enough. Water the newly seeded area twice a day for ten minutes until the grass is at least an inch tall. Then water the newly seeded area three times a week for ten minutes. Don't mow the newly seeded area until the grass is at least 4 inches high. Newly growing grass is fragile, and foot traffic or mower blades could rip the new grass seedlings out of the ground.

Four to six weeks before your county's average last frost date, start seeds of basil and fennel indoors. You may also sow seeds of other herbs inside, if you haven't already.

Sow seeds of borage, caraway, cilantro, leaf lettuce, and mustard in the garden two to three weeks before your area's last frost. That may mean March or April, depending on where you live.

Many perennial herbs (and parsley) don't mind chilly weather, so if you find them growing outdoors at nurseries, it's fine to take them home and plant them in your garden. (Annual herbs such as basil are planted after the frost-free date because they don't like cold weather.)

Start seeds of Swiss chard and eggplant indoors. You may still start seeds of tomatoes to be set out in May. (See page 38 for tips on seed starting.)

Divide chives if necessary. Replant about 8 inches apart in good soil. Or plant some of the chives in containers. They are excellent container plants and, with their purple blooms, look nice among ornamentals.

LAWNS

Patch bare spots. Although it's best not to start a cool-season lawn in spring, there's no reason you can't repair small sections of your lawn this month or next.

1. Remove all grass and weeds from the area.

2. Square off the edges.

3. Dig the soil to a depth of 6 inches, removing any roots, rocks, and debris.

4. Mix compost or other organic matter (rotted leaves, fine bark) with the soil.

5. Rake the area and then water.

6. Sow grass seed at the rate recommended on the bag or box.

7. Using the back of a rake, the back of a hoe, or your hand or foot, make sure the seed comes into contact with the soil.

8. Cover with a light layer of straw.

9. Water often to keep soil most.

PERENNIALS AND ORNAMENTAL GRASSES

Before they've started growing, divide those ornamental grasses that need it—early in the month for zones 7 and 8, late in the month for zone 6. Cut the foliage back so that only one-fourth is left. Dig up the plant with a shovel, and then use an ax or a saw or garden forks to divide the roots into three or four equal sections. Leaving as much soil as you can on the roots, replant quickly so the roots don't dry out.

For dividing perennials, wait till your frost-free date has arrived and the plants have grown to about 4 inches tall. That may mean the end of March for the warmest sections and April (or early May) in cooler areas.

1. The day before you plan to divide a plant, water the soil.

2. Dig up the plant.

3. Wash the soil from the roots so you can see what you're doing.

4. For clumping perennials and those that develop a mass of crowns, use two spading forks, back to back, to break the roots into smaller sections.

5. For perennials that grow from rhizomes, such as bearded irises, see page 131.

6. Use a sharp knife to divide in half plants that grow from fibrous roots.

7. As quickly as possible, replant divisions in new spots or in pots.

8. Firm the soil and water thoroughly.

HOW TO DIVIDE PERENNIALS OR ORNAMENTAL GRASSES

1. *Cut back the foliage on an overgrown perennial by about one-fourth to reduce water loss in the transplanting process.*

2. *Use a sharp spade to cut around the plant and gently lift as much of the root ball out of the ground as possible.*

3. *Smaller rootballs can usually be cut into pieces using a sharp knife. Larger clumps can be sliced with a sharp spade or pried apart using two back-to-back garden forks.*

4. *Remove excess soil from the rootball so you can see what you are working with and remove any rotted or damaged roots.*

5. *Replant the new plants as soon as possible at the same depth the plant was growing at or slightly higher to allow for settling, and water the soil thoroughly. If you can't replant the same day, pot up the divisions and keep well-watered until they are established.*

ROSES

Here's how to plant a bare-root rose:

1. First, prune any broken roots from the plant. The canes don't need pruning unless they were damaged in some way.

2. Dig a hole 24 inches deep and 24 inches wide.

3. Mix the soil removed from the hole with organic matter—compost, fine pine bark, old mushroom compost—in a ratio of two parts soil to one part organic matter.

4. Use the soil mixture to build a firm cone or pyramid in the center of the hole.

5. Place the rose on top of the cone with the roots draped down the sides. The bud union (swollen area) should be 1 inch above the level of the surrounding ground or, for the coldest parts of the state, at ground level.

6. Carefully pour the soil mixture into the hole around the roots, packing it around the roots.

7. Pour into the hole some of the water in which the roots soaked.

8. After the water soaks in, add more soil till the hole is filled.

■ *Dig a hole for your new bare-root rose, then build a cone of soil in middle and spread the bush on top, with the rose's roots positioned over and down the sides of the cone.*

9. Pour the remainder of the soaking water into the hole. (If you are planting many roses at once, there won't be enough of the water in which roses were soaked. In that case, substitute water mixed with transplant solution.)

10. Cover the bud union with a mound of soil or mulch until the chance of frost has passed.

SHRUBS

To plant a container-grown shrub or one that is balled and burlapped, water the shrub well, then:

1. Move the shrub by the rootball, never by the stem.

2. Dig a hole two to three times as wide as the rootball and about the same depth. (Measure a rootball that is balled and burlapped before digging so that you don't have to keep moving it in and out of the hole to see if it fits.)

3. Mix the soil that's removed from the hole with fine bark, compost, peat moss, or another organic material. Add one-fourth to one-third organic matter to the soil, depending on how bad your soil is. (You can skip this step if you're planting in an area where the soil has been amended or where it's naturally of high quality. Or, some horticulturists now recommend just planting in whatever soil you have.)

4. Remove the shrub from its container. If the roots are tightly wound around the rootball, loosen them. Place the shrub in the hole. For a plant that's balled and burlapped, loosen the top of the covering, toss away the twine, and place the shrub in the hole.

5. Check to be sure that the shrub is growing at the same level it did before.

6. Remove the covering from around the roots of a shrub that's balled and burlapped and slide the wrapping out of the hole. Discard the wrapping.

HOW TO PLANT A SHRUB

1. *Dig a planting hole 2-3 times as wide as the rootball, but no deeper. The plant should sit at the same place it was growing in the container or maybe an inch or so above the surrounding soil to allow for settling.*

2. *Place the container on its side and roll it on the ground while tapping it to loosen the roots. Upend the container and gently pull it off of the plant roots. Do not pull a plant by its stem.*

3. *Use your fingers to loosen any roots that may be matted, gently untangling them. Roots that are tightly coiled should be cut apart and loosened. Gently spread the roots wide so they are pointing outward as much as possible*

4. *Set the shrub into the hole.*

5. *Backfill the hole with the original soil. Mound the soil to create a ridge around the plant to hold water. Water well and cover the soil with organic mulch, keeping it a few inches from the shrub.*

7. Fill the hole halfway with the soil mixture.

8. Water, using a transplanting solution (available at garden centers).

9. Add the rest of the soil.

10. Water again, using a transplanting solution.

11. Using the extra soil, make a rim or saucer around the hole and fill that with water.

12. Mulch around the planting area, but not in the saucer, which will hold water for the shrub during its important first year in your yard.

VINES AND GROUNDCOVERS

If your area's last-frost date is sometime in April, you may start seeds of these quick-growing annual vines indoors. (See pages 38 and 44 for details.) They all require about four weeks from sowing seed to setting the plant out in the yard. (Seeds of these vines may also be planted outdoors in May or June; see page 114.)

WATER GARDENS

If you have a pond or water garden, buy a water thermometer if you don't already own one, so you can measure the pond's temperature. It's important to know for certain whether the water's warm enough to put in plants or if you should wait a while longer. You can't go by what the weather gurus report as the air temperature. When your handy thermometer tells you that the water is at least 60 degrees Fahrenheit, you may plant hardy water lilies and hardy marginal plants. (For tropicals, wait till the water warms up to 70 degrees Fahrenheit.)

It's fine to put underwater plants in the water garden late this month. Plant oxygenating or submerged plants in 1-gallon containers filled with sand or pea gravel, then lower them to the bottom of your pond.

When water plants, particularly lilies and lotus, have been in the same pots for several years, they often become potbound and bloom less. Here are two quick ways to tell if your plants need repotting:

- You see lots of shoots coming from the rhizomes. These are potential new plants that will crowd the main plant in the container.

- The rhizomes grow over the edge of the pot, as if they're looking for somewhere to root. They need more space to expand.

March through May are the best times of year to divide and repot your water plants. The procedure is simple:

1. Buy containers and make sure you have enough soil. (Plain old clay loam from the garden is best. Don't use packaged potting soil. It washes away.) You can find special pots for water garden plants, but you may also use tubs and black plastic pots that you already have on hand—provided they don't have holes in the bottom. The best containers for water lilies and lotuses are wider than they are deep (10 inches wide for small plants and about 16 inches for larger ones; 6 or 7 inches deep is fine for both widths). Many people like the fabric pots sold specifically for water gardening.

2. Do your dividing in the shade, not out in the sun, to avoid having the plants dry out.

3. If any of the extra containers you're repotting into have been used, wash them well. Fill each about half-full with soil.

WATER GARDENS NEED SPECIAL FERTILIZER

Beginning in spring and continuing until one month before the first expected fall frost, fertilize your water garden using fertilizer specially made for water gardens. Too much nitrogen from regular fertilizer in the main part of the pond unbalances the water.

4. Remove the plants from their pots (you may have to cut the container) and hose the soil off the rhizomes.

5. With a sharp knife, cut the rhizomes into 4- to 6-inch sections, each having an eye that looks like a potato eye.

6. Wrap the cut rhizomes in wet newspaper or paper towels while you're working with the others.

7. Replant, adding 10-20-10 fertilizer tablets to the pot, according to directions. (If you're new to water gardening and you've been helping a friend divide plants in return for some of the extras, see the full planting directions given in the April chapter.)

CARE

ANNUALS AND EDIBLES

If you're growing seedlings in natural sunlight, such as on windowsills, give the containers a quarter turn to a half turn each time you water. This keeps them growing straight.

BULBS

Cut a few early daffodil flowers to bring indoors. They have such a cheery presence. If you don't have enough daffodils to spare any for cutting, make a note in your garden notebook or on your October calendar to buy more. These are perfect bulbs for Kentucky and Tennessee. Not only aren't they bothered by wildlife but, if given the conditions they like, they come back year after year, always increasing in number.

Although bulbs are tough and can generally tolerate quite a bit of cold weather, extreme cold snaps can make flower stalks fall over if the bulbs have already started blooming. If a warm spell is followed by temperatures in the low 20 degree Fahrenheit range, you may:

- Accept some minor foliage damage (if there are no flowers yet).

- Mulch with pine straw deep enough to cover the entire plant.

- Pick the flowers the afternoon before the cold weather arrives, so you can continue to enjoy the blooms indoors.

When dwarf crested iris (*Iris cristata*) has been in the same place for several years, the center of the rhizome tends to die out. There are two ways of overcoming this. After growth has started this month, dig up the rhizome, remove the unproductive portion, and replant. See directions on page 131. But the easiest way is to cover the underperforming portion of the rhizome with a thin layer of rich compost, which you keep moist. This encourages new shoots and roots.

When crocus and snowdrop foliage browns, cut it off and remove it from the garden. If you'll be planting annuals or other plants in the same bed, mark the location of the early bulbs so they won't be damaged when you add more plants.

Once early daffodils have bloomed, let their foliage begin to fade naturally. Do not braid it, fold it over, or hold it down with a stone. These methods interfere with photosynthesis, which is how the bulb renews itself for next year.

EDIBLES

About the middle of the month, prune back perennial herbs such as rue, sage, and thyme to fresh green wood. This removes dead stem tips, helps shape the plants, and encourages new growth.

HOUSEPLANTS

March is a good time to pinch back plants that have grown a bit lanky or that need to be shaped. Those may include aluminum plant, arrowhead, English ivy, grape ivy, peperomia, heartleaf philodendron, pothos, purple passion, and Swedish ivy.

LAWNS

Set the lawn mower blade to its lowest position this month. Normally, mowing cool-season grasses high is the best thing you can do for them. But that's not true for the first two mowings of the season. That's when you want to cut close—in order to remove winter damage and to stimulate new growth.

Newly seeded grass seems so fragile that you may hesitate to mow it. But mowing is good for it. Wait till the soil is dry, though. Cut an inch off newly sown Kentucky bluegrass when it reaches 3½ inches tall and tall fescue when it reaches 4 inches high.

PERENNIALS AND ORNAMENTAL GRASSES

If you have mulch over the crowns or tops of plants, remove it. Gardeners in zone 8 should begin doing this the first to the middle of the month; those in zones 7 and 6 should do this the middle to the end of the month. But leave mulch around the plants.

The first week of the month, cut back all ornamental grasses. (See the February chapter.) When grasses have been in place several years and have grown large, pruning them becomes increasingly difficult. If you have trouble cutting through the thick base, consider using electric hedge shears or a small chainsaw.

If perennials weren't cut back in the fall, do so now—before they begin growing. Shear creeping phlox (often called thrift) after blooming to keep the plants compact and to encourage new growth.

SHRUBS

Warm spells in February may cause premature blooms in March or early April, before frosts have truly ended. If you find that sometimes happens in your yard, listen to the weather forecast nightly and keep near the door an old blanket, mattress pad, spunbonded fabric such as Reemay, or some other protection so you can gently cover plants and flowers threatened by cold. Remove the covering the next day once temperatures have risen above freezing. Don't cover sensitive plants with plastic; plants get much too hot when the sun shines through it.

If you didn't cut your butterfly bush back to about a foot tall last month, do so now. Because butterfly bush blooms on new wood—that is, stems that it grows this year—pruning it severely causes increased new growth and therefore an abundance of flowers.

HOW TO CUT BACK GRASSES

1. *The main maintenance task with ornamental grasses is cutting back the browned foliage each spring.*

2. *You can use an electric hedge trimmer, hand pruners, or even a string trimmer, depending on how big your plants are and how many. Cut back to about 2 inches from the ground.*

3. *Be sure to cut the clumps back early enough so that you don't cut off any new green growth. Avoid cutting back grasses in the fall as winter injury may result and the winter beauty of the plants and their value to wildlife is lost.*

Remove one-third of the old stems of overgrown bottlebrush buckeye, beautyberry, bush cinquefoil, and Carolina allspice. Cut them back to ground level. On *Hypericum* and summersweet, cut only one-fourth of the canes annually.

ROSES

Once you have pruned and planted, renew mulch on the ground around your rosebushes so that it's about 3 inches deep.

Even though there may be a warm spell, don't begin pulling back the winter-protection mulch from over the bud union until closer to the average last-frost date for your county. (You want to avoid damage by a hard freeze.)

VINES AND GROUNDCOVERS

Direct new growth of young vines onto the trellis or support, if needed. Remove excess debris from groundcover beds—leaves that are covering the plants, small tree branches, and so forth.

Remove dying or damaged stems on all vines in the yard. Cut back overgrown vines. Also prune passionflower. See February, Care for more information on pruning.

Give established Japanese wisteria the first of its three annual prunings. Prune all new growth from the previous year back to two buds.

WATER GARDENS

There's plenty to do this month in your water garden:

- Feed the fish when water temperature reaches about 50 to 55 degrees Fahrenheit. Start with a low-protein food, and feed from three to six times weekly, depending on how hungry your fish seem and how they're growing. Scoop out any food that remains in the water after five minutes.

- Buy a water-testing kit, if you don't own one, and check your pond's pH monthly from now through November. (It should range from 6.8 to 7.4.)

- Add water if the weather has been unusually dry and the pond's level is down several inches. Use a dechlorinator to remove chlorine from municipal water and test again to see whether the additional water has upset the pond's balance. Treat as necessary.

- Avoid fertilizer runoff from your lawn. It can be harmful to fish and also cause algae growth.

WATER

ANNUALS AND EDIBLES

Remember that seeds need constant moisture to germinate. Once sprouted, young plants shouldn't be allowed to dry out. Check the soil's moisture level *daily*.

HOUSEPLANTS

Near the end of the month, return cactuses to their usual places in the house, and begin watering them again. Don't water a cactus (or any other houseplant) by giving it a tiny drink of water occasionally. Instead, water the plant thoroughly—until the excess drains out the hole in the bottom of the pot—and then don't water again until the soil dries out. If you're growing a bromeliad, keep water in the plant's cup at all times.

Toward the end of the month, light gets brighter, temperatures become warmer, and houseplants may need to be watered more frequently. If you have a regular schedule for watering, begin checking plants to see whether they should be watered at least a day earlier than usual.

LAWNS

If rainfall is lacking, you may have to water any grass seed you sowed to repair bare spots in cool-season lawns. Don't let the seeds dry out; otherwise, they won't germinate. Once the seeds have sprouted, continue to water about every other day—if there's no rain—so the young grass doesn't wilt.

ROSES

Regularly water miniature roses being grown indoors as houseplants. They tend to dry out quickly.

FERTILIZE

ANNUALS AND EDIBLES

About six weeks after transplanting seeds or cuttings indoors, fertilize young annuals and vegetables with a plant food that's formulated for flowering plants. Feed pansies. Whenever the soil is not frozen and pansies are blooming, give them a drink of fertilizer-enriched water.

HOUSEPLANTS

Begin fertilizing houseplants again about the middle of the month. Some gardeners prefer to mix a soluble fertilizer in water and apply it monthly during the growing season. Others like to use one-fourth the recommended fertilizer when they water each week. Either way works fine. Or you can mix into the soil the same 14-14-14 or 20-20-20 timed-release fertilizer that you use outdoors.

LAWNS

About the middle of the month, fertilize Kentucky bluegrass and tall fescue with ½ pound of nitrogen per 1,000 square feet of lawn. See the chart on page 84 to determine how much of various fertilizers is needed to supply 1 pound of nitrogen. Shady lawns that consist mostly of fine fescues may be fertilized lightly now or not at all until fall.

PERENNIALS

Fertilize perennials very lightly as soon as you notice new growth. In zones 7 and 8, that's likely to be this month. Ornamental grasses rarely need fertilizing after their first year in your yard. With perennials, you have a choice of fertilizer types— granulated 10-10-10 or 6-12-12, pelleted slow-release fertilizer, water-soluble fertilizer, or organic products such as cottonseed meal. Granulated and water-soluble types produce quick results,

■ *Pansies grow well in the cooler months of the year.*

but the effects aren't lasting. With slow-release and organic fertilizers, the plants are fed over a longer period. That saves you work and is better for the plants.

The main thing to know about fertilizing perennials is that if you prepared the soil well, the plants need little fertilizer. Too much can lead to lanky growth that easily falls over and needs staking. Many perennial gardeners use as fertilizer a yearly or twice-yearly application of 2 inches of sifted compost around each plant. For most, that's all that's needed.

ROSES

See the February chapter (page 45) for a discussion of whether to start seasonal fertilizing at pruning time or afterward. Fertilizers made especially for roses are a good choice. There are a number of them, including an organic mixture, Mill's Magic Rose Mix, which is made in Tennessee. Other organic choices are alfalfa meal and fish emulsion (the latter is usually mixed with water and applied later in the season to supplement the alfalfa meal). Roses respond well to both. Some growers also like to sprinkle a handful of Epsom salts around the base of roses first thing in the spring. It helps produce very green leaves.

SHRUBS

March, April, and May are the best months in which to fertilize shrubs in this area. Water the shrub after fertilizing. Azaleas and rhododendrons prefer an acid fertilizer. Fertilize butterfly bush (*Buddleia*) after pruning it.

WATER GARDENS

Insert fertilizer tablets made especially for water gardens in containers as you pot or repot hardy lilies and marginal plants. For plants that are staying in last season's containers, begin fertilizing again when water temperatures begin to rise above 55 degrees Fahrenheit.

PROBLEM-SOLVE

ANNUALS AND EDIBLES

It's difficult to space small seeds evenly when you sow them, so they may sprout in clumps or end up growing much too close to one another. Then your plants are all competing for space, moisture, nutrients, and light. So it isn't cruel to thin your seedlings; it's cruel *not* to.

When thinning seedlings, try not to disturb the root systems of the plants you're keeping.

- Gently tug extras out by hand or with tweezers.

- Use cuticle scissors to cut the unwanted plants off at soil level.

- Gently firm any disturbed soil back into place.

EDIBLES

Watch out for cabbage loopers this month. Prevent them by covering cabbage and other cole crops with row covers when they're planted, or you

HERE'S HOW

TO FERTILIZE ROSES

- Follow the directions on the label for the correct amount to use. Smaller bushes (miniatures and those 12 inches tall) should receive a smaller serving.

- Sprinkle the fertilizer around the bush in a spiral beginning near the base and continuing out beyond the roots.

- Always water thoroughly after applying dry fertilizer.

- Roses are generally fertilized each time a flush of blooms fades (every four to six weeks) until late summer, when most fertilizing stops to allow growth to slow in preparation for cold weather.

can dust or spray the loopers with Bt (*Bacillus thuringiensis*), an organic control.

HOUSEPLANTS

A wilting houseplant may be the result of too little water. But if the soil is damp around a wilted plant, the problem may be overwatering. If you catch the problem in time, you may be able to save the plant by removing it from its current container and potting it in another container filled with moistened (but not wet) potting mix. Don't water the plant again until the soil has dried. If the plant is still wilted at this point, it was probably too far gone to save.

LAWNS

Crabgrass, which in hot summers seems to grow as fast as kudzu, is more easily prevented than killed. In spring, any garden center will have lawn fertilizers that contain a pre-emergent crabgrass preventer. As an alternative to the chemical products, corn gluten meal is a natural and organic pre-emergence herbicide. It contains slow-release nitrogen (which will fertilize the lawn) and should be applied at the rate of 20 pounds per 1,000 square feet. Expect one application to work for five to six weeks, and then you may need to apply again.

- Pre-emergent crabgrass herbicides must be applied before the seeds of this annual weed germinate in the spring. That can happen from mid-March into early April, depending on the weather and the area of the region. Many gardeners apply a pre-emergent crabgrass control when forsythia bushes bloom in their neighborhood. Or you can ask your local Extension service what the best time for your area is.

- It's important for you to know, however, that these products work by preventing crabgrass seeds from germinating. In most cases, you cannot apply this product and then sow grass seed—it won't germinate either.

- Once or twice? In the warmer parts of the region, you may have to apply a pre-emergent herbicide once in March and again in late spring.

TREES

Tent caterpillars may become active and visible this month. You'll notice the white fuzzy webs, or tents, in the crotches of trees. The best way to get rid of these pests is to wait till dusk and pull the tents down by hand if you can reach them. (Wear gloves.) Drop the tent in a bucket of soapy water. When the tents and caterpillars are still small, you may also control them by spraying with Bt in early evening. Make certain that you wet the tent thoroughly with the Bt mixture. Do *not* set fire to the tents to get rid of them. That's harmful to the tree.

If you have fruit trees, pick up a spraying schedule from the Extension service. Follow it throughout the year.

VINES AND GROUNDCOVERS

Groundcovers that grow next to lawns may invade the grass. Many, such as bugleweed, are easily mowed down. Others may be kept inbounds by edging the beds this month. (Use an edging tool, or stick a sharp spade into the soil where the groundcover and grass meet.) If the problem becomes severe, install heavy edging 12 inches deep as a barrier between the grass and groundcover.

WATER GARDENS

Use Mosquito Dunks or other biological controls (one per 100 square feet of water surface) to prevent mosquito larvae from hatching in your water garden. Start your preventive measures now and continue until frost, even in container water gardens.

April

April wouldn't be spring without bulbs—sunshiny daffodils, jewel-toned tulips, fragrant hyacinths. They are year-round residents but really shine in spring.

If you love the flavor of a just-picked tomato on a summer's day (and who doesn't?) or the taste of pesto from basil grown in your own garden, then April is your month to get things going. But don't worry— growing herbs and vegetables is *easy* in our climate!

The easiest way to have a great-looking summer yard is to plant plenty of annual flowers in the spring. They provide instant color, they're simple to grow, and they require little attention. Best of all, even those who consider themselves nongardeners can be successful with annuals. Now's the time to plant lots of annuals.

A lush, green lawn is one of the most versatile elements in the landscape, many homeowners believe. It's useful, it's beautiful, and it serves as the perfect complement to everything in your yard—trees, shrubs, flowers, vines—while letting them be the center of attention.

Or maybe you prefer not to have to mow the grass week after week anymore. If so, replace the lawn with beds of groundcovers interspersed with evergreen or flowering shrubs and small trees such as Carolina silverbell or redbud, that dependable old standby that brightens the yard spring after spring.

And perennials! For many people, daylilies, coneflowers, black-eyed Susans and other perennials are the fun part of gardening. They're a wonderful way to express your creativity and individuality, and April is the perfect month for a number of perennial chores.

No group of plants can make as much difference in your landscape as shrubs. This is the time to get them into shape.

It's hard to imagine a world without trees. Every month brings something new, but in April it's the flowering trees that make a statement.

Put a vine or groundcover to work in your yard this month. They aren't the "stars" of your landscape, but they're great character actors.

When summer brings sticky heat, you'll be glad you spent a little time this month working on your water garden. Later on, nothing in the yard will make you feel cooler or more peaceful.

ALL

Take your list of desirable plants with you when you head out to nurseries and home stores this time of year. While everyone buys a few plants on impulse, remember that they have to fit into your overall design. Read labels carefully when deciding between plants; especially note the height. Various cultivars of the same plant may vary quite a bit in height and spread.

ANNUALS

Balmy temperatures and sunshine can be seductive. Even those of us who know that our average frost-free date won't arrive for another couple of weeks need to be cautious. We convince ourselves that warm weather has arrived for good at the first string of pretty days. We rush off to the garden center, buy plants, and set them out all across the yard. What frequently follows is a few nights of temperatures in the 30-degree range.

Even if we manage to keep all the transplants covered so they aren't harmed by frost, warm-season annuals don't like temperatures that cold—and they will sulk. If you want to rush the season, invest in plenty of protective coverings and listen to the local weather forecast each evening, ready to take action if needed.

BULBS

Get out your camera and take pictures throughout April, usually the prime month for bulb beauty in this area. You'll enjoy these in years to come, but they can also help you with planning your fall bulb purchases. Do you need more early daffodils around the kerria and forsythia shrubs? Do the color combinations work well, or do your tulips and azaleas clash?

Don't make all of the photos of your entire front yard or backyard. If you try to get everything in one shot, you won't be able to spot the details later. Take time for some photos of just one bed and one border, which record helpful details that will guide you to making your spring landscape as glorious as you always hoped it could be.

EDIBLES

The next time you're at a garden center, look at all the different kinds of radishes in the seed rack.

While you may want to stick with your old favorite for your main crop, it's fun to experiment with various types, from 'French Breakfast' to daikon.

LAWNS

While you may be tempted to install bermudagrass sod or sprig zoysia during April, it's best to wait until the weather's at least 60 degrees Fahrenheit, day and night. Most years, that means at least May. Have you measured your lawn, or the portion of it you're going to plant, to determine the amount of sod, plugs, or sprigs you need? Do that this month; then you can arrange delivery for later.

PERENNIALS AND ORNAMENTAL GRASSES

If you've had perennials and ornamental grasses in your yard for some time, check back through your garden journal or notebook to see how they've performed for the past several years. The best rule of thumb on perennials is to give a new plant three years to prove itself. If at the end of that time it hasn't performed as well as you expected, dig it up and give it to someone else or move it to another spot in the garden if you suspect that it doesn't have just the right conditions it needs where it is now.

With all the wonderful perennials out there, there's no point in giving room to a problem plant. Instead, move on to something that will thrive. This advice especially applies to those plants that have been attacked by insects or disease two of the past three years; they're more trouble than they're worth. If you love the particular species of plant, check to see whether less pest- or disease-prone cultivars are available.

ROSES

Stick with your landscape plan for roses, and don't be seduced by boxed roses being sold inexpensively at grocery and discount stores. These roses are not of high quality.

Many roses grow nicely in containers—miniatures, polyanthas, and some smaller shrub roses, for instance. If this idea intrigues you, start shopping for large pots as you make the rounds of garden centers and nurseries this month. A 5- to 8-gallon container will hold a full-sized rose, although larger containers are better. A miniature should go in at least a 3-gallon pot. It will quickly outgrow anything smaller and will need repotting.

If yellow roses are favorites, and you have an entire bed of them, consider bordering the bed with creeping thyme. Woolly thyme and sedum are nice edging plants with pink roses.

SHRUBS

One of the delights of evergreen azaleas is the wide range of flower colors. But beware if you're mixing lots of different azaleas in close proximity in your yard, especially over a period of several years. If you buy two different cultivars of azaleas—both with red flowers—they often won't be the same hue. And the same is true of the various shades of red, orange, and pink—which, unfortunately, don't combine harmoniously. What seemed like red at the nursery may appear to be more orange or pink when you get it home and put it next to the red azaleas you already own. One solution is to buy azaleas only when they're in bloom. Buy one plant, take it home, and see whether its flowers harmonize with the azaleas you already own. Then go back and buy as many as you want.

Another way to solve this common problem is to save the labels of all the plants you buy, especially shrubs and trees. Keep them in a manila envelope with your garden notebook so that you can find them quickly. Then you'll be able to tell the nursery owner what you have in your yard now.

April is probably the month in which homeowners buy the most shrubs. It's the time when warm weather calls to us, and we feel the need to get out and plant. So we end up at the garden center, bowled over by the plants. We can't wait to get them home. If you buy a few flats of annuals that you don't need, it won't matter much; you can always find a spot for them. But a shrub purchased on impulse is a different story. How does it fit into your landscaping plan? Do you have the right conditions for it in your yard? Instead of buying it on the spot, write down the name of the shrub that impresses you, come home, and look it up in the *Tennessee & Kentucky Garden Guide*. Then maybe you'll discover it's exactly the plant you need in your yard. If it isn't, that's valuable knowledge, too. And you've been saved from making an expensive and time-consuming mistake.

■ *When possible, buy evergreen azaleas and other spring-flowering shrubs when they're in bloom so you make sure that your colors match and don't clash—one with orangish flowers next to one with fuchsia, for example.*

TREES

Flowering trees bring so much beauty to our yards in early to mid-spring. But then what? Does the flowering stop in your yard? It doesn't have to. Consider planting some trees that bloom in late spring or early summer. These include:

- Chinese fringe tree (*Chionanthus retusus*), which has white flowers

- Yellow-blooming Chinese flame tree (*Koelreuteria bipinnata*), highly recommended for urban areas

- Yellowwood (*Cladastris kentuckea*)

VINES AND GROUNDCOVERS

If you have a shady yard and acidic clay soil, you're likely to have one or two spots where moss is growing. You may have tried to get rid of it but found that it returned.

For permanent moss control, you have to correct the conditions that caused the moss. The soil may be too acidic; correct the pH by liming. The soil may be damp; improve drainage. The area may be too shady; if possible, prune nearby trees or shrubs to allow more light to reach the ground. Or the soil is poor; mix soil with one-third organic matter, such as fine bark or compost.

An alternative is to join the if-you-can't-beat-'em school of thought and cultivate moss as a groundcover. When you visit garden centers this time of year, you'll likely find several different types of moss if you want to add more or plant some mosses that are different. Recently, moss has turned out to be quite a trendy plant!

Take a moment to jot down in your garden journal or notebook the names of any ground covers and vines you're planting, the date on which you plant them, and the store where you bought them. This will come in handy when you want to buy the same variety next year and can't seem to find it anywhere.

WATER GARDENS

You've chosen a site for your water garden, but after you start digging, you find a big boulder or two. You may want to switch sites, but you can also dig the pond around the rocks, using them as part of your design.

PLANT

ANNUALS

If your last-frost date has occurred this month (your local Extension office can tell you the date, if you don't know it), you may begin planting annuals, perennials, vegetables, and herbs. You can plant them over several evenings or weekends or do it all in one day.

- If seedlings or bedding plants have been growing in a greenhouse or indoors, they need to be hardened off, or acclimated to outdoor weather, before being planted. Place the plants outdoors during the day in a shady, protected spot, then take the plants indoors—to an unheated area—at night. Gradually move them into a part of the yard where they receive more sun and wind, and leave them out all night. Depending on the temperatures, hardening off can take as little as a week or as long as ten to fourteen days.

- Prepare the soil. Water the flower bed the night before planting, if it's dry.

- If rain has been abundant recently, test the soil to see whether it's too wet for planting. Form a ball of soil in your hand and squeeze it. If it crumbles and falls apart, it's fine to plant. If it remains a lump, wait a few days.

- Choose an overcast day to plant, or do it in early evening.

- Water the plants thoroughly about twelve hours before you plan to plant.

- Remove plants from their containers and gently loosen excessive roots that wind around and around the soil.

- Dig individual holes and place plants in them at the same depth they grew in their pots.

- Replace the soil around the plants and water.

- Mulch the bed about 1 inch deep. Keep the mulch away from the stems of the plants. For one thing, mulch may overwhelm a tiny seedling. And second, keeping the mulch a few inches from the stems allows the soil to warm up, which is good for the plants at this time of year.

BULBS

Wait till all chance of frost has passed to plant your Easter lily outdoors in a sunny spot. Do not place it in the same bed as other lilies, because it can transmit a disease to them.

Plant or replant bearded, dwarf crested, and Siberian irises. Selecting them when they're in bloom allows you to choose favorite colors. But you have other options: Siberian irises may be easily transplanted just before and after blooming, and bearded irises transplant well about six to eight weeks after they've finished blooming (midsummer). Here's how to plant irises:

- Bearded iris, or German iris, needs a sunny spot. Well-rotted mushroom compost is a good soil amendment for them. Cut the leaves back in a fan shape about 4 inches high. Dig a hole and make a mound of soil in the center that's slightly lower than the surrounding soil. Place the rhizome on top so that its roots radiate over and down the side of the mound. Cover the roots firmly with soil. The rhizome should be sitting at soil level or no more than ¼ to ½ inch below. If a bearded iris rhizome is planted too deep, it will rot.

- Siberian irises like a spot with moist but well-drained soil and light shade. Although they tolerate clay soil, it's best to mix rotted leaves, compost, or fine pine bark into the soil before planting. Also incorporate slow-release fertilizer into the soil mixture. Place the rhizome so that the top of it is about 1 inch below the soil surface.

- Dwarf crested iris prefers the shade of a woodland, but doesn't want competition from other plants and shouldn't be allowed to dry out. An acidic soil rich in humus is ideal. Plant it the same as bearded iris.

HOW TO TEST SOIL QUALITY

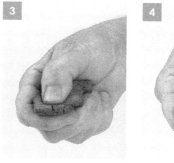

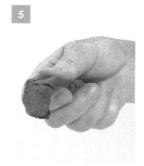

1. *Take a handful of soil and dampen it with water until it is moldable, almost like moist putty.*

2. *Roll the soil into a ball, as if working with cookie dough.*

3. *Using your thumb and forefinger, gently press the soil until the ball begins to roll out of your closed hand. The ribbon will begin to form, and will eventually break under its own weight. If the soil crumbles and doesn't form a ribbon at all, you have sandy soil.*

4. *If a ribbon more than one inch long forms before it breaks, you have silty soil.*

5. *If a ribbon 1–2 inches long forms before it breaks, you have clay soil.*

6. *If a ribbon greater than 2 inches forms before it breaks, you have very heavy and poorly drained soil. It will not be suitable for a garden without some major amendments.*

Lilies like soil enriched with organic matter (rotted leaves, compost, fine bark). Dig the soil 8 inches deep, mix in the organic matter and a timed-release fertilizer, and plant the bulbs. Asiatic lily bulbs should have 4 to 5 inches of soil over the tops of them, and Oriental lily bulbs should be covered by 1 to 2 inches of soil.

Gladioli appreciate a spot that's out of the wind. To have a long succession of blooms, plant corms 4 to 6 inches deep in a sunny location with well-drained soil every two weeks until midsummer.

Plant blackberry lily and crocosmia in well-drained soil that's been amended with organic matter. Blackberry lily grows nicely in light shade. Crocosmia needs full sun and doesn't like to be moved.

Although it's best not to plant caladiums outdoors until May, you can certainly start them indoors about the first of April, if you like. Here's how:

- Moisten a commercial potting mix and fill a flat or several plastic pots about three-fourths full with the mix.

- If there's a shoot growing in the center of the tuber, scoop it out with a small pocketknife. This encourages many side shoots to develop, which will produce more foliage.

- Place the tuber on the soil, with the roots down.

- Cover the tubers with 1 to 2 inches of soil and water them well.

- Keep the planted tubers in a warm location. Bottom heat (from a heating mat sold to aid seed germination, or from simply placing a few pots or one flat on top of your water heater or refrigerator) will encourage faster germination and growth.

- As soon as growth is evident, move the plants into bright light.

EDIBLES

When the frost-free date for your area has passed, plant just about any vegetable or herb in the garden except those that are true heat lovers. Wait till May or later for melons, okra, eggplant, Southern peas, pumpkins, and sweet potatoes. Don't plant basil till you're sure that there's no frost in the forecast—it's very sensitive to cold. Harden off transplants grown indoors before moving them to their final homes in the garden. (See page 70.)

After chance of frost has passed, sow seeds of these herbs where they are to grow: basil, caraway, chervil, dill, hyssop, lovage, marjoram, summer savory, thyme, and fennel. You may also plant parsley seeds, but soak them in water twenty-four to thirty-six hours first or nick the hard seed covering with a knife.

The first week of the month, continue sowing seeds or setting out plants of cabbage, spinach, broccoli, English and edible-podded peas, potatoes, onions, mustard, turnips, and beets. You can't wait longer because it will be too hot when the plants mature, and you won't get much of a harvest.

For best pollination, sow corn in blocks rather than one or two straight rows. Continue sowing seeds of radishes and different kinds of leaf lettuce. To extend the harvest and not end up with too much one week and not enough later in the month, sow a small amount of both every ten days during April.

There are many ways to plant a tomato seedling, and it's fun to see what works best for you. You can plant it the way you plant a pepper plant—at the same depth it grew as a transplant. Or you can strip off all but the top four leaves and lay it on its side or bury it up to its top leaves in an extra-deep hole (to develop a better root system).

When you plant vegetables, install supports—trellises for cucumbers, poles for beans, and cages for tomatoes. In fact, it's best to install beanpoles and cucumber trellises first, then plant the seeds at the base. Tomato cages should be at least 5 feet tall and 2 feet in diameter and anchored well at the base.

Divide chives, bee balm, lemon balm, mint, and tansy this month, if needed. Slice through the center of the plant with a sharp shovel, or dig up the plant and divide it with two spading forks. Replant the divisions at the same depth they grew before, and water well.

■ *Dig out weeds and patch bare spots in cool-season lawns this month. Keep the area well watered, then plan a full renovation in fall, if needed.*

LAWNS

Continue patching bare spots in cool-season lawns. (See directions on page 54.)

If your cool-season lawn looks awful, and you dread the idea of living with it until September, you could overseed it now. It's not an ideal solution—and you may have to water weekly from now through August. But it will give you a green lawn. Directions below.

PERENNIALS AND ORNAMENTAL GRASSES

Begin planting ornamental grasses and perennials about the time of your area's average last frost. Plant container-grown perennials at the same depth they grew before unless the plant's label instructions direct otherwise. (See page 74 for more information.) Give the plants plenty of room to grow—spacing them close may look better now, but it means dividing plants or grasses much sooner than you would otherwise have to.

Should you receive a bare-root perennial from a mail-order catalog, dig a hole at least 6 inches deep and 6 to 8 inches wide in a prepared bed. Mound the soil in the middle of the hole, and place the roots over the top so that they drape down the sides. Holding the plant in place, fill the hole with

---

HERE'S HOW

TO OVERSEED A LAWN

- Set the mower blade at its lowest setting and mow the grass.

- Rake up the clippings.

- Mow again. Rake again. This exposes more of the soil, so the grass seed can come into contact with it.

- Rough up the soil with a hard metal garden rake.

- Sow one and a half to two times more seed than recommended on the label for new lawns. The reason you need more is that some of it won't germinate because it won't come into contact with the soil.

- Rake lightly to help the seed get next to the soil.

- If possible, sprinkle a ¼-inch layer of sand, topsoil, or compost on top.

- Water daily to keep the soil moist till most of the seeds germinate.

HOW TO MAKE A PLANTING BED

1. Measure the area where you're planning to plant the garden. Take length and width measurements and multiply them to get the square footage of the planting bed. You'll use these when calculating the amounts of soil, mulch, and plants to purchase for the garden bed.

2. Add two inches of soil or compost to the bed. To determine the total cubic feet needed, multiply the area of the bed (length × width) by two and divide by twelve. (For three inches of mulch, multiply the entire area of the bed by three and divide by twelve.)

3. Use a 4 tine claw or hard rake to mix the soil into the planting bed. In new housing developments, topsoil is scraped off and sold. Adding compost or garden soil replenishes nutrients and helps plants grow.

4. Set the plants out where you want to plant them. Stagger the plants so that they aren't arranged in straight lines. You can also create groupings with one of each type of plant and repeat the groupings in several places throughout the flower bed. If you know you'll have time to plant on the same day that you set out the plants, take all of the plants out of their containers before you set them in the planting bed—you'll save yourself a lot of time.

5. Dig the planting holes just as deep as the rootballs of the plants. If you're planting larger perennials (plants in gallon-sized containers), use a spade or shovel for quick work. Really pay attention to the depth of your planting hole. Perennials can't handle being planted too deep. The top of the rootball of a plant should be level with, or just slightly higher than, the ground around it.

soil so that the crown of the plant is at the level of the surrounding ground. Water with a transplant solution, and add more soil if necessary.

In cooler areas, you may still divide ornamental grasses if they haven't yet begun to grow. When it comes to dividing perennials, some gardeners go by the rule of dividing spring-blooming plants in the fall and summer- or fall-flowering ones in the spring. But much depends on the weather and how busy you are. You may also divide spring-blooming perennials after they finish blooming, provided you keep them watered throughout the summer as needed. See the March chapter for directions on dividing perennials.

Don't dig up and transplant or try to divide perennials, such as butterfly weed, that have deep taproots. They don't transplant well.

ROSES

Homeowners in the cooler parts of zone 6 can plant bare-root roses about the middle of the month. It's important to plant bare-root roses early so they can develop a good root system before hot summer weather arrives. That doesn't mean that if you've missed the March 15 to April 1 planting window for Memphis, for instance, you have to forego roses this year. Instead, buy roses planted in containers.

■ *It's fine to plant irises in April, when local growers often offer them from their fields. Cut the leaves back into a 4-inch fan before planting. Leave the rhizome at ground level or no more than ¼ inch below, or it can rot.*

HERE'S HOW

TO PLANT A LOTUS

When you buy a lotus, get a recommendation on a container size from the seller. Small ones may fit in 3-gallon pots, but others may require a pot ten times that size. Lotuses won't bloom well unless they have enough room. You also need clay loam soil, fertilizer tablets, and a stone that will fit into the pot with the lotus.

1. Fill the pot halfway with soil and place several fertilizer tablets in the soil. (Use additional fertilizer for bigger containers.) Add more soil to within a few inches of the pot's rim.

2. Handle the tuber very carefully, since it's brittle. Place the tuber on top of the soil with the cut edge against the inside of the container. Put the stone on top of the tuber to hold it in place.

3. Add more soil, but don't cover the growing tip.

4. Carefully place ½ inch of gravel over the soil—but not over the growing tip.

5. Place the pot on the edge of the pond so that it's initially covered with only a few inches of water. Then gradually lower the container as the plant grows.

In most parts of Tennessee, you can buy container roses this month—but don't plant them in the ground yet. They were probably potted up in February and March and haven't yet developed enough roots to be removed from their pots. If the soil ball falls apart when you're removing it from the container, it can harm the roots, and the plant may not live. There's no rush. Wait until you see some roots growing through the drainage hole. In Kentucky, buy potted roses in May or June.

SHRUBS

This is an excellent month to plant shrubs—deciduous, evergreen, flowering—whatever your yard needs most. See March for shrub planting instructions. One important key is to make sure that the shrub isn't planted any deeper than it grew before. Before planting, see whether the soil is dry enough to work. Pick up a ball of soil and squeeze it in your hand. If it forms a hard ball, the soil is too wet. If it forms a ball that then falls apart, it should be fine.

TREES

Tree planting continues in April. See pages 182–183 for planting advice. If you're planting a tree that's balled and burlapped, always remove the wrapping around the rootball (even if you're told that it's natural burlap and will rot). These can prevent the roots from growing out into the soil.

Also toss away the twine or wire that fastens the covering to the trunk.

Large trees (often installed by the nursery) are sometimes sold in wire baskets that hold the rootball together. These are left in place, since they are designed with plenty of room for roots to make their way through the cage.

VINES AND GROUNDCOVERS

All vines and groundcovers may be planted this month. Choose plants that like the light and soil requirements of the planting area. Here's how to plant a container-grown vine or groundcover:

1. Dig a hole that's as deep as the rootball and twice as wide.

2. Remove the plant from its pot. If roots are growing around and around the rootball, loosen them so they will grow out into the soil.

3. Place the plant in the hole at the same level it grew before.

4. Mix the soil removed from the hole with fine bark or compost and a slow-release fertilizer.

5. Add the soil mixture to the hole until it's about half-full.

HERE'S HOW

TO PLANT CLEMATIS

- Clematis prefers to be planted with its leaves in the sun and its roots in the shade. You can accomplish this with mulch or a stone over the root area. Or you can plant it where a nearby shrub or building will cast a shadow on the root zone. Or plant it behind the trellis and let it grow forward.

- Instead of planting a clematis vine at the same depth it grew previously, plant it 2 to 3 inches deeper. It will send out new roots, which help it survive clematis wilt.

- Clematis prefers alkaline soil (pH above 7.0), but will grow in neutral to slightly acidic soils. In very acidic soils, you must apply lime several months before planting. (If you don't know the pH of your soil, have the soil tested.) If your soil is acidic, place some cold fireplace ashes around your clematis vine once or twice during the winter.

HERE'S HOW

TO PLANT HARDY WATER LILIES

1. Have all your supplies on hand before you begin: pea gravel, clay loam soil (dug from your yard), water garden fertilizer tablets, and containers. You can buy a soil substitute at water garden stores, but it may be expensive. Because hardy lilies grow horizontally, their pots should be 14 to 16 inches wide and 7 to 9 inches deep. You may also need some bricks to place beneath the pots on the bottom of the pond.

2. Prune damaged roots and dead leaves.

3. Fill the container about half-full of soil, and add two water garden fertilizer tablets. Add more soil so the container is about three-fourths full.

4. Position the rhizome so the cut end rests against the inside of the container and the growing tip is held out of the soil at a 45-degree angle, facing the opposite side of the container. Add more soil to within 2 inches of the container's rim, making sure the growing point is not covered.

5. Carefully add 1 inch of pea gravel. This keeps the soil from washing out of the pot and helps prevent fish damage.

6. Water the container gently.

7. Lower the pot into the pond so the growing tip is covered by 3 inches of water.

8. Over the next few weeks, gradually lower the pot so that it's beneath 12 to 18 inches of water. (You can put water lilies into deep water right away, but many gardeners believe they grow faster early in the season if they're gradually lowered to the correct depth.)

6. Water, using a transplant solution.

7. Finish filling the hole with soil, firming it around the roots.

8. Water thoroughly, using a transplant solution.

9. Mulch with 2 to 3 inches of organic material.

WATER GARDENS

Most gardeners in our region will plant hardy water plants this month (as soon as water temperature is 50 to 55 degrees Fahrenheit) and tropical ones next month, after temperatures are reliably warm. The time to add water lettuce and water hyacinth to your water garden is after all chance of frost has passed. In much of the area, that will occur by the end of April. For those in the colder sections, it could be early next month.

CARE

ANNUALS

One of the best things you can do for all annuals is to pinch off any flowers before you plant seedlings or set out bedding plants. Seems like heresy, doesn't it? But a young plant has only so much energy. If it spends most of that energy producing flowers, it doesn't develop as good a root system as it should. And that root system is essential to a strong, healthy plant that can tolerate hot, dry weather. So clip off any flowers before planting. You'll reap the rewards later in the season, when your plant grows larger and performs better than those whose blooms were left in place.

BULBS

When bulbs are in flower, mark their locations so you'll know where to fertilize in the fall. Some people use short stakes, others golf tees. Or you can draw the bulbs' location on a plan of your yard. As the weather warms up across the region this month, pull back the protective mulch you placed over the cannas, glads, and dahlias you left in the ground last fall. After Siberian irises finish blooming, divide the clumps if they need it and replant. Be sure to keep the new divisions watered.

Continue to remove the faded flowers from bulbs flowering outdoors. It makes the garden look better and prevents seeds from forming. (Seed formation takes energy away from the bulb, which reduces the vigor of the bulb the following year.)

Remove all faded daffodil flowers. If you don't, the bulbs may set seed. Instead, let that energy go to the bulb, which is where next year's flowers come from. If you see seedpods, snap them off and toss them away.

EDIBLES

Thin radishes, beets, carrots, Swiss chard, and other seed-sown vegetables. See the seed packet for correct spacing. Thinning is tough work, mentally— it's hard to pull up and throw away a perfectly good vegetable. But think of it as something you're doing to help the plants that are left. They'll have more room to grow to their full potential.

Even if asparagus puts up stalks the first year in your garden, don't harvest them. Wait till the second year and then cut them only when they reach 8 inches high. Once the new stalks are about as thick as a pencil, stop picking and wait till next year. Being patient helps the plant renew itself and ensures a larger harvest in the future.

Harvest beets when the roots reach 2 to 3 inches in diameter. Pull carrots when the tops or shoulders are ½ to ¾ inch across. If you want to pull some green onions to use in spring salads, do so whenever they reach the size you like. Cut rhubarb stalks when they become 8 to 15 inches long.

When planting herbs and vegetable transplants, remove any damaged leaves. Also pick yellow or brown leaves from plants when you see them in the garden. The garden will look better and is more likely to remain insect- and disease-free when you practice good sanitation.

LAWNS

Keep debris picked up. As you walk in the yard, make it a habit to pick up leaves, small branches, and trash that may have blown onto the lawn. Not only does it look better, but it makes mowing go more quickly.

Some types of grass stand up to repeated foot traffic better than others. Avoid the damage, though, by creating a pathway where people and pets are already traveling across the lawn.

GRASS	BERMUDA	CENTIPEDE	FINE FESCUE*	KENTUCKY BLUEGRASS	TALL FESCUE	ZOYSIA
Type	Warm-season	Warm-Season	Cool-Season	Cool-Season	Cool-season	Warm-season
Zone	6-8	7b-8	5-6	5-6	6-8	6-8
Method of Planting	Sod, sprigs or seed	Sprigs, sod	Seed	Seed	Seed, sod	Sprigs, plugs
Heat tolerance	Good	Good	Poor	Poor	Fair	Good
Cold tolerance	Fair	Poor	Good	Good	Good	Good
Drought tolerance	Good	Fair	Fair	Fair	Fair	Good
Shade tolerance	Poor	Fair	Good	Fair	Good	Fair
Traffic (wear) tolerance	Good	Poor	Varies	Fair	Fair	Good
Mowing Height (inches)	½ to 1½	1 to 2	1½ to 2½	½ to 2½	2 to 3	½ to 1½

*Fine fescue = chewings, hard, and creeping red fescues

Dethatch or aerate warm-season lawns after the grass has completely greened up and has been mowed several times. Depending on where you live, that may be late this month or in May. See page 169 for information.

If bermudagrass and zoysia lawns have greened up completely this month, mow them with the blade at its lowest setting to remove any winter damage and to encourage new growth. If they're still brown, wait till May.

After the second mowing of the season, for fescue and bluegrass lawns, raise the height of the mower blade.

Mowing makes a difference. Mowing is the most frequent lawn activity—and it's also the most important. When you mow a lawn, you're doing more than cutting the grass. If done properly, mowing can prevent and kill weeds, conserve water, and reduce the need for fertilizer.

- **Follow the one-third rule.** Instead of mowing the lawn every Saturday morning, cut the grass when it has grown one-third taller than the recommended mowing height. (See the chart above for the correct mowing height of your grass.) If you're trying to keep your lawn at a recommended 2 inches tall, remove 1 inch when the grass has grown to 3 inches tall. The

one-third rule of lawn mowing encourages a deep root system and helps avoid stress on your grass.

- **Don't scalp your lawn.** While warm-season grasses need to be mowed short, cool-season lawns should not. Many people cut their cool-season grasses very short because they think it will take longer for them to grow back. Just the opposite is true. The advantages of mowing fescue and Kentucky bluegrass at the high end of the suggested height range are many: Taller grass helps keep moisture in the soil and moderates soil temperature. And because, generally, root growth mirrors top growth, taller grass means deeper roots. Deeper roots withstand drought, heat, and cold. And here's the best part: Taller grass crowds out weeds naturally. Try it, and find out for yourself.

- **Leave the clippings on the lawn—most of the time.** Those clippings provide valuable nutrients to your soil. Why toss away free fertilizer? But there are times when it's not a good idea to leave the clippings where they fall. And that's when—after a long rainy spell or you've been out of town—the grass has grown quite tall before you got around to mowing it. Then the excess clippings will lie on the lawn in big clumps. That doesn't look good, and it isn't good for your lawn. So for those times only, collect the clippings. Add them to the compost pile, or spread them in a single layer to dry and use them as mulch.

PERENNIALS AND ORNAMENTAL GRASSES

Protect tender plants from frost. (See page 24.)

If you have oak trees, you'll often see squirrels rummaging around in flower beds to dig up acorns. Check the beds several times a week to make sure the squirrels didn't dig up any plants too. They don't usually harm the plants, but exposed roots can dry out, causing the plant to die.

Renew all mulches so they're 3 inches thick. Don't pile the mulch right up to the stem of perennial flowers. Instead, start it 1 or 2 inches away.

Put stakes or supports in place for peonies and foxgloves. Tall foxgloves can get knocked over in April or May showers and thunderstorms, and peonies often end up trailing their blooms in the mud when it rains as they're flowering. It's best to get the supports in place early in the season so the plants grow up through them and their foliage hides the metal or wood. Check garden centers and catalogs for the various types of supports available for perennials; you're not limited to wood stakes.

In areas with colder climates, perennials that have not yet begun growing should be pruned back now. Even if new growth has started at the base of the plant, carefully cut off any dead flower stalks from last year. This improves the garden's appearance.

If you didn't prune ornamental grasses last month, do so right away. It's a more difficult job once the plants have begun to grow because you can't just lop off all the old leaves; you have to be careful not to damage the new growth. But a mixture of brown and green stalks detracts from the grass's appearance.

Remove faded flowers from early-blooming wildflowers such as Mayapple and bleeding heart.

ROSES

If you've been growing miniature roses indoors, begin to acclimate them gradually to the outdoors about two to three weeks before the last frost date. First, place them outside all day in a shaded, protected place, and bring them indoors at night. Then gradually move them into more and more sun, but still bring the pots back in if frost threatens. After two weeks, prune the roses to 8 inches tall and plant them in the ground, just as you would any other container-grown rose. (See page 100.)

As soon as the chance of frost has passed, remove mulch mounded over the bud union and rake it into the rose bed. Mulch the rose bed with 3 inches of organic matter if you haven't yet. This helps the soil retain moisture.

In zones 7 and 8, you may still prune roses the first two weeks of this month if they weren't pruned earlier. Pruning later than mid-April, though, will delay blooming considerably. If you didn't get around to pruning your roses in time, prune only lightly. Remove all deadwood and crossing or rubbing branches, as well as suckers and growth at or below the bud union. Prune all canes back lightly (no shorter than 24 inches on regular bushes, 18 inches on miniatures), and then, during the growing season, cut stems longer than usual as you cut roses to go indoors.

In zone 6, wait until April 15 to prune most roses. Climbers, ramblers, and species or old garden roses flower only once a year and are pruned after they flower.

SHRUBS

The easiest way to damage your shrubs is with a string trimmer. Next is with a lawn mower. Why take a chance on harming a good shrub? Remove weeds and grass in a wide circle around shrubs, fill it in with 3 inches of organic mulch, and then it won't be necessary to mow or trim grass close to shrubs.

If the winter was colder than normal, wait until crapemyrtle begins to leaf before pruning what you think are dead stems. Before leafing, it's very difficult to tell which portions were killed and which are alive.

If they need it, prune deciduous magnolias, such as star magnolia (*Magnolia stellata*), by thinning within a month after they have finished flowering. Not all shrubs need pruning every year—many need minimal pruning—but for spring-flowering shrubs, the best time to prune them is right after they finish blooming.

If a hedge has become overgrown or straggly, you can rejuvenate it by cutting it down to about 6 inches high. Or you can cut one-third of the stems back to the ground each year.

TREES

Rarely is it necessary for homeowners to stake a tree. Leaving it unstaked helps the tree develop a stronger root system. But should you be planting a tall tree, or the site is very windy, staking might be necessary since the root system may not be large enough in the beginning to keep the tree upright in strong winds. Trees planted on a steep hill may also need to be staked.

If staking is needed, cover the guy wires with rubber hosing, flexible plastic, or soft cloth where they will touch the tree. Attach the hosing to the lowest part of the limbs, allowing some room for the trunk to be able to sway slightly. Stakes should never be left in place more than a year. It's better to remove them even sooner—when the roots have taken hold and can support the tree on their own.

If there's been a lot of rain this month, mulch may have washed close to tree trunks. Take a moment to rake it back so it isn't touching the trunk, which can lead to disease or borers.

Be careful when using string trimmers near trees. They can quickly cause trunk damage, which is an open invitation to insects. Dogwood borers, which often kill trees, get into a tree through a wounded trunk. It's better to encircle lawn trees with mulch so it's not necessary to trim near trees.

Once trees have leafed out, stop pruning unless it's to remove dead, diseased, or damaged limbs.

VINES AND GROUNDCOVERS

Clean up groundcover beds if you didn't do that last month. Remove excess leaves and tree debris, and cut back cold-damaged stems and leaves.

PLANT MAINTAINENCE TIPS

■ *Water flowers gently at ground level so the moisture is aimed at the plants' roots, which is where it's needed. Be sure to water long enough that the soil is wet several inches deep.*

■ *Place cages around peonies when the plants are just sprouting.*

■ *If lavender needs pruning, do it in the spring before new growth starts. You may also neaten it up shortly after it flowers.*

Harden off annual vines that were started indoors in February or March so they can be set outside after the chance of frost is past. See page 70 for more details.

Tie vines lightly to their supports so the tie won't cut into the vine's stem as it grows. Check monthly during the growing season to make sure that vines are attached securely to the structure on which they're growing.

Although March is a better month to prune vines than April, it's not too late to trim back dead leaves or stems and thin crowded vines. (See page 44.) If you haven't cut back a vine that flowers on this year's growth, you may still do so. (See page 43 for a list of these vines.) The vine may flower later than it did last year. On the upside, a vine that blooms on the current season's wood and is pruned to 12 inches high the first to middle of April will bloom much more bountifully than if it isn't pruned at all. Prune Carolina jessamine this month or next—after it has finished flowering. To encourage new growth, cut back creeping phlox (thrift) after the flowers fade.

WATER GARDENS

Increase fish feeding. Once water temperatures rise reliably above 60 degrees Fahrenheit, switch to a high-protein fish food and use it one to three times a day the first week.

Remember to feed only an amount that the fish will consume in five minutes. Scoop out any food they don't gobble up. Never feed catfish food to goldfish or koi. It's not good for them.

Prevent mosquitoes. Even though fish eat mosquito larvae, it's a good idea to regularly use a natural control made for water gardens. This needs to be renewed every thirty days. Since it's a monthly chore, you may want to mark it on your calendar so you don't forget.

Leaves fall in spring, as well as in autumn. Some trees keep their dried leaves all winter and then drop them in spring. So your pond may be picking up a few leaves about now. If you have many such trees, you may want to spread netting over the water's surface for a week or so. But most people take care of the debris by skimming it out two or three times a week.

Thin out your supply of oxygenating plants such as anacharis. Too many will clog the pond and prevent growth of flowering plants. Toss the excess on the compost pile.

WATER

ANNUALS

Young transplants have small root systems that can't absorb a great deal of water at once. For the first few weeks in your garden, they may need to be watered every couple of days (or even daily if the weather is hot). *Don't let them wilt*, which will stunt their growth. The ideal time to water young plants is first thing in the morning. That allows any water that splashed onto the foliage to dry during the day, which cuts the risk of fungus diseases.

BULBS

Should April showers not arrive on schedule, water bulbs if there's been no rainfall in the past two weeks. If bulbs are in bloom, try to keep the water from touching the flowers so they'll last longer.

EDIBLES

Seeds must be kept moist, but not soggy, until they germinate. If rainfall is irregular, water the seeds you've sown daily. The usual rule of 1 inch of water per week holds true for vegetables, although there are times when that water is essential and other times when the plant may be able to slide by a few extra days, if necessary. But remember that if plants are stressed from lack of water, they aren't going to produce well, and they're more likely to be attacked by insects.

LAWNS

If Mother Nature doesn't supply plenty of rainfall this month, you may need to water. It's especially important for newly seeded areas and lawns that have been renovated in the past year.

PERENNIALS AND ORNAMENTAL GRASSES

Newly planted perennials may need watering several times a week if there's little rain. Be sure the soil around them doesn't dry out.

Ornamental grasses are mostly drought tolerant, but they, too, should be watered regularly during dry spells that occur the first year after planting.

ROSES

Once roses have started growing, they will need 1 to 1½ inches of water per week in cooler weather and up to 3 inches when the weather's really hot. Drip irrigation, soaker hoses, or in-ground irrigation—which keep the moisture at the base of the plant and don't splash it up on the foliage—are best for roses. If possible, water early in the day so that any plant part that got wet will dry quickly.

SHRUBS

Keep an eye on newly planted shrubs. They will need watering more frequently than established shrubs—maybe as often as twice a week in the first month they're in your yard, even if rainfall is about 1 inch a week. Water slowly enough that there's no runoff and the ground gets soaked 6 to 10 inches deep. If you have a border of shrubs or new foundation shrubs, consider using a soaker hose or putting drip irrigation at the base of the plants. It will water efficiently without your spending a great deal of time doing it by hand.

TREES

Frequently check trees that have been planted recently to make sure their soil doesn't dry out. Drying will be quicker in fast-draining soils than in clay, but all young trees may need watering a couple of times weekly the first few weeks they're in your yard, if rainfall is less than normal or it doesn't rain weekly. During dry spells, pay attention to the watering needs of trees that have been planted in the past year or two. Most mature trees don't require extra watering except during drought.

VINES AND GROUNDCOVERS

After vines and groundcovers have been growing in your yard for a year or so, they won't need much supplemental watering unless there's no rainfall for two weeks. Plants that have been set out this year will generally need water whenever rainfall has not totaled 1 inch per week.

Soaker hoses and drip irrigation are excellent methods of watering vines because they deposit the water at the root zone, where it's needed, and keep it off the foliage.

FERTILIZE

ANNUALS

Before the weather is warm enough for your seedlings to go outdoors, continue to fertilize them about every ten days with a water-soluble fertilizer made for blooming plants.

Water annuals well before planting them outdoors in a bed or into hanging baskets or containers and then fertilize. Your options include:

- Sprinkle around the plants a balanced timed-release fertilizer according to package directions. This will feed plants for up to three months. Water after applying.

- Use 10-10-10 granular fertilizer, being careful not to drop any on the plants, because it will burn them. Keep a hose handy to wash accidental spills. Water the fertilizer in.

- A third alternative is to use a water-soluble fertilizer. But the effects of a water-based fertilizer don't last nearly as long as with granular or timed-release fertilizer. That means you will need to fertilize much more often—which isn't going to be fun when temperatures and humidity levels begin to climb toward the stratosphere.

- Organic gardeners should mix compost liberally with the planting soil and nurture young seedlings with manure tea or compost tea (manure or compost soaked in water until it's the color of weak tea, then strained). Or, even easier, buy an organic fertilizer made especially for flowers.

BULBS

Feed amaryllis with a water-soluble fertilizer made for houseplants. Spread a timed-release fertilizer around summer-flowering bulbs as they emerge from the soil. These fertilizers slowly release nutrients to the plants over a long period, so you don't have to apply them more than once or twice a season.

HERBS AND VEGETABLES

Mix fertilizer with the soil when preparing the vegetable garden for planting. (See page 94.) Herbs generally need little fertilizer if they're grown in soil that's been enriched with organic matter.

Side-dress asparagus, broccoli, cabbage, and cauliflower with fertilizer when they've been planted about a month, and Irish potatoes after they have sprouted. Side-dressing is the practice of applying a band of fertilizer about 3 inches away from plants. Use half the amount recommended on the fertilizer container.

LAWNS

Feed all lawns this month. About April 15, spread ½ pound of nitrogen per 1,000 square feet fescue and Kentucky bluegrass lawns. Use ¼ pound of nitrogen for fine fescues and 1 pound of nitrogen for bermudagrass and zoysia. See the chart at right to figure out how much you'll need for the type of fertilizer you've chosen.

COOL-SEASON GRASSES (FESCUES, KENTUCKY BLUEGRASS)	
APPLICATION DATE	TOTAL POUNDS OF NITROGEN PER 1,000 SQUARE FEET*
March 15	¼ to ½
April 15	¼ to ½
September 1	½ to 1
October 15	½ to 1
November 15	½ to 1

*Tall fescues usually require the higher amount; chewings and red fescues, less. If your lawn is mostly shady and sown primarily with fine and chewings fescues, you may want to fertilize only in September, October, and November.

WARM-SEASON GRASSES (BERMUDA, CENTIPEDE, AND ZOYSIA)	
APPLICATION DATE	TOTAL POUNDS OF NITROGEN PER 1,000 SQUARE FEET
April 15	1
June 1	1
July 15	1
September 1	1

The dates to fertilize seem clear enough, but you may be wondering what "total pounds of nitrogen per 1,000 square feet" means? How does that translate into the amount of fertilizer you should spread on your lawn? Here's another chart to help.

TYPE OF FERTILIZER	PERCENT NITROGEN	POUNDS FERTILIZER*
15-5-5	15	6½
20-10-10	20	5
24-8-8	24	4
27-3-3	27	4
Milorganite**	6	17

*Total pounds of fertilizer to supply 1 pound of nitrogen
**processed sewage sludge

PERENNIALS AND ORNAMENTAL GRASSES

Fertilize perennials lightly as they begin growing. Grasses don't need fertilizer except at planting time. A couple of inches of compost or Milorganite (processed sewage sludge) are often better for the plants and soil than chemical fertilizer.

ROSES

Begin fertilizing roses after new foliage appears, if you haven't earlier. Use the amount of a granular rose fertilizer recommended on the label and water it in. Or spread pellets of a slow-release fertilizer, which will fertilize the bushes all summer with one application.

SHRUBS

If you didn't fertilize shrubs last month, do it now. If you applied one-third of the recommended amount of granular fertilizer at the end of March, do the same at the end of this month, too.

TREES

Fertilize hollies, southern magnolias, and other young evergreen trees if you didn't in February. Use 1 pound of 10-6-4 or a similar high-nitrogen fertilizer per 1 inch of trunk diameter or use an organic tree fertilizer. Spread it in a spiral outward—starting about 12 inches from the trunk and continuing beyond the tips of the branches. Water.

What about pounding fertilizer spikes into the ground? If you like them, fine. But it's much easier to spread granular or pellet fertilizer by hand than it is to pound spikes into the ground. Besides, the spikes don't evenly distribute the fertilizer.

Also fertilize trees planted in large tubs. It's best to use a slow-release fertilizer for container-grown trees since it provides a constant replacement for the nutrients in the soil that may be washed away through frequent watering.

VINES AND GROUNDCOVERS

An alternative to using a slow-release fertilizer on ground cover beds is to mix a water-soluble plant food (14-14-14 or 20-20-20) in a hose-end sprayer and spray all the plants thoroughly once or twice a month from now until mid-August.

Never, *ever* fertilize wisteria, even if you're trying to get it to bloom. Instead of encouraging flowers, fertilizer produces excessive leaf and stem growth on wisteria—and fewer flowers.

WATER GARDENS

This month, begin fertilizing hardy water lilies and marginal or bog plants using special compressed fertilizer tablets made for water gardens. Larger plants need several tabs inserted in each pot. See package directions for the number of tablets required for the size containers you have.

■ *Aphids suck the juices out of plants' stems. They're especially attracted to rapidly growing plant parts in spring. Knock them off with a hard stream of water.*

PROBLEM-SOLVE

ANNUALS

Watch out for aphids (tiny, pear-shaped insects, above) on new growth. If there are only a few, knock them off with a blast of water from the hose. If there are more than a few, spray them with insecticidal soap. Repeat every five days until they're gone.

When plants are cut off at ground level, suspect cutworms. Paper or cardboard collars around the stems can help. So does a sprinkling of Bt.

BULBS

If any irises didn't flower, or if they produced flowers that collapsed, the problem is probably rhizome rot. Dig up the rhizome and remove all soft spots. Before replanting the rhizome, you may want to dust it with sulfur. Preventive measures include shallow planting and removing all dead foliage.

EDIBLES

Lemon verbena is one of the last herbs to leaf out. After cold winters, it may not return, but be patient: it could be next month before you know for sure.

Each time you visit the garden in April, take a hoe or hand weeder with you and chop down a few weeds. It's easier to control weeds when they're young.

■ *Watering wands dispense moisture gently but thoroughly.*

■ *Fertilizers may be organic or chemical; liquid or granular.*

PLANTING DEPTHS FOR VEGETABLE SEEDS

• Bean	1 to 1½ inches	• Okra	1 inch
• Cantaloupe	1 inch	• Peas	1 to 2 inches
• Carrot	¼ inch	• Radish	½ inch
• Collards	½ inch	• Southern peas	1 to 2 inches
• Corn	1 to 1½ inches	• Spinach	½ to ¾ inch
• Cucumber	½ to ¾ inch	• Summer squash	1 to 2 inches
• Kale	½ inch	• Turnip	½ inch
• Lettuce	⅛ inch	• Watermelon	1 to 2 inches
• Mustard	½ inch	• Winter squash	1 to 2 inches

FIXING PET DAMAGE

Does your pet—or a neighbor's—always wet on the same place in the lawn, causing the grass to turn yellow or brown? You have several solutions:

1. Put up a barrier so the animal can't reach the spot. Sometimes a large overturned flowerpot will cause pets to move on to another location.

2. Use a product sold to repel cats and dogs. (It will have to be resprayed periodically, especially after rain.)

3. Water the area frequently to dilute the urine.

4. Replace the damaged grass, water and fertilize it, and start again with Steps 1 to 3, if needed.

PERENNIALS AND ORNAMENTAL GRASSES

If it's been a wet spring, slugs may become troublesome around hostas. See page 108 for tips on controlling them.

Ignore ants on peonies. They're attracted by a sweet sticky substance and do no harm.

If mums that had been in the garden for more than a year didn't return this year, the reason is usually that they weren't divided and replanted regularly. On the other hand, when mums planted the previous fall don't come back, you can usually blame cold weather.

ROSES

Aphids are attracted to tender new growth of roses. If not controlled, these pear-shaped insects suck the juices from the leaves and buds or blooms. Wash off as many as possible with a spray of water from a hose. If that doesn't get them all, use insecticidal soap. Cut off and destroy any damaged plant parts. If they're present in the garden, ladybugs and syrphid fly larvae will consume aphids.

Tiny yellow speckles on evergreen azalea leaves may indicate that lace bugs are present. Ask the Extension service or a good garden center for advice on controlling lace bugs.

How do you know whether a perennial needs dividing? If it isn't blooming as well as it used to, and the plants are crowded, it should be divided. This shows you the importance of spacing correctly when you plant so the plants don't become crowded too quickly. Some perennials, such as hostas and peonies, rarely need dividing, but chrysanthemums should be divided at least every other year. Most other perennials should be divided every three to five years. See page 55 for more information.

TREES

Leaf miners leave what look like tunnels in the leaves of hollies. These are easier to control when you can spray (with pyrethrin) the small black flies or gnats as they fly around before laying eggs. But if you don't catch leaf miners at that stage, consult the local Extension service office for control advice.

Once temperatures have warmed up, put away the dormant oil and apply a light horticultural oil to fight scale and mites on holly. They suck the juices from the leaves.

In a wet spring, sometimes dogwood flowers and foliage may be covered with small disfiguring spots. This is called leaf anthracnose (not to be confused with the much more serious dogwood anthracnose). It doesn't do any lasting harm; it just looks ugly. Spraying with a fungicide is an option if you've had the problem several springs in a row. It won't cure the disease, but can help keep it from returning. Check with the Extension service for advice. You may also want to consider whether your dogwood is in too much shade; if it is, prune some larger surrounding trees to let in some sunshine.

Brown spots on crabapple leaves are signs of cedar-apple rust. Since the spores are produced by eastern red cedar trees, it's important never to plant crabapples anywhere near red cedars. If this is a recurring problem in your yard and you're determined to grow a crabapple, consider planting a resistant variety. A nurseryman should be able to

recommend a number of them. The list of options includes 'Adams', 'Adirondack', 'Centurion', 'Donald Wyman', 'Indian Summer', 'Molten Lava', 'Red Jewel', 'Sargent', 'Sugar Tyme', and 'White Cascade'.

Caterpillars and what we often call worms (which are really caterpillars) may be a problem on flowering forms of fruit trees—flowering cherry, peach, plum. Spray with Bt if the damage is severe.

VINES AND GROUNDCOVERS

TWO PLANTS
FOR THE PRICE OF ONE

Groundcovers are usually purchased a flat or more at a time. Sometimes they were just rooted in flats, and sometimes they're growing in six-packs or 2- to 4-inch pots. If the plants are in six-packs or individual containers, gently lift a few out to see what kind of root systems they have. You want plenty of roots, because that will help the plants take off. When you find plants where the roots cover the rootball and there's vigorous top growth, buy them; when you get them home, divide each into two plants—you'll get two plants for the price of one.

WATER GARDENS

If you have fish in your water garden, don't use any chemical controls, since they may be toxic to koi or goldfish. Check with a water garden dealer or your local Extension service office for recommendations; there are natural products made especially for water gardens that may help.

WATER PLANT TIPS

Before you pile soil into the pot, put a rock in the bottom of the containers of tall plants to help prevent them from getting blown over by strong winds. Wide pots also help keep tall plants from toppling.

Lotus tubers are easily damaged in transit, because they're brittle. You may want to look for a local supplier instead of ordering them by mail.

May

Suddenly it feels like summer in our part of the world. Joy! That makes it prime gardening time. You can dig in the dirt, plant almost any warm-season flower or vegetable that you want to, improve your zoysia or bermudagrass lawn, or act on ideas to create exciting new areas in your landscape—maybe create a section of the yard to attract small wildlife, butterflies, or bees (those buzzing pollinators that continue to have such a tough time and therefore aren't able to pollinate as much of our food as they used to).

Annual flowers—in beds and containers—are beginning to put on a show that will last until fall. Early vegetables—including snap peas, which are rarely available unless you grow your own, planting them very early in the season—are appearing. It won't be long before every day you're eating the freshest vegetables possible, straight from your own backyard. Probably your family is already enjoying lettuce, radishes, and your favorite kind of greens. But the nicest part is that in May you still have time to plant more so you can enjoy more—maybe heirloom tomatoes and gold cherry tomatoes to go with the regular tomatoes you usually plant? It's always such fun to try something new, and often that experiment turns into a new favorite.

If the pleasant memories of spring's flowering trees still lingers in your mind, what about considering a tree for your yard that blooms in summer? Because it's a bit unusual, a summer-flowering tree will add a new note of interest in your landscape. You can plant your choice now—if you are careful to keep the young tree watered all summer—or wait till early fall.

By this time of spring, you may want to add more colorful plants to the yard—roses, tall annuals, a small shrub or two—but feel as though you've run out of energy to dig any more holes. That's okay—plant in containers instead. There's hardly any plant that can't be grown in a container if the container is big enough. And another advantage of containers is that you can move them around—from the front porch to the back deck if you're having a party, for example. Sometimes grouping a number of containers together can make quite a show.

PLAN

ALL

Visit several garden centers to get an idea of the variety of flowers available—colors, types, and sizes that you may not have expected. Branch out a bit. Try something new to you. You may be delightfully surprised.

It's a busy time in the garden, but you'll be happy later that you took time to write down this year's last-frost date. While you have your garden notebook open, why not note the total rainfall for each month?

LAWNS

How much of your lawn is weeds? If the answer is half or more, you need to start over. For warm-season lawns, that can be done beginning this month. (See the Plant section for May.) For cool-season lawns, wait till September. With four

months to plan, you can investigate some of the new varieties of tall fescue. Maybe one will be the improvement you've been looking for.

Are you noting in your garden journal the times when your perennials and roses bloomed? It's helpful for future reference to write down the date blooming started and also how long it lasted.

PERENNIALS AND ORNAMENTAL GRASSES

Look over your perennial beds: Do you need a few plants of a certain color? Are there bare spots? Is there at least one group of perennials in bloom all the time from spring through fall frost? That's a good goal, though sometimes it takes a few years to achieve. Late spring and early summer bloomers are the most common, so you may need to think more about adding plants that flower in the hottest part of summer (perennial hibiscus and yarrow, for example) or those that flower in late summer or fall (everything from *Chelone* to Joe-pye weed).

When possible, choose perennials with interesting leaves. They add interest to the flower bed or border even when they're not in bloom.

ROSES

Want to honor Mom in a special way on her day? Instead of buying her a dozen roses, why not invest in several rosebushes that have flowers in her favorite color? Container roses are an especially good choice. Deliver them with big bows tied to the pots and with a promise to dig the holes and plant the bushes for her. Then get them in the ground the weekend after Mother's Day. Rather than having a dozen roses that last for maybe a week, she'll have dozens each month from now until November.

SHRUBS

Want to attract more butterflies to your garden? Shrubs can help. There's still time to plant shrubs that are favored by these winged jewels. Some that you'll want to consider are:

- Azalea (*Rhododendron* spp.)

- Blue mist shrub (*Caryopteris* × *clandonensis*)

- Butterfly bush (*Buddleia* spp.)

■ *Attractive garden ornaments attract a lot of attention in the landscape. They also make good gifts for a gardening mom or grandmom.*

■ *Plant shrubs that attract colorful butterflies to encourage these winged jewels to visit your yard. Masses of flowers are more likely to attract butterflies than one or two bursts of color here and there.*

- Button bush (*Cephalanthus occidentalis*)

- Daphne (*Daphne* species and hybrids)

- Glossy abelia (*Abelia × grandiflora*)

- Lilac (*Syringa* species and hybrids)

- Mock orange (*Philadelphus* species and hybrids)

- Privet (*Ligustrum sinense*)

- Snowball (*Styrax* species and hybrids)

- Summersweet (*Clethra alnifolia*)

- Virginia sweetspire (*Itea virginica*)

Think about moving beyond purple or lilac flowers when you buy your next butterfly bush. You can now find butterfly bushes with red, pink, white, or yellow blooms.

TREES

Have you thought about adding a summer-flowering tree to your landscape? Admittedly, there aren't as many of them as there are trees that bloom in spring, but they're all the more welcome—and admired—for that reason. Some to consider:

- Chaste tree (*Vitex agnus-castus*)

- Franklin tree (*Franklinia alatamaha*)

- Japanese pagoda tree (*Styphnolobium japonicum*)

- Sourwood (*Oxydendrum arboretum*)

- Southern magnolia (*Magnolia grandiflora*)

- Stewartia (*Stewartia ovata* var. *grandiflora* and *S. pseudocamellia*)

- Sweet bay magnolia (*Magnolia virginiana*)

HOW TO PLANT A CONTAINER GARDEN

1. *Select your plants. Container gardens need three types of plants: thrillers, fillers, and spillers. The pink SunPatien® in this group is the thriller, a stand-out plant. White angelonia is the filler, planted in odd numbers. Purple scaevola and chartreuse sweet potato vine are the spillers in this container.*

2. *Fill your container halfway with potting soil. (The bag will be marked "potting soil.") After you have the container half-full, you can begin placing your plants. Some plants will have larger rootballs than others, so you might should place the largest plant first then add additional soil to the container and place additional plants.*

3. *Finish placing your plants and add more soil to fill in the spaces between them. It's important that the plant stems aren't buried in soil so they don't rot. That's why you need to be careful when placing plants in the pots and place larger plants first. Don't be afraid to really pack the container full of plants. Because you usually grow them for only one season, their spacing doesn't matter as much.*

4. *Push the soil down at the edge of the container so that it is at least one inch below the edge of the pot. This leaves room for water to sit and soak in when you water the plant. If you fill the soil to the top of the container, it will all run out when you water the pot and will make a big mess. This is also a good time to sprinkle some slow-release fertilizer into the pot. Add it around the edges and on top of the soil—don't sprinkle it on top of the plants.*

5. *When you've finished planting, water the container. Give it a good soaking and let the water run out the bottom of the container. Then, wait several days to water again. A good rule of thumb is to water containers when the soil down to the second knuckle on your index finger (if you stick your finger in the pot) is dry. You should also water if the plants look droopy or saggy. Once the plants have grown to fill the pot, you'll need to water once or twice a day.*

PLANT

ANNUALS

As spring-flowering bulbs begin to fade, plant annuals in front of them to hide browning foliage. If the cuttings you took of overwintered annuals have enough roots, pot them up and move them outdoors, gradually getting them acclimated to the weather outside. (See page 70.)

Sometimes containers filled with flowers supplement a garden's in-ground beds and borders, and sometimes—in the case of condo dwellers—it may be the only way you can grow flowers at all. Choose containers that have drainage holes in the bottom or that you can easily drill holes in. Plastic pots and large containers will require less watering than small

containers and clay pots. If you don't have room to bring containers indoors in freezing weather, consider some of the new clay-look pots made from lightweight materials. They aren't harmed by being left outdoors, as terracotta may be.

BULBS

Any spring-flowering bulbs may be moved when their foliage has yellowed and fallen over or begun to brown. Don't wait too long, or you won't be able to locate the bulbs. Replant immediately.

Once both days and nights are reliably warm, it's fine to plant tubers of caladiums and elephant ears outdoors. (Caladium plants that have already started growing—either started indoors or bought in pots—may go out early in the month in the warmest areas.) Both like rich, moist soil that's been amended liberally with organic matter (Nature's Helper™ soil conditioner, compost, rotted leaves, or aged mushroom compost). Both will also perform nicely in containers. Caladium shines in the shade; elephant ear will grow in full sun or partial shade. Continue to plant caladiums all month, if you like.

■ *A container of geraniums and purple lobelia pops with the first colors of summer.*

Dahlias are so impressive – the colors as well as the size of the blooms—that everyone needs a couple to show off in the garden. They're as easy to grow as vegetables, but planting is a bit different.

HERE'S HOW

TO GROW DAHLIAS FROM TUBERS

1. Plant tubers after all chance of frost has passed. You may continue to plant in June and early July in the warmer parts of the area, for fall flowers.

2. Choose a spot with good soil, full sun, and access to water, the sort of location you'd put a vegetable garden. In fact, a former vegetable garden is an excellent place for tall dahlias.

3. Till the soil 8 to 10 inches deep, and incorporate plenty of organic matter into the bed—composted leaves, fine pine bark, compost, and so forth. Mix in slow-release fertilizer.

4. Dig holes 10 to 12 inches deep and 5 inches wide.

5. Space small dahlias 8 to 10 inches apart, medium ones about 18 inches, and large ones 24 to 36 inches from one another.

6. Spread the tuber in a hand shape on the bottom of the hole.

7. Place a stake in the hole now because putting it in place later is likely to damage the tuber.

8. Add 3 inches of soil on top of the tuber, firming it around the stake, so the stake will stand up.

9. As the tuber grows, add more soil until the hole is filled.

10. If you are growing many dahlias, install drip irrigation or soaker hoses since they need plenty of water during the steamy days of summer.

11. Top the soil with 2 to 3 inches of mulch.

Bedding plant dahlias are small and may be planted just as you would any annual. (See page 70.)

Plant cannas in a bed that's in full sun and has moist, rich soil or in containers filled with potting soil mixed with dry bagged manure. Because cannas are heavy feeders, incorporate timed-release fertilizer into the soil as you plant, so you won't have to fertilize as frequently throughout the summer.

Continue planting glads and lilies, if bulbs are available. Because lily bulbs lack a protective coating, plant them quickly so they don't dry out.

Plant annuals and perennials in and among bulbs to hide the bulb's ripening foliage. Daylilies and daffodils are an excellent combination. As the daffodils begin to fade, daylily foliage comes on strong.

HOW TO PLANT VEGETABLE SEEDLINGS

1. *Prepare the planting area by adding compost. You can buy bagged compost at garden centers and home-improvement stores. Use a hard rake or 4-tine claw to incorporate the compost into a prepared vegetable bed.*

2. *Set out your plants. It is always tempting to cram a lot of vegetable plants into a small space, especially when they're little transplants. Resist that urge! Follow instructions on the plants about spacing. You can always thin seeds, but transplants are too expensive to throw away.*

3. *Plant tomatoes deep and plant everything else so that the plant's rootball matches the soil level surrounding the planting hole. You don't need to put fertilizer in the planting hole.*

4. *Spread mulch around the plants. Mulch is just as important in vegetable gardens as it is in flower gardens because it helps keep water in the soil, moderates the soil temperature, and prevents weeds from sprouting. Use wheat straw or grass clippings in vegetable gardens. Our climate is already hot.*

5. *Place stakes and supports around newly planted vegetables right after you plant them. Tomatoes have brittle stems, so it is difficult to maneuver them into cages after they've started growing. Tomato cages are the best support for tomato plants.*

6. *Water the plants by directing the watering wand or hose nozzle at the base of the plant. Count to ten while watering each plant and then go back and repeat the process. If you have the time and money, put soaker hoses around your vegetable garden beds. It will be much easier to water—you can just turn on the hoses and let them run for a while while you do something else.*

■ *If your soil isn't appropriate for herbs, plant them in small containers.*

EDIBLES

Once the temperature is consistently 70 degrees Fahrenheit or above (55 degree nights), plant the crops that need heat. These include eggplant, melons, okra, pumpkins, Southern peas, and sweet potatoes.

Plant sweet potato slips so that the top two leaves are above soil level. Space them about a foot apart in rows that are 3 feet apart or in hills or mounds 4 feet from one another. Avoid wet spots and don't mix fertilizer in the soil when planting.

HERE'S HOW

TO SPACE VEGETABLES IN CONTAINERS

It's fun to grow vegetables in containers, but it isn't always easy to know exactly what size container to use and how many seeds or plants to put in it. Here's a handy guide for regular-sized plants. You may be able to fit more in if you use dwarf varieties:

- Beans: two plants per 8-inch pot

- Beets: four plants per 8-inch pot

- Broccoli: one plant per 12-inch pot

- Brussels sprouts: one plant per 12-inch pot

- Cabbages: one plant per 10-inch pot

- Carrots: one plant per inch of diameter (The pot must be deep.)

- Cauliflower: one plant per 12-inch pot

- Cucumbers: one plant per 8-inch pot (The pot must have a trellis or support.)

- Eggplant: one plant per 12-inch pot

- Lettuces: one plant per 8-inch pot

- Onions: one plant for each 3 inches of pot diameter

- Peas: one plant per 6-inch pot (The pot must have a trellis or support.)

- Peppers: one plant per 8-inch pot

- Radishes: one plant per inch of diameter

- Spinach: two plants per 8-inch pot

- Squash: one plant per 12-inch pot

- Swiss chard: one plant per 12-inch pot

- Tomatoes: one plant per 12- to 18-inch pot (The pot must have support.)

Continue planting all herbs and all warm-season vegetables—beans, corn, cucumbers, pepper, summer squash, tomato, and zucchini. You may also plant more leaf lettuce in May, but sow the seeds in a spot that will be shaded some in the afternoon. Also, choose a heat-tolerant cultivar of lettuce.

Some herbs—lavender, artemisia, and santolina, for instance—require well-drained soil. If you haven't been able to grow these herbs but you really want to, consider planting them in containers. They look especially nice grouped together, so look for containers that match but are different sizes.

If you have a sunny place in the garden where you'd like to plant herbs, but it isn't close enough to stretch a hose there easily, these herbs like dry soil, once they're established: dill, hyssop, lamb's ear, rosemary, sage, and santolina.

University research has shown that tomatoes planted in cages bear more fruits than those that are staked, but they do begin bearing slightly later. If you're trying for the earliest tomato harvest in your neighborhood, you may want to stake a couple of 'Early Girl' plants and put the main-season tomatoes in cages.

HOUSEPLANTS

All during May, continue repotting houseplants that need it. How do you know if a plant needs to move to a larger pot? Signs include:

- The plant has stopped growing or blooming.

- The plant needs watering frequently.

- Roots are growing through the drainage hole.

- Roots completely cover the surface of the rootball, growing around and around.

What can you do about plants that have grown too large and heavy to be repotted? It helps to remove the top 1 or 2 inches of soil and replace it with fresh new soil annually. This is called topdressing.

As you move plants outdoors or repot them this month, it's also a good time to expand your plant collection by taking cuttings (see box, right).

HERE'S HOW

TO PROPAGATE HOUSEPLANTS BY CUTTINGS

1. Fill a 2½- to 3-inch pot with moistened commercial potting mix.

2. Using pruning shears or a sharp knife, cut off a 3- to 5-inch stem.

3. Pinch off all but the top two leaves.

4. Dip the end of the cutting into a rooting hormone, such as Rootone.

5. Use a pencil to poke a hole in the soil, and then stick the cutting in it.

6. Firm the soil around the cutting.

7. Water the planted cutting.

8. Cover the pot with a plastic bag and seal.

9. Place the pot in a place that receives medium light but not direct sun.

10. When new growth appears, open the top of the plastic bag permanently and water enough to keep the soil moist.

11. Remove the plastic bag within two weeks.

Houseplants that are easily propagated by cuttings include African violet, angelwing begonia, aluminum plant, arrowhead plant, Chinese evergreen, croton, dieffenbachia, English ivy, flowering maple, grape ivy, heart-leaf philodendron, lipstick plant, peperomia, polka-dot plant, pothos, prayer plant, purple passion plant, rubber plant, snake plant, Swedish ivy, wandering Jew, and weeping fig.

LAWNS

Sodding is the fastest—and most expensive—way to install a new lawn. Often it's the only way for warm-season grasses. But increasingly in our region, fescue sod is also widely available.

When's the best time to sod? For warm-season grasses, wait till the soil has warmed up to

HERE'S HOW

TO INSTALL SOD

1. Estimate the amount of sod you need. First, measure the dimensions of the area you plan to plant and convert those figures into square feet. (100 feet by 50 feet equals 5,000 square feet.) Most sod is sold by the square yard (9 square feet). Divide the square footage of the lawn area by 9 to arrive at the amount of sod you need. (For 5,000 square feet, that will be at least 556 square yards. Some experts recommend ordering 5 to 10 percent more, to be certain you have an adequate amount.)

2. Have your soil tested.

3. Prepare the soil by removing all existing grass, roots, and rocks.

4. Apply fertilizer as recommended by the soil test. Till fertilizer and a 1-inch layer of compost, well-rotted manure, or fine wood chips into the top 6 to 8 inches of the soil.

5. Rake the soil so it's level.

6. When the sod is delivered, place it in the shade and water it.

7. Begin laying sod near a straight edge such as a walkway.

8. Fit the strips together so that there are no gaps between them.

9. Use a sharp knife to cut any strips that must be divided.

10. Roll the lawn to make sure the sod comes into firm contact with the soil.

11. Water well.

12. Keep the sodded area moist for two weeks. Then gradually cut back on watering, but watch the edges—they're the first to dry out.

Bermudagrass, centipede grass, and zoysia are also available as sprigs—pieces of grass stems. To sprig these grasses, follow Steps 1 through 6 for installing sod. The quickest way to plant sprigs is to broadcast them over moist soil (1 bushel of sprigs per 200 square feet). Cover them with soil, roll the surface, and water. Keep them moist for at least two weeks or until most have begun to grow. Then water regularly.

70 degrees Fahrenheit in spring, and don't install it any closer than two months before your estimated fall frost. May and June are the best months for bermudagrass, centipede grass, and zoysia. From early September to mid-October are best times for fescue.

PERENNIALS AND ORNAMENTAL GRASSES

Continue planting perennials and ornamental grasses in all parts of the region. After woodland wildflowers finish blooming, divide them if needed.

You may also divide other perennials, especially in zone 6, but it's best to wait till early next spring to divide ornamental grasses. If the perennials you plan to divide have gotten taller than 4 or 5 inches, cut them back by one-third before you start.

ROSES

It's too late in the year to plant bare-root roses, but you should find a good selection of container-grown roses at local nurseries and garden centers. Before you plant, make sure the roots have grown enough that they fill the rootball. If the rootball falls apart during planting, the rose may not survive.

HERE'S HOW

TO PROPAGATE PERENNIALS BY TIP CUTTINGS

Want to increase your stock of perennials? Division (discussed in the March chapter) isn't the only way. Some perennials root easily from tip cuttings. For asters, catmint, dianthus, penstemon, and salvia, take tip cuttings:

1. Using sharp pruners, cut a 3- to 4-inch piece from the tip of a healthy, actively growing stem.

2. Remove the lower leaves.

3. Fill a pot or flat with moistened potting soil, and poke holes in it with a pencil.

4. Wet the stem ends of cuttings, and dip them in a rooting hormone.

5. Insert the cuttings into the holes, and firm the soil around them.

6. Water.

7. Cover the pot with a plastic bag, and place it in a warm spot that has bright light but doesn't receive sun.

HERE'S HOW

TO PROPAGATE PERENNIALS BY STEM CUTTINGS

Perennials with pithy or hollow stems are more easily propagated by stem cuttings. These include *Campanula*, *Chelone oblique*, chrysanthemum, gooseneck loosestrife, obedient plant, phlox, rose campion, veronica, and yarrow. Catmint may also be propagated by this method.

1. When new shoots are about 3 or 4 inches tall, use hand pruners or a sharp knife to cut stems close to the ground (so some of the woody part of the stem is included).

2. Wash any soil off the cutting.

3. Follow steps 2 through 7 of taking tip cuttings.

After cuttings start to grow, let them develop adequate new roots so they can live on their own, then pull the cuttings away from each other and replant them individually. Fill in bare spots in the perennial border with annuals, if necessary. Be patient; your young plants will soon begin growing together.

SHRUBS

May is a good month to transplant shrubs that you have been growing in containers. Once these have been in their containers for two or more years, they're either ready for a larger pot or they need fresh soil. Because packaged potting mix is too lightweight for outdoor shrubs, you should make your own mix. One mix recipe to consider is two parts topsoil, one part Nature's Helper™, one part commercially composted cow manure (from a 40-pound bag), and one-fourth part sand. Add a water-holding polymer, such as Moisture Mizer™, according to package directions. (Never use more than called for on the label.) That will help hold moisture in the soil so you don't have to water quite as often. Then mix in a timed-release fertilizer. Place a piece of screening (or a coffee filter) over the drainage hole, pour in the moistened soil mix, then place the shrub in the container. Water and then fill the

HERE'S HOW

TO PLANT CONTAINER ROSES

1. Twenty-four hours before planting, water the rose until the excess drains freely from the bottom of the container.

2. Choose a spot for the rose that receives at least six hours of daily sunshine and has well-drained soil.

3. Dig a hole 2 feet wide and 2 feet deep.

4. Mix the soil removed from the hole with organic matter—aged mushroom compost, fine pine bark, rotted leaves, and so forth. Use two parts soil to one part organic matter.

5. Wearing thorn-proof gloves and long sleeves, place the container on its side and grasp it just below the bud union to remove it from the pot. If it doesn't release easily, use a knife or tin shears to make three or four cuts from the rim to the base of the container.

6. If roots are growing around and around the rootball, gently pull them apart or score the rootball with a sharp knife.

7. Place the rose in the hole so that the bud union is 1 inch above ground level or, in the coldest parts of the state, exactly at ground level. You don't want to plant too deeply.

8. Refill the hole about halfway with the amended soil mixture. Water with a transplanting solution.

9. Fill the hole to the top and water again, using a transplanting solution.

10. Mulch around the rose with 3 inches of organic matter, starting 3 inches away from the base of the bush.

container to within an inch of the rim with soil. Water again.

Plant all types of nursery-purchased shrubs in the yard this month. Tips for planting are on page xx.

VINES AND GROUNDCOVERS

Once the weather has warmed up and stays that way, seeds of these annual vines may be planted outdoors where they are to grow: black-eyed Susan vine, cardinal climber, cypress vine, gourds, moonflower, morning glory, and Spanish flag. See page 114 for advice on sowing seeds outdoors.

WATER GARDENS

Once all chance of frost has passed, and air and water temperature stay about 70 degrees Fahrenheit, you may plant tropical water lilies.

CARE

ANNUALS

It's fine to gradually move the overwintered tropical plants you grew as annuals back outdoors. Angel's trumpet is a good example. Do this over two weeks or so once the weather is reliably warm. Start by moving the plants to the shaded part of the porch or other shady spot, taking them back inside if nighttime temperatures threaten to fall below 50 degrees Fahrenheit. Then gradually move them into more sun.

BULBS

Anytime this month, it's fine to move your potted amaryllis outdoors for the summer. If you didn't get to it last month, mark bulb plantings in some way so that you'll know where they are when fall fertilizing time arrives.

HERE'S HOW

TO PLANT TROPICAL WATER LILIES

1. Have everything ready before you start: clay loam soil, fertilizer tablets, pea gravel, and plenty of containers. Pots for tropical lilies should be plastic, about 10 to 12 inches in diameter. You may also need some bricks to place under the pots so they'll be at the proper depth.

2. Make sure the water temperature is at least 70 degrees Fahrenheit. Colder water will stunt the plant. Fill containers about half-full of soil, add two fertilizer tablets and more soil, stopping about 2 inches from the rim.

3. Place the tuber of a tropical lily on top of the soil in the middle of the container with its roots spread out. Gently push the roots into the soil and make sure the growing tip or eye is not covered by the soil.

4. Gently add 1 inch of pea gravel to prevent the soil from washing away and so fish won't muddy the water by poking around.

5. Water the container gently but thoroughly.

6. There are two theories about placing plants in water gardens. One school says to immediately lower them to the correct depth (12 inches of water over the growing tip for tropical water lilies). But some water garden experts think it's better to first place the plants in more shallow water—with about 6 inches of water over the growing tip—then gradually lower it to 1 foot deep as the plant grows. You may want to see which works best for you.

■ *Watch out for cabbage loopers in the late spring vegetable garden. They can be prevented by covering small cabbages with row cover fabric.*

Leave the ripening foliage of tulips, daffodils, and other spring-flowering bulbs in place until it begins to turn brown, usually about eight to ten weeks after flowering. Don't braid the yellowing foliage; that isn't good for the plant. Cut back iris leaves that have developed spots.

EDIBLES

To have the baby lettuce leaves that are so popular—and so pricey—start snipping leaf lettuce when the plants reach about 6 inches high. Cut them with sharp scissors and leave about 1 inch at the base of the leaf on the plant so it will resprout. You will get several cuttings from each plant.

Depending on when you planted cauliflower, it may need blanching the first of the month. When small heads form, pull the outer leaves over the head and fasten them with string or a rubber band. This keeps the cauliflower white. It won't be necessary with self-blanching types of cauliflower, though.

If the soil is warm, mulch vegetable and herb plants with 2 to 4 inches of organic matter—straw, hay, shredded leaves, and so forth.

Pick peas when the pods are deep green and the peas are small- to medium-sized. They may not be ready till next month. Cut cabbage when the heads are good-sized but still firm, and the leaves are tight around the head.

HERE'S HOW

TO ACCLIMATE PLANTS TO THE OUTDOORS

- Move the plants to a shady spot first, on the porch if you have one.
- Then move them to a semi-shady spot that's not quite as protected from wind.
- Finally, move the plants to where they will stay for the summer.

HOUSEPLANTS

Many indoor gardeners like to let their houseplants vacation outdoors in the summertime. It's a matter of personal preference, but if you'd like to move your plants outside, wait till temperatures are consistently 60 degrees, even at night. Gradually get plants used to outdoor conditions—wind, rain, and much brighter light.

Remember that even shady spots outdoors are likely equal to medium or bright light indoors. An hour or two of filtered morning sun is fine for plants that like high light levels, but those that normally grow in medium or low light should be kept in shade.

Amaryllis and poinsettia plants may also be moved outdoors now, if you'd like. Poinsettias should be cut back and repotted. Don't do anything to amaryllis, which prefers to stay in the same pot for three or four years. Both will appreciate a few hours of morning sun.

When houseplants are outdoors, sometimes watering or rain causes soil to splash up on the undersides of leaves. To prevent this, cover the soil with a very thin mulch of aquarium gravel, decorative stones, pea gravel, or Spanish moss.

LAWNS

Remove sticks and trash from the lawn the day before you mow. Or maybe you can have the children take over this weekly job.

If your warm-season lawn has at least ½ inch of thatch, you should remove it now.

How often do you need to mow the grass? In spring, when rainfall is usually abundant and temperatures moderate, grass grows fast—especially if you've fertilized it. Sometimes it may need mowing twice a week instead of the usual once. The decision to mow should be made by the height of the grass, not by the day of the week. This time of year it's not always easy to follow the one-third rule; nevertheless, you should try to mow when the grass gets one-third taller rather than at the recommended mowing height and then remove only one-third of the grass blade. If you use that as your general guide most of the time, your lawn will improve.

PERENNIALS AND ORNAMENTAL GRASSES

Are all flower beds covered with about 3 inches of mulch? Be sure the mulch isn't piled up against the plants themselves, but starts 1 to 2 inches away from the stems.

Stake or support peonies if you haven't already. Earlier is better because it is easier when plants are small. Unsupported peony flowers—especially doubles—often end up falling over and getting muddy if it rains when they're in bloom.

Thin asters and garden phlox by removing some plants from the stand. This enables the remaining plants to receive more sun and helps avoid mildew problems.

Remove faded flowers from perennials and wildflowers that have already bloomed. Pinch back all or some of your bee balm, Shasta daisies, obedient plant, phlox, and spiderwort. This helps control the height and also—if you pinch some plants and not others—produces flowers over a longer period.

Pinch all stems of mums monthly between now and the middle of July. This ensures a more compact plant that blooms in the fall, not in the summer.

ROSES

Check climbing roses every ten days or so, and tie the canes to their supports. When flowers wilt and turn brown, cut them off. Not only can decaying blossoms attract insects, but the bush won't start growing a great crop of new blooms until the old ones are removed.

■ Some vines will need pruning in early to mid-May. Trim out dead or damaged stems and brown or yellow leaves. Then cut off the tips of a few stems to make the vine bush out.

SHRUBS

May is last call for pruning bridalwreath spirea, deutzia, flowering quince, forsythia, and mock orange, as well as azalea. If you prune these spring-flowering shrubs later than the end of May, you'll be lessening or eliminating next year's flowers.

To prune an overgrown forsythia each year for three years, cut one-third of the stems back to the ground. That preserves the shrub's attractive shape but makes it a more manageable size. Snap off faded blooms of lilacs, rhododendrons and mountain laurel. This should increase next year's bud count.

Each time a hedge has 3 to 4 inches of new growth, use hedge trimmers to shear the top and sides back to just about the place where you trimmed it the last time. Start at the bottom and work up so that the base is wider than the sides.

VINES AND GROUNDCOVERS

As soon as nighttime temperatures remain above 60 degrees Fahrenheit, move mandevilla, bougainvillea, allamanda, and other potted tropical vines back outdoors for the summer. Don't place them in full sun immediately. Instead, acclimate them (see page 102).

Pinch the stems of perennial vines so they will grow fuller and not just straight up. After wisteria blooms, cut back leafless shoots and shorten long

HERE'S HOW

TO PRUNE A ROSE AS YOU REMOVE OLD FLOWERS

Each time you cut a rose from the plant—whether to take it indoors or to remove it from the plant because it has faded—you're actually pruning. And how you do it makes a difference in how the bush grows and blooms. The correct procedure is simple:

• Make the cut ¼ inch above a cluster of five leaves that's facing the outside of the bush. This causes a dormant bud to break or begin growing outward. You want the new stem to go toward the outer portion of the bush so as not to crowd the interior, which can create favorable conditions for fungal diseases.

• Always make the cut at a 45-degree angle.

• Using white glue or shellac, seal any cuts that are ¼ inch in diameter or larger.

twining side branches. Remove any growth that's coming from below the graft union (a swollen area near the base) on a grafted vine.

Prune Carolina jessamine if needed. Cut back some of the stems near the bottom of the vine to encourage them to fill out. Prune and shape gold-flame spirea and trumpet honeysuckle after they stop blooming.

WATER GARDENS

If your fish don't seem hungry when you toss food into the pond, the reason may be that they're eating plenty of insects and larvae. Cut back on feeding frequency and amount. Keep the water garden tidy by removing damaged foliage and debris knocked into the water by storms.

WATER

ALL

Plants in containers need water more often than those planted in the yard, so feel the soil frequently and water them before it dries out completely. The larger the container, the longer it takes for the soil to dry. Plastic will hold moisture longer than clay

■ *Plants growing in containers will need watering more often than those planted in the ground. They'll also need more fertilizer since all that water washes nutrients out of the pot. At the height of the season, plan on daily watering and twice-monthly fertilizer.*

or terracotta. But once temperatures start to climb, all container-grown plants need frequent watering.

ANNUALS

For successful annuals, pay careful attention to watering in the early part of the growing season. Stick your finger 1 or 2 inches into the soil. If you don't feel moisture, water.

If you have spots in your yard that are difficult for you to water, consider planting annuals that can tolerate soil on the dry side once they've gotten established. These include celosia, cosmos, globe amaranth, moss rose, and sunflower.

BULBS

Any bulbs, corms, rhizomes, and tubers that were divided, moved, or planted this spring should be watered anytime this month that rainfall is less than ¾ to 1 inch weekly.

EDIBLES

All vegetables need 1 inch of rain weekly. When rain doesn't total that much, it's up to the gardener to supply the shortfall. Vegetables that need water, particularly when buds and fruits are being formed, include cucumber, melons, peas, and squash. Vegetables that need an even supply of water throughout their growing season are beets, carrots, eggplant, greens, peppers, radishes, and tomatoes.

HOUSEPLANTS

Houseplants that are outdoors need watering much more frequently than when they were indoors—especially those in 6-inch pots and smaller. Get in the habit of feeling the soil of your outdoor houseplants at least every other day. Or invest in a moisture meter and stick it into the soil of smaller plants every other day and big plants at least twice a week. Water when indicated.

PERENNIALS AND ORNAMENTAL GRASSES

All newly planted, divided, or transplanted perennials and ornamental grasses should be watered enough that their soil doesn't dry out—once or twice a week if there's no rain. Established perennials generally don't need much watering unless rain fails to fall for two or three weeks. There are exceptions, though: don't let plants that prefer moist soil (foxgloves, hardy begonia, and most ferns, for instance) dry out. Established ornamental grasses rarely need watering except in a drought.

ROSES

Now that new roses are growing well, see that the soil is kept moist. If you have just a few rosebushes, consider buying a bubbler to place on the end of your hose. Then you can put the hose at the base of the plant and the bubbler prevents water from getting on the foliage. It also allows the water to slowly penetrate the soil. If you can't find a bubbler attachment, look for a watering wand, which has many small holes in the head and lets you direct the water to the root system but not so that it splashes up on the leaves.

TREES

With newly planted trees, the rule is this: Keep the soil moist but not wet. Because the root system of a young tree is still small and can absorb only so much moisture at a time, it's best to water frequently—enough to thoroughly wet the rootball each time.

The rule is different for established trees (those that have been planted for more than a year). For bigger trees, apply larger amounts of water, but do it less frequently. That helps them develop deep root systems. For more information, see page 154.

VINES AND GROUNDCOVERS

A sprinkler is the easiest way to water a ground-cover bed. The first time you use one, set up clean tuna or small cat food tins in various areas of the groundcover and keep track of how long it takes the sprinkler to deliver 1 inch of water. The next time you turn the sprinkler on, you can set it on a timer or just note the time that you need to come back and turn it off.

Few established vines or groundcovers need watering unless there's a drought. But look for signs that a plant needs more moisture—dull foliage and leaves that turn yellow or fall off prematurely.

Tropical vines grown in pots like lots of water. Check their soil daily to make sure it doesn't dry out more than 1 or 2 inches deep.

FERTILIZE

ANNUALS

If you used a timed-release fertilizer when you planted, you won't have to worry about fertilizer for some time. If you applied a water-soluble plant food instead, use it again about every three weeks for plants in beds. Exceptions are plantings of cosmos, globe amaranth, and melampodium, which don't like much fertilizer. Use a water-soluble plant food on all container-grown annuals twice this month.

BULBS

Fertilize container-grown amaryllis bulbs outdoors about twice a month since they will need more frequent watering than when they were indoors, and that washes the nutrients from the soil. Use a water-soluble fertilizer made for blooming plants.

As you continue to plant summer-flowering bulbs, mix a slow-release fertilizer into their soil. For bulbs such as dahlias and cannas that were left in the ground over winter, spread the label-recommended amount of the fertilizer over the soil around the plants, if you didn't feed them in April. Place mulch on top and water. If you used a water-soluble fertilizer on cannas, glads, dahlias, or other summer-flowering bulbs last month (instead of a slow-release fertilizer), repeat the application this month.

Fertilize irises after they finish blooming. Don't fertilize any spring-flowering bulbs until fall.

EDIBLES

Fertilize vegetables at planting time, mixing granular 6-12-12, 10-10-10, or organic vegetable fertilizer with the soil. Side-dress corn with 6-12-12 or 10-10-10 when it reaches 6 inches high.

Fertilize rosebushes with a granular rose food after the first flush of blooms has faded. Apply the amount recommended on the label, starting in a spiral near the base of the plant and working outward to just beyond the ends of the canes. Then water well. If you applied a timed-release fertilizer to rosebushes last month, you may want to use a water-soluble fertilizer this month, after flowers fade.

SHRUBS

Those who fed their shrubs one-third of the recommended amount of granular 10-10-10 fertilizer the last weeks of March and April should finish the regimen by applying the last third at the end of the month. Spread the fertilizer in a spiral outward from the main trunk. To avoid burning, keep the fertilizer off the leaves or stems. (Wash it off quickly if it accidentally falls onto the shrub.) Water the soil after fertilizing.

With container-grown shrubs, homeowners have several choices when it comes to fertilizer. As noted in the Plant section for this month, a timed-release fertilizer that feeds all season is one option. You may also use a granular fertilizer this month, as you do with shrubs that are planted in the ground. Or you may use a water-soluble fertilizer every other week from now through the middle of July.

TREES

When you plant a tree (see pages 182–183), don't fertilize it. It won't need food until next February or March.

VINES AND GROUNDCOVERS

If you didn't fertilize the vine that you planted this spring, or if you haven't yet fertilized those vines planted in the past year, do so now. Use a slow-release or a granular fertilizer for vines and shrubs.

Exceptions: Very vigorous vines *never* need fertilizer. Trumpet creeper and wisteria are among these.

Apply a slow-release fertilizer to the soil in which young groundcovers are planted or spray a water-soluble fertilizer on the foliage, as well as the ground. Avoid using a granular fertilizer on groundcovers—it can burn the leaves.

WATER GARDENS

Insert fertilizer tablets into the containers of any new plants before placing the pots in the pond. Also fertilize hardy water lilies and lotuses that were planted last month and are already growing.

PROBLEM-SOLVE

ALL

Be aware that many insecticides, even organics, are toxic to bees. Read the label of the product you're planning to use; if it isn't safe around bees, apply it at dusk when bees are no longer active in the garden. Or choose another product.

EDIBLES

Aphids and whiteflies are common problems in the yard this time of year. If they turn up in the vegetable or herb garden, or on roses or shrubs, try hosing them off with water. Then, if necessary, spray with insecticidal soap. If whiteflies are a persistent problem, buy yellow sticky traps at the garden center and put them next to susceptible plants. The insects are attracted by the yellow color and get stuck in the goo.

If the first tomato blossoms aren't pollinated, you can do the job yourself. Gently but firmly tap the flower as soon as it is completely open.

Mexican bean beetles may become a problem on all types of beans, turning the leaves into clear skeletons. The beetles can be picked off by hand.

Don't be concerned when the first few squash blossoms fall off without producing any fruit. The early blossoms are usually male, and it's the female blossoms that produce the squash.

LAWNS

The grubs of Japanese beetles and June bugs are close to the surface of the soil twice a year—in May and in September. That's the time to get rid of as many as you can by treating the lawn. Check with your local Extension office for specific advice. If you've had severe problems with Japanese beetles in the past, consider spreading milky spore, an organic control that continues to work in the soil for up to fifteen years. It's most effective if you get your neighbors to treat their yards, too. Getting rid of the grubs helps prevent lawn damage and also reduces the number of beetles that will hatch and affect your garden all summer.

Dig dandelions out of your yard by hand or use a long-handled weeder. Be sure to get all of the long

Japanese beetles attack plants in the sun more than those in the shade. Never put up traps to ctach them. That only attracts them to your yard.

Spreading milky spore over your lawn and landscape may help deter Japanese beetles for the next decade or more.

taproot. If you aren't able to get to this as soon as the plants have bloomed, pick off all the flowers—that will prevent seeds being formed and scattering about.

PERENNIALS AND ORNAMENTAL GRASSES

Slugs are often a problem around hostas. See the Vines and Groundcovers section for control techniques.

Some spring wildflowers (such as trillium, Virginia bluebell, twinleaf, or hepatica) begin to look awful about now. Don't worry, this is normal—many native plants go dormant in the summer. (They're called ephemerals.) If possible, keep them watered during dry spells until the end of June; this is especially true during the first two years they're in your yard. But if one day you look and there's bare ground where a spring wildflower was, it's usually all right. Be careful, though, about planting something else in that area since you don't want to damage the native plant's roots.

ROSES

Japanese beetles may become a problem by the end of the month. They are very fond of roses—some roses seem to attract them more than others, but it varies from location to location. Pick them off by hand daily, and drop them in a jar of soapy water.

SHRUBS

If spring was wet, you may notice what appear to be hard green, brown, or white growths on your azaleas. These are galls. Remove them by hand and dispose of them away from the garden.

TREES

It's easy to overlook a few bagworms on arborvitae, hemlocks, Leyland cypress, and spruce trees. They're perfectly camouflaged. But once there are dozens, even hundreds of them, you notice. The most effective way to get rid of bagworms is to wait until dusk and pick them off by hand. Pick as many as you see, and then go back a few nights later. You'll probably find a few more that you missed in out-of-the-way spots. Continue this for a week or two, and you should get them all. But look over the affected plant occasionally in the next month or two to make sure the bagworms are all gone.

VINES AND GROUND COVERS

Why didn't my wisteria bloom? Wisteria is a beautiful vine, but not easy to grow. There are many reasons it may not have ever flowered. These include:

1.   The flower buds (usually formed in summer) were inadvertently pruned.

2.   The plant was overfertilized, especially with too much nitrogen (the first of the three numbers on the label of the fertilizer container). This usually causes lush leaf growth at the expense of flowers. In reasonably good soil, wisteria needs no fertilization.

3.   The flower buds are killed by low temperatures or late frosts.

4.   The vine isn't mature enough. Vines grown from seeds take many years to reach blooming stage. Grafted vines flower sooner.

If none of those causes are accurate with your wisteria, the usual remedy is to root prune the vine. Wait until after flowering, then with a spade cut vertically into the ground in a circle out from the plant but within the root zone.

If euonymus has scales (they look like tiny bumps on stems, branches, or leaves), spray with a light horticultural oil. It may be necessary to repeat the application in a few weeks.

Slugs and snails become a problem in ground cover plantings when spring weather has been wet. You'll see slime trails and large, ragged holes in the leaves. You can control them by:

- Picking the snails off by hand (after dark, with a flashlight).

- Putting out eaten grapefruit or orange halves (for the slugs to crawl under and you to gather up the next day and destroy).

- Placing saucers of water mixed with 1 teaspoon of yeast around the area (the slugs crawl in and drown). Beer also works, but it is more expensive.

- Applying slug bait. Until recently, many gardeners avoided this because it was toxic. But an organic product, Sluggo, which is just iron phosphate, is nontoxic to pets and wildlife. Ask at a garden center about this or a similar product.

If a newly planted clematis droops, the cause is usually clematis wilt. It tends to strike during a vine's first two years. Prune off all the

REASONS TREES DO NOT BLOOM

Why didn't my spring-flowering tree bloom this year?

1.   Not enough sun: Although some flowering trees are considered shade-tolerant, most require about half a day of sunlight to produce a good crop of blooms.

2.   Too much fertilizer: This may be a problem when trees are planted in lawns fertilized five times a year. Large amounts of fertilizer produce lots of leaf and shoot growth, but can diminish development of flower buds. Also, early fall fertilization can cause a tree not to go dormant before cold weather arrives—and therefore kill new growth.

3.   Pruning at the wrong time or incorrect pruning: Prune spring-flowering trees right after they've finished blooming. For summer-flowering trees, you may do the same, or wait until late winter.

4.   Diseases and insects: Note the symptoms or cut off an infected part and talk with a knowledgeable person at your favorite nursery about how to control the problem.

5.   Freeze damage: Late spring frosts may kill flower buds.

wilted stem—even if you don't reach good wood until you're below ground—and put the affected material in the trash. Quite often, the vine grows back from those underground roots it formed when you planted it deeply. If it doesn't, do *not* plant another clematis in the same spot.

WATER GARDENS

If fish in your pond munch up all the young submerged plants, you can buy plant protectors to place over the plants. These allow the plants to become established.

One morning you may wake up and find that you no longer have fish in your water garden—or you may find that the number of your fish is gradually diminishing. Blame wildlife predators such as raccoons, blue herons, turtles, and occasionally, a neighborhood cat. What can you do?

- Place a plastic net securely over the pond for several weeks.

- Although their effects aren't long-lasting, try noisemakers, scarecrows, and other devices sold to keep wildlife at bay.

- Remove large turtles to another home.

- Stack cinderblocks in several places in the pond to provide hiding places for the fish.

- If the problem is persistent, you could consider redigging the edges of the water garden. Ponds with edges that go straight down are less likely to have problems than those with shallow "shelves" built into the sides.

- Let the dog stay outside in the yard at night.

CARING FOR VINES

Now that vines planted this spring are beginning to grow and to climb, May is a good time to think about how to care for them.

1. Cut back the vine by one-third to one-half when planting it. This encourages faster growth and branching.

2. Help young vines reach their supports, if needed.

3. Regularly attach stems of climbers to their supports. The easiest fasteners are soft cloth, twine, and plastic-covered wire. Screw hooks and special masonry fasteners may be used on wood and brick.

4. Pinch the tips of shoots to encourage the vine to fill out.

INVASIVE WATER PLANTS

Beware of gift water plants. Accept all water lilies that a buddy is dividing and giving you, of course. But sometimes the plants that gardeners most readily share—because they have an abundance of them—are aggressive plants that grow quickly. Watch out for some of these. They can take over even a medium-sized water garden, or the area next to it, before you realize what's happening. These include:

- Horsetail (*Equisetum hyemale*)

- Duckweed (*Lemna minor*)

- Bamboo

- Chameleon plant (*Houttuynia cordata* 'Chamaeleon')

- Water hyacinth (*Eichhornia crassipes*)

ATTRACT BUTTERFLIES TO WATER GARDENS WITH PLANTS

These plants will attract butterflies to your water garden: cardinal flower (*Lobelia cardinalis*), water mint (*Mentha aquatica*), and water snowball (*Gymnocoronis spilanthoides*). Cardinal flower and water mint also attract hummingbirds.

June

Summer is in full swing, and so is gardening. Although there are plenty of garden-related things to think about and do this month, consider stopping and smelling the roses occasionally, rather than just pruning them. All you need is a hammock or comfortable lounge chair in which to occasionally rest and feast your eyes on how good your property looks. Sometimes we're all too caught up in making our yard look better and don't take any time to appreciate how great it—or, at least, portions of it—actually looks. Even if it doesn't look great yet, you can relax a little and plan ways to improve it in the future.

June is the month when we reluctantly bid goodbye to the pansies that have brightened the yard since fall. They've given us our money's worth, and more, but pansies don't perform well in heat, and the hot weather typically begins in earnest in June. But you can sow seeds of other popular annual flowers—marigolds or zinnias, for instance—outdoors where they will grow. It will take them a little longer to bloom than if you'd started the seeds indoors, but they will be wonderful late-summer replacements if needed or will just supply fresh flowers when others have succumbed to heat.

As bounty from the vegetable garden begins to show up on the dinner table, you'll be thrilled to know that you may be picking the first warm, ripe tomato in less than a month. And you can continue to plant warm-season crops such as eggplant, as long as you keep the young veggies well watered.

Roses will look wonderful this month. After enjoying old-fashioned and climbing roses that bloom just once a year, it's time to give them an annual pruning. Make sure you share some of the flowers with others. Or display them at a meal you've planned for friends. Another conversation starter when people are visiting your house is a water lily floating in a bowl of water. How to keep it open is a simple trick appreciated by any water gardener.

If you'd like free perennial plants—and who wouldn't?—take cuttings to root this month. Next year they'll start blooming.

PLAN

ALL

The best thing any homeowner can do at the beginning of summer is to go buy a large, comfortable hammock and suspend it between two big trees. When the temperature and humidity climb toward the stratosphere, or you're tired from watering or spreading pine straw, it's refreshing to be able to collapse into a hammock, grab a glass of lemonade, and enjoy the shade for a while.

All too often gardeners don't make time to truly appreciate the landscape that they've designed and nurtured. There's always one more little task, one or two weeds to pull, the hose to move from one side of the yard to another . . . the list can seem endless. Why should the neighbors be the only ones to enjoy the beauty your hard work has produced? Take time to enjoy the shade of your trees, the acrobatics of the squirrels jumping from branch to branch, the cardinals darting here and there among the limbs. Children instinctively know how to do this. They can sit and watch a line of ants for hours. But as we adults grow older, we often lose the ability to do nothing. Make a vow that this is the summer you slow down and notice what's going on in the natural world that surrounds you.

LAWNS

Did you know that your state's Extension service tests many different species and cultivars of grass? Often these are new ones that promise improvements over other grasses. Check with your local Extension agent to find out where grass trials are being held. These can be quite interesting to visit if you're not pleased with the grass you're currently growing.

ROSES

Cut a bouquet of roses and take it to cheer someone up or to say thank you. Then go to the library and check out a book about the history and lore of roses. It's fascinating.

PLANT

ANNUALS

Since they don't like heat, pansies will look bad by the end of the month. Realize that this happens every year, and replace them at the beginning of the month, when a wider variety of bedding plants is available than at the end of June.

It's not too late to plant any and all summer bedding plants this month. Visit a local nursery and add moss-lined hanging baskets of 'Wave' petunias to the porch and a wooden tub of coleus by the driveway, or plant a bed of salvia out by the mailbox to welcome guests and cheer the spirits of passersby.

BULBS

There's still time to plant dahlias, caladium, and gladioli. See page 72 for instructions. The dahlias and glads won't bloom until the end of summer, but that's not necessarily a bad thing, since few flowers except annuals are blooming at that time of year. It's nice to have fresh flowers in fall, and both glads and dahlias make excellent cut flowers to take indoors or to the office with you.

HERE'S HOW

TO PROPAGATE HERBS BY CUTTINGS

The herbs that are most easily propagated by cuttings are artemisia, bay, French tarragon, lavender, lemon balm, rosemary, rue, santolina, scented geraniums, and winter savory. Cut off 3 to 5 inches of new growth, strip off all but the top leaves, and dip the end of the cutting in a rooting hormone such as Rootone. Plant the cuttings in a flat or pot of moist potting mix. Place in the shade and keep the soil moist until the cuttings have rooted (three to four weeks, usually). Remove the rooted cuttings and pot them individually or plant them in the herb garden.

HOW TO PLANT SEEDS

1. Use a trowel to dig a row in the garden soil outside. Dig the row about one to two inches deep.

2. Sprinkle the seeds in the row according to spacing instructions on the seed package. Some seed packets will advise you to sow the seeds "thickly." That means to sprinkle a lot of seeds in one area because the seeds don't sprout consistently. You can always snip off seedlings at the soil line to make room if more seeds than you need sprout and grow too close together.

3. Sprinkle seed starting mix over the seeds. While you can cover seeds outdoors with regular garden soil, seeds sprout more easily when they're covered with the lightweight seed starting mix. After covering the seeds, water them. Do not let the soil dry out until you see the seeds starting to sprout. If the seeds dry out while they're sprouting, they'll die.

4. Label the rows where you've planted seeds. Seed leaves can look similar to one another when they're sprouting, and you don't want to forget what you planted, where.

TO PLANT ANNUALS FROM SEED OUTDOORS

Many annuals can be grown from seeds sown directly in the garden. This doesn't provide instant color, as bedding plants do, but it's inexpensive, it gives you a sense of accomplishment, and it's fun to do with children.

The easiest annuals to sow outdoors are those with fairly large seeds and quick germination and growth rates. Marigolds, sunflowers, and zinnias are ideal for your first try.

Prepare the soil just as you would for setting out bedding plants, but rake the surface so it's relatively smooth. See page 113 for directions.

Sow your flowers in rows or broadcast them—scatter the seeds about the whole area. When you sow in rows, it's easier to space them correctly, and you can tell which are weed seedlings and which are your annuals. But the look is more formal. When you broadcast seeds, you'll have to thin them, and it will be easy to confuse flowers and young weeds, but the appearance is informal. Experience is the best teacher in this case. To sow seeds outdoors:

1. Read the seed packet for recommended spacing and follow it.

2. Cover the seeds with an amount of soil to equal the diameter of the seed. Firm the soil (with a trowel or the back of a hoe) to ensure good contact between seeds and soil.

3. Gently water the area.

4. Keep the soil moist until most of the seeds germinate.

5. Gradually cut back on watering as the plants begin to grow.

6. Thin the flower bed—remove plants that are growing too thickly.

7. Fertilize with a water-soluble fertilizer after the plants have two sets of true leaves.

8. Remove weeds and then apply 2 inches of mulch.

EDIBLES

Plant sweet potato slips the first of the month if you haven't earlier (see page 96). To avoid disease problems, don't plant them where they grew last year. They take about four months to reach maturity. Continue planting beans, cucumbers, eggplant, melons, okra, pepper plants, pumpkins, Southern peas, summer squash, tomato plants, and zucchini.

You may also sow seeds of annual herbs such as basil, caraway, chervil, and dill where you want them to grow.

HOUSEPLANTS

Most cactuses don't need repotting more often than every three or four years. But if you have a cactus that has definitely outgrown its container, summer is a good time to repot it. Because this is a sticky job, you may want to recruit a friend or family member to help you.

1. Use a special potting mix made for cacti, or make your own by adding one part sand to two parts commercial potting soil.

2. Water the plant and moisten the potting mix the day before transplanting.

3. Buy thorn-proof gloves. (These are also good when you're working around roses.)

4. Fill a clay pot about half-full of potting mix.

5. For a large cactus, get three or four full-sized pages of newspaper and fold them into a strap. For a small cactus, use a pair of tongs.

6. Tighten the newspaper strap around the cactus, and use it to move the plant from the old container to the new. Or use the tongs.

7. Place the cactus at the same depth it grew before.

8. Fill in around the plant with soil.

9. Water thoroughly.

10. Place the plant in bright light, but no sun, for two weeks, then move it to a sunny location.

Continue repotting any houseplants that need it.

LAWNS

Sod and sprigs (see page 98) aren't the only ways to establish a new warm-season lawn. Zoysia is also available as plugs, which are small pieces of sod (including soil and roots). They establish a lawn more quickly than sprigs, but more slowly than sod. Plant them this month or from May until early July. Plugs can be placed anywhere from 6 to 12 inches apart, but the closer they are, the faster they will grow together.

PERENNIALS AND ORNAMENTAL GRASSES

It's all right to divide or transplant perennials in the first half of the month, if necessary. Cut them back by about one-half first. Keep the new plantings well watered. To increase your chance for success, rig up a way to keep the plants shaded for a week after dividing.

As plants begin to grow well, some crowding may occur in a perennial flower border that's several

HERE'S HOW

TO PROPAGATE FERNS

If you see brown or green spots in a regular pattern on the back of your fern fronds, don't panic. They're just spores, and you can use them to grow more ferns, if you like. It's a slow process, but it isn't difficult.

1. Cut off a frond covered with spores. Place it in an envelope or on a piece of paper (spore side down).

2. Collect the spores when they fall off the frond.

3. Fill a large pot or small flat with moist potting mix and sprinkle the spores over the mix.

4. Mist with water.

5. Cover the surface with a piece of glass or enclose the container in a plastic bag.

6. Place the container in a warm spot that receives bright light, but no sun. Outdoors is fine this time of year.

7. Keep an eye on the container and mist again if needed to keep the soil moist.

8. In a few months, you'll see something that looks like moss. This is an intermediate growth stage. Keep the soil moist.

9. Move the container back indoors in early September if you've started the spores outdoors.

10. When little ferns have developed two or three fronds, transplant them to individual pots.

years old. Remove some of the excess plants when the weather is moderate. Give them to friends, put them in pots (to be shared later or planted in a new bed in the fall) or transplant them to another

PLUG SPACING	NUMBER OF ZOYSIA PLUGS NEEDED PER 1000 SQ. FT.
6 inches	4,000
8 inches	2,250
12 inches	1,000

HERE'S HOW

TO PLANT GRASS PLUGS

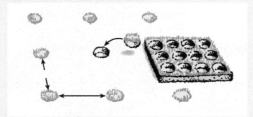

1. Follow steps 1 through 5 on page xx.

2. Using a plugger or trowel, dig holes in a checkerboard pattern 6, 8, or 12 inches apart.

3. Lightly water the plugs when they arrive, and keep in the shade those not being used.

4. Place plugs in the holes so that the bottoms of the grass blades are level with the ground.

5. Firm the soil around the plugs.

6. If you're planting just a few plugs, step on the newly planted plugs to make sure they come into contact with the soil. If you're planting an entire lawn, it's best to roll them instead.

7. Water.

8. Keep the area constantly moist for twelve to fourteen days, and then water regularly.

part of the garden right away, cutting the tops of the plants back by half. Continue to propagate perennials by taking stem or tip cuttings (see page 99) or by layering (below and page 132).

VINES AND GROUND COVERS

During the first part of June, you can still sow seeds of annual vines outdoors: black-eyed Susan vine, cardinal climber, climbing snapdragon (*Asarina scandens*), cypress vine, hyacinth bean, moonflower, morning glory, and sweet potato vine.

If you'd like to increase your stock of groundcover plants, it's easy:

- Some ground covers, such as bugleweed, English ivy, and wintercreeper, form roots along the stems. Cut off the tips of plants that have rooted and replant them where you need them. They'll need to be watered frequently until they settle in.

- Layering is a method of propagating that works on most perennial groundcovers—also vines—that have woody stems. In early summer or late spring, bend a stem over to the ground (if it isn't already growing horizontally). Make a ¼-inch cut or scrape a spot in the bottom surface of the stem. Cover the stem with rich soil, and weigh down the cutting. When new growth is apparent, cut the rooted cutting from the parent plant.

- Here's how to root cuttings of pachysandra, ivy, and clematis. Using a sharp knife or pruners and cutting at a 45-degree angle, take 4- to 6-inch cuttings. Remove the bottom leaves, dip the base of the stem in a rooting hormone, and insert it in a flat or pot of moistened peat moss, peat, and sand, or just commercial potting soil. This time of year it isn't necessary to cover the pots with plastic. Just keep the soil moist until the cuttings begin to grow.

CARE

ANNUALS AND PERENNIALS

Deadheading—pinching off faded flowers—makes a big difference in how your flowers perform.

Some annuals, such as Madagascar periwinkle, never need deadheading because the plants shed their dead blooms themselves. But many others—from geraniums to petunias to marigolds, and practically all perennials—should be deadheaded. That makes the plants and yard look better, of course. But removing dead flowers also keeps your annuals blooming nonstop and prevents perennials from forming seeds. Each time you walk by your flowers, take a few moments to snap off old flower heads.

BULBS

As dahlias grow, continue to add enough soil to the holes in which the tubers were planted so that you barely cover the new growth each time. Do this until the soil in the hole reaches the level of the ground around it, then stop. Once the hole is filled with soil, water well and add 2 to 3 inches of mulch on top.

Tie dahlias and other tall bulbs such as lilies to stakes as they grow taller. Sometimes staking is a

Neaten the appearance of bearded irises by cutting ratty-looking foliage back to a fan shape about four inches high. Remove excess from the garden.

chore we tend to postpone, but it's important to get it done. Summer thunderstorms can quickly topple tall plants and snap their stems.

The best time to pick flowers is first thing in the morning. They'll stay fresher. With glads, wait till the second floret has opened before cutting the stalk.

When bearded iris foliage begins to look bad, cut it back in a fan shape about 4 to 6 inches high. If you don't get to it, it doesn't make much difference to the plant, but your garden does look neater if you get rid of the damaged tips of the leaves. When cutting gladiolus flowers, leave as much foliage as possible to help the plants grow more corms by fall.

EDIBLES

Pick peas and harvest broccoli, cabbage, carrots, and other cool-season crops regularly. Once hot

Acid soil produces blue hydrangea flowers, and alkaline soil causes pink blooms. But you can treat the soil to change that.

HOW TO STAKE PLANTS

1 Place several stakes in and around the plant clump to serve as a framework and as individual supports. If one branch is particularly large and floppy, put one of the stakes next to it, about an inch away from the plant stem.

2 Start creating a web of string between the stakes. Try to pull the string as taut as possible between stakes, without bending the stakes. You can create as many crisscrossing strings as you'd like. The more string, the more support for the plants growing through the web.

weather is here to stay, they will rapidly deteriorate. Harvest garlic when the majority of the leaves have turned yellow.

Mulch all garden plants with 2 to 4 inches of organic material—anything from pine straw or cocoa hulls in the herb garden to weed-free straw in the vegetable plot. Remove weeds and water the soil deeply before mulching. One trick to get more moisture-retention from your mulch is to water the soil, lay two or three sheets of newspaper on top, water the paper, and then spread your usual mulch on top.

Regularly tie tomatoes to stakes or other supports. Put netting over peach, cherry, and other fruit trees if birds are usually a problem.

When growing tomatoes on stakes, pinch out the suckers that develop between the main stem and branches since they grow into branches on their own and make the plant too heavy on the stakes. These suckers can be used to start a fall crop of tomatoes. Root them as explained in the Plant section (page 112). (It's fine to leave the suckers in place if your tomatoes are caged, rather than staked.)

HOUSEPLANTS

During dry spells, occasionally hose down outdoor houseplants with a light mist to keep their leaves clean. Do this in the morning so the foliage will dry before dark. Consider giving plants inside the house a shower every few months. Clean plants grow better.

A poinsettia grows quite large outdoors (the ones you buy at Christmas have been treated with a growth retardant), so you may want or need to cut it back some this month or next. Wear rubber gloves so the white sap doesn't irritate your skin.

LAWNS

Let the grass be your guide to how often to mow. If temperatures have been high and rainfall low, your grass may not be growing much. But if June sees plenty of rain and moderate temperatures, your grass could be growing rapidly and need frequent cutting.

PERENNIALS AND ORNAMENTAL GRASSES

If you'd like to increase your collection of coreopsis, cut or pinch the mature seedheads off and scatter them on top of the soil wherever you'd like the new plants. They grow easily.

Pinch back mums once this month so the plants don't grow too large and to encourage them to develop a compact shape.

Prune back spring-flowering perennials and wildflowers that look ratty. Cut or pinch off any yellow or brown foliage.

ROSES

Remove flowers when they fade. Don't delay too long, because it slows down the next round of blooms.

Would you like larger flowers on your grandiflora or floribunda roses? Pinch off the center bud in a flower cluster, and the two side buds will put on quite a show.

Old garden roses that bloom once a year (in May or June, depending on where you live) are pruned more like shrubs than like hybrid tea roses. Remove any dead or diseased wood, as well as suckers, whenever you see them. After they flower, cut the main canes back lightly, if needed to shape the bush. Once the rose is four or five years old, begin cutting one-fourth of the oldest canes back to the ground every year.

After flowering is finished, lightly prune climbing roses that produce just a single flush of blooms each year, to remove unproductive and too-small canes. Don't start pruning climbers or ramblers—except to remove damage—until they're four years old.

SHRUBS

You probably know that the color of some bigleaf hydrangea flowers depends on the pH (acidity or alkalinity) of the soil in which the shrub grows. Low pH, which indicates acidity (6.5 and lower), produces blue flowers. High pH, which indicates alkalinity (7.0 and above), produces pink flowers.

The problem comes when your soil's pH is in the middle and the flowers don't have a distinct blue or pink cast. You can change that by adding dolomitic lime to the soil to make it more alkaline or aluminum sulfate (soil sulfur is another choice) to make it more acidic. Ask at a nursery about this technique. There are also several hydrangeas that produce flowers that stay pink, no matter what your soil is like.

Trim hedges when shrubs have 3 to 4 inches of new growth. If you have a short hedge that consists of broadleaf evergreens (Japanese holly or boxwood, for example), you'll get better results with hand pruners than with an electric trimmer, since the pruners won't cut the leaves in half.

■ *Prune a hedge each time it produces four inches of new growth. Prune a hedge so it's wider at the bottom than the top.*

TREES

Prune needled evergreen trees this month by using hand pruners to cut back by half the candles (new growth) on the top and sides of the tree. The result is a more compact shape. Always make these cuts at a 45-degree angle.

If, during cold weather, you put off pruning trees that bleed (exude sap) when they're pruned in winter, June is the time to tackle them. These include elm, dogwood, golden chain tree, maple, walnut, river birch, and yellowwood.

VINES AND GROUNDCOVERS

Keep an eye on annual vines as they begin to grow, and guide them to the trellis. One way to do this is to place a string or small bamboo stake from the vine to the support when you plant. Otherwise, just do it by hand.

If one of a vine's holdfasts or aerial roots comes loose from its support, it will not reconnect. If that happens, cut it off above a bud that's below the stem that has become unattached. It will grow and reattach.

Very vigorous vines may need to be cut back several times during the growing season to keep them inbounds. Don't let them get away from you.

Pinch back the tips of annual vines to make them bushier.

WATER GARDENS

If the water in your pond is 1 inch below normal, very slowly add more. A flexible liner that's exposed to sunlight because it's not covered with water has a shorter life.

Trim back plants to keep one-third of the water garden's surface open. Having no more than two-thirds of the water covered allows built-up gases to escape from the water and beneficial oxygen to get into it.

It's time to test your water and renew your organic mosquito larvae control. Feed fish sparingly.

Remove damaged, browning, or yellowish leaves whenever they appear on plants in water gardens.

■ *Don't overcrowd the water garden with too many plants. Leave at least one-third of the surface clear to allow plants to grow and look better.*

Also deadhead regularly—cutting off dying or spent flowers close to the crown. But if you want to have those interesting brown lotus pods to use later in dried arrangements, don't remove spent lotus flowers.

WATER

BULBS

Cannas, dahlias, and elephant ears grow best with plenty of water. Make sure the soil they're planted in doesn't dry out.

Gladiolus and blackberry lily like to be watered when rainfall is less than 1 inch a week. If you don't have a rain gauge so you can be certain of how much rain your yard really received, lift the mulch and stick your index finger several inches into the soil. If you don't feel dampness 2 or 3 inches down, water is probably needed.

Plants in containers need watering much more often than those planted in flower beds. Depending on the size of the pot, and whether you used a water-holding polymer, it may be necessary to water container-grown bulbs every other day or even daily. Water in the morning, if possible, so the foliage won't stay wet overnight.

DIVIDING WATER LILIES

If you weren't able to get water lilies divided in the spring, and all of a sudden you notice they're not blooming as much as they once did, it's still possible to divide and replant them now or anytime during the summer. You'll miss out on a few weeks of flowering as plants recover, but you should be able to skip dividing next year, which will give you something to look forward to.

■ *Use sprinklers to water the lawn early in the day to avoid excess evaporation. Also watch and move the sprinkler if its water pattern escapes into streets, driveway, and paths, wasting money and water.*

Water dahlias at the base of the plants to help prevent mildew and other fungal diseases.

EDIBLES

An old-fashioned way to water the larger plants in the vegetable garden is still effective. Wash plastic milk jugs and then, using a nail, poke holes in the sides of them. Bury the jugs up to their necks in the soil next to plants (this works best for individual plants, such as tomatoes and squash, rather than row crops such as beans). Fill the jugs with water, or water mixed with a soluble fertilizer, and replace the cap. The water drains out slowly near the plants' roots.

Check a couple of times a week to see if you need to add more water to the jugs. Typically each plant of cucumber, eggplant, melons, peppers, and squash needs 1½ gallons of water per week. Give tomato plants about 2½ gallons. Start with these figures and adjust according to your soil, the amount of rainfall, the temperature, and the size of the plants. You may find that some plants need two or three times these amounts in the hottest part of summer, others only half when they're small.

HOUSEPLANTS

If bromeliads are outdoors, you may need to pour water in their cups daily or every other day.

LAWNS

The amount of water your lawn needs depends upon:

- Recent rainfall—or the lack thereof

- The type of soil in your yard (Clay holds more moisture than sandy or rocky soil.)

- The type of grass you're growing (Some are thirstier than others.)

- Whether the grass is in the sun or in the shade

- Whether the area is sloped or level

- The temperature and humidity

To figure out how long you need to leave your sprinkler on to wet the soil to the desired depth,

TO TELL WHETHER YOUR LAWN NEEDS WATER

- The grass isn't as green as usual or has a grayish cast.

- When you walk on it, your footprints remain.

- The grass blades fold up vertically.

How often you water isn't as important as *how* you water. In order to develop deep roots (which help grass withstand heat, cold, and drought), grass should be watered slowly and enough to wet the soil 6 to 8 inches deep. Watering lightly but more frequently causes grass to develop shallow roots, which aren't drought proof.

set out clean tuna or cat food tins (or aluminum pie plates) at intervals around the area to be watered. Let the sprinkler run for thirty minutes. Then measure how much water is in the containers. That will tell you how long you have to run the sprinkler to give your grass the needed 1 to 1½ inches of water each time. Here are some water-saving tips:

- Get rid of weeds, which compete with grass for the available moisture.

- Increase the mowing height. Taller grass shades the soil and conserves water.

- Water early—before 8:00 a.m.—to avoid excess evaporation.

- Dethatch the lawn if the thatch layer is ½ inch thick or thicker.

- Go easy on fertilizing, which causes grass to grow faster and use more water.

PERENNIALS AND ORNAMENTAL GRASSES

Gardeners usually think of daylilies as plants that need very little watering. And it's true. Still, like other plants, they bloom better if watered when rainfall has been lacking. The one time you definitely want to water daylilies is after rebloomers finish their first flowering. Water weekly if rainfall isn't regular, so the reblooming buds form.

ROSES

As temperatures climb in June, monitor the soil around your roses to see that it doesn't get too dry. Roses need a great deal of water and perform much better when they get it. Water early in the day, and be sure to keep the water off the foliage.

SHRUBS

As temperatures rise, shrubs are more likely to need occasional watering if rainfall doesn't measure 1 inch per week. Many mature shrubs can go several weeks without receiving moisture, but some can't—and these are the ones that should be watered first if there are no water restrictions. Which shrubs are most vulnerable to lack of moisture?

- Shrubs planted in the past year (check them twice weekly)

- Shallow-rooted shrubs (such as azalea, pieris, and hydrangea)

- Shrubs that are developing fall berries or flowers for next spring

- Plants that need constantly moist soil

The mature shrubs most likely to need supplemental watering during summer dry spells are: aucuba, beautyberry, butterfly bush, camellia, evergreen azalea, fothergilla, redvein enkianthus, hydrangea, leucothoe, pieris, rhododendron, summersweet, and witch hazel.

TREES

When there's been no significant rainfall within a week, water trees that you've planted in the past year. Those set out in the past six months may need watering twice or more a week, depending on the type of soil, the temperature, the type of tree, its size, and whether the tree is growing in full sun or partial shade.

FERTILIZE

ANNUALS

Continue regular fertilizing about once a month (with a granular or water-soluble product) for annuals in flower beds and once a week (with a liquid) for container plants. If you used a timed-release fertilizer at planting time, you can skip additional fertilizer for beds and borders. But because frequent watering washes nutrients out of hanging baskets and pots, feed them twice monthly with a water-soluble plant food for flowering plants.

EDIBLES

Lightly fertilize eggplant, peppers, and tomatoes after they set their first fruits.

HOUSEPLANTS

Houseplants indoors and out that are actively growing should be fertilized about every four to five weeks if you use a water-soluble or liquid plant food. Although those in the yard or on an outside porch are being watered more frequently than those indoors—and therefore losing more nutrients—the extra light and fresh air outdoors compensate for the difference. Don't overfertilize. Not only will it cause too-quick growth that isn't good for the plants, it also causes them to outgrow the spots you have for them in the house.

Plants in low-light situations—peace lilies in bathrooms without windows, for instance—may not need fertilizing each month, because they probably aren't growing much. Every other month may be sufficient. Don't try to force growth by fertilizing too much. Without good light, the new growth will be spindly and unattractive.

LAWNS

On June 1, spread 1 pound of nitrogen over bermudagrass and zoysia lawns. See the chart on page 84 to determine how many pounds of various fertilizers it takes to equal 1 pound of nitrogen. Apply the fertilizer when the lawn is dry. The best time is just before rain is forecast. Otherwise, you need to water the fertilizer into the soil after you've applied it.

Do not fertilize cool-season lawns during the summer. High temperatures can burn fertilized grass, and fertilizer stimulates the growth of crabgrass and other weeds in hot weather.

After they finish blooming, fertilize roses that flower just once yearly. Fertilize them first in the spring and then once or twice more, lightly, between June and September with a balanced granular fertilizer, such as 10-10-10, or with an organic fertilizer such as Rosetone or Mill's Magic Rose Mix. Or you can fertilize them once with a timed-release fertilizer. That will help them grow strong stems, which will produce next year's blooms.

■ *Wait to fertilize warm-season lawns such as Bermuda and zoysia until after the weather has warmed up. June is ideal. Apply evenly when the ground is dry, then water in.*

WATER GARDENS

Feed plants more frequently. When air temperature is 75 degrees Fahrenheit or below, fertilize water lilies once a month using special water garden fertilizer tablets. Once temperatures head higher than 75 degrees, many experts recommend that you feed twice a month. Fertilize lotuses twice a month throughout the growing season.

PROBLEM-SOLVE

ALL

Do not put up traps to attract Japanese beetles. True, the traps may lure these pests away from your roses and crapemyrtles, but they will attract many more of the pests to your yard than would have come otherwise. And while many are caught in the traps, plenty of others that aren't caught lay eggs in your yard, which stay over winter in your lawn or soil as grubs and then hatch the next spring to plague you again. Handpick Japanese beetles and drop them in a jar of water.

Weeds are no one's favorite subject, but it's easier to remove them when they're young than after they've grown larger and have more extensive root systems. Weeding also goes faster after a soil-soaking rain.

BULBS

If newly emerging leaves on cannas are distorted or won't unfurl, this is a sign of canna leaf rollers. Cut off the affected foliage and spray remaining leaves with Bt, an organic control. Jot a reminder in your garden notebook to clean up all canna foliage from the ground in fall so no leaf roller caterpillars will overwinter to plague the plants again next year.

Aphids are fond of new gladiolus foliage. Wash them off with a hose. If that doesn't clear up the infestation, spray with insecticidal soap at three-day intervals. However, don't spray in the hottest part of the day or when the sun is shining on the plant.

EDIBLES

A leathery patch on the end of tomatoes is a symptom of blossom-end rot. It occurs after too much rain (or watering) followed by a dry spell. Remove the affected fruit and toss it away. Try to provide a more even moisture supply in the future. Next spring, two months before planting tomatoes, apply lime where tomatoes will grow. That helps prevent blossom-end rot. So does using 6-12-12 fertilizer instead of 10-10-10.

HERE'S HOW

TO WATER HOUSEPLANTS

Help! My houseplant needs watering every day!

It could be because it's very small and has an immature root system or doesn't have much soil from which to draw water. Or the plant is potbound and needs repotting (see page XX). But the most common cause is that the soil has been allowed to completely dry out on some occasion, and now the water runs right through; it isn't absorbed. There are two ways of overcoming this:

1. Place a small- or medium-sized plant in a bucket or sink of tepid water that's deeper than the container is tall. Hold the pot under the water until the bubbling stops.

2. For a large plant, add two drops of a mild dishwashing liquid (such as Ivory) to 1 gallon of tepid water. Pour the water slowly over the soil, trying to stay away from the edge where the soil has pulled away from the pot (otherwise the water will go directly to the saucer). Do the same thing the next two or three times the plant needs watering. (The dishwashing liquid helps the soil absorb the water.)

3. Once the soil has been thoroughly moistened, don't let it dry out completely again.

HERE'S HOW

TO HARVEST HERBS

The best time to harvest herbs is just before they bloom, because their essential oils are strongest then.

Cut herbs by midmorning (when there's no dew on the leaves). Don't cut more than one-fourth or one-third of the plant, especially in very hot weather. Avoid harvesting herbs in rainy weather.

Rinse briefly in cold water, if needed, and let them air dry. Place in a plastic bag and refrigerate until dinnertime. Do not refrigerate basil, though. It will turn brown.

There are several methods of freezing herbs:

- Rinse them briefly and pat dry. Strip the leaves from the stems. Chop the leaves in a food processor, mix with stock or water, and freeze in ice cube trays. Add to soups or stews in place of other liquid.

- Rinse briefly, pat dry, and strip leaves from stems. Chop the leaves in a food processor, gradually adding about ½ cup oil for each 2 cups of herbs. Spoon into small containers and freeze. Use as the oil portion of a salad dressing or marinade, or use to sauté meat.

- Rinse and dry herbs; remove the leaves from the stems, and place them in a small plastic container with a lid. Fill the container as full as possible, and place it in the freezer.

- See page 128 for tips on drying herbs.

HOUSEPLANTS

Keep an eye on houseplants that are summering outdoors. They may be knocked over by wind, thunderstorms, or dogs. Their leaves may be nibbled by cats or insects. If you're in the habit of checking them every day or two, though, the damage will usually be negligible because you catch and correct the problem in time. Sometimes, if wildlife is troublesome, moving a plant to a different location—or up off the ground—can help. Other times you need to build a temporary barrier of chicken wire or hardware cloth.

PERENNIALS

Prevent the spread of mildew by increasing air circulation among the plants and picking off infested leaves the minute the first few show the telltale white blush. Avoid using sprinklers or other overhead watering equipment around plants susceptible to mildew. If the infestation gets too bad, cut the plants back and consider planting more mildew-resistant cultivars next year. If you can't bring yourself to replace mildew-prone plants, you may want to transplant them to the back of the border so their condition won't be as noticeable.

ROSES

Spider mites may attack rose foliage in hot, dry weather. The leaves will appear speckled, spotted, or bronzed. Try spraying with insecticidal soap or light horticultural oil. Ladybugs, lacewings, and predatory insects also control mites.

SHRUBS

If bermudagrass grows over into shrub beds, try pulling it out by hand. If you spend ten minutes early in the morning weeding, it won't be a burden.

TREES

To control woolly adelgids on hemlocks, spray the trees twice a year with horticultural oil—regular horticultural oil in cool weather and light oil ("sun oil") in summer. The first spraying of the organic oil comes this month. The second one can take place from October through March.

People in our area typically expect July to be a hot month, but it isn't always. What you do know is that it will produce high humidity—and a wonderful display of beauty and bright color from annual and perennial plants and a few flowering shrubs and trees that don't mind the heat or humidity.

So it's a good month to look closer at others' yards and at professional gardens, including university test gardens. They're filled with ideas that you can use, and it's instructive to see how new varieties or cultivars of plants are coping with current weather conditions. (If it's especially hot, make a note of their names because plants that laugh at heat are valuable in home gardens. They make it possible for you to visit other gardens and return home, knowing that your landscape will look as good as it did when you left. Test gardens—usually at universities and seed companies' headquarters—often include the latest vegetables too. Now, just as your long-anticipated vegetable garden is beginning to produce well, it's time to start thinking about a fall garden, so it would be helpful to see what the experts are growing that you haven't.

If weather is moderate instead of steamy, you can continue to plant annuals early this month; maybe add a new container or two to the porch or patio. You can also continue succession planting in the vegetable garden—replacing a crop that's been harvested with a new planting—and install sod of a warm-season grass such as zoysia or bermuda. And watering is a constant activity in the garden this month—from keeping the soil moist in containers of all sizes to making sure that veggies, annuals, and newly planted shrubs or trees have enough water to keep them growing through the heat and bright sun.

But when temps and humidity levels reach for the stratosphere, pull up a chair in the shade and chill out by the water garden. Is there anything that makes you feel cooler and more peaceful than listening to the sound of water? That's when you enjoy the pleasures of gardening. That's when you're delighted that you undertook the various chores that it took to bring the water garden—and plants surrounding it—to completion.

PLAN

ALL

Get out the camera and take lots of photographs. First of all, shoot your yard and what you planted—even if it doesn't look quite as good as you'd hoped. (This step can help you improve next year.) But also slip your camera into your pocket or purse so you can record ideas when you visit public gardens or see a commercial landscape that you really like. It's much easier to remember what impressed you if you have a photo to look at.

BULBS

Are you adding to the list of spring-flowering bulbs you'd like to plant in fall? Even if you plan to buy bulbs from a local nursery, where you can see exactly what you're getting, it's fun to read bulb catalogs. Place your lawn chair in a shady spot on a hot July weekend, and spend some time reading through a couple of bulb catalogs, marking the plants you like.

EDIBLES

If you want to grow a fall vegetable garden, begin planning now.

1. Think about varieties—some grow better in the spring and some in the fall. Consider how long it takes a particular variety to reach maturity (this information is available on seed packets and in catalogs. Because fall days may be cool, add ten days to that number.

2. See page 229 for the average first frost in your area (or check with your local Extension service if you live at a higher elevation than most of your county). All warm-season vegetables (beans, cucumbers, and so forth) will need to reach maturity at least two weeks before frost. Crops that don't mind some cold weather (broccoli, carrots, cabbage, cauliflower, collards, kale, kohlrabi, mustard, radish, spinach, turnip greens) can mature about two weeks after the average first frost date.

3. To determine the last possible planting date for warm-season vegetables, subtract the number of days to maturity (don't forget to add ten

HERE'S HOW

TO DRY HERBS

1. Rinse herbs briefly and pat dry.

2. The best way to dry herbs is on a screen. With very small herbs or seedheads, cover the screen with paper towels. (Leave basil leaves whole, and place them between paper towels.) Place the screen indoors in a well-ventilated place. (Never dry herbs outdoors in the sun.) Stir the herbs with your hands three or four times daily so they'll dry more evenly. Complete drying takes from three days to a week.

3. If drying herbs in a microwave, use the lowest power setting. Place herbs on a paper towel or paper plate and cover with a paper towel. Start with one minute and see what results you get. Increase or decrease time by a few seconds as needed for the next batch. If herbs turn brown, they've been dried too long. Parsley and chives often dry well in the microwave.

4. Herbs for craft use are often air dried by tying them into bunches and hanging them upside down in a warm, dry spot for one to two weeks. (This isn't recommended for herbs you plan to use for cooking; they can get dusty, and it's often difficult to separate the leaves and stems.)

5. A really easy trick, if you have a frost-free refrigerator, is to place herbs in a single layer on a paper towel in the fridge. They'll dry in 24 hours.

days) from the date of two weeks before the first frost. For cool-season vegetables, subtract the number of days to maturity (plus ten) to find the date two weeks after the average first frost.

LAWNS

Avoid water runoff. If you find that when you water your lawn, you're also watering the street, the driveway, and the front walk, you may just need to position your sprinkler more carefully. But sometimes the soil can't absorb the water at the rate it's receiving it, and the water just runs off. If you find this is happening, turn the sprinkler off for fifteen minutes, then on for half an hour—or whatever combination of times works over a period of a couple of hours to avoid runoff and wet the soil deeply.

PERENNIALS AND ORNAMENTAL GRASSES

Keep notes of those periods when no perennials are in bloom. Fill in the gaps in the fall or next year.

Visit good gardeners and public gardens to see how others' plants cope with the heat and humidity. Jot down the names of the plants that look good, and then look them up in this book or in the *Tennessee and Kentucky Garden Guide* to see whether they'll perform well in your yard's conditions too.

Flower beds and borders aren't the only places to grow perennials and ornamental grasses. If you need more places for these delightful plants, consider placing them in a shrub border or a rock garden, or beside a water garden or pond. Shade lovers are right at home in a woodland garden.

ROSES

Are you happy with how your roses have performed so far this year? Take time to sit on the screened porch in sight of the rosebushes and record your impressions in your garden notebook—the good, the not-so-good, and what you'd like to do differently next year. If you have any unsolved rose problems, now's the time to track down one of your area's consulting rosarians. These are local experts who give free advice about rose selection and growing.

Before you head out on vacation, check the website of All-America Rose Selections (http://www.rose.org) for a list of more than 130 accredited public rose gardens around the country. They're well worth visiting, because they contain such a wide variety of roses, including the latest award winners. You can see for yourself how tall and wide various roses get—how the flowers really look (not just in a photo)—and you get to sniff the fragrance for yourself, which is much better than reading about it.

If you like fragrant roses, they're becoming more common, thank goodness. But rose scents vary greatly—from spicy to sort of lemony to musk. Once you learn your favorites, begin to look for more roses whose fragrance is described that way in catalogs and books.

VINES AND GROUNDCOVERS

Is July a vacation month in your household? Since you know it's going to be hot, and you have no way of telling how much rain will fall, plan to water all your vines and ground covers a day or so before you leave (unless they're already wet from rain). That should hold them for absences of up to two weeks.

WATER GARDENS

When the temperature and the humidity levels are both headed for the stratosphere, no one wants to work in the garden. So don't. Relax beside your water garden and read a book—about water gardening, what else? It's a great way to plan ahead for next year.

PLANT

ANNUALS

Zinnias are among the easiest flowers to grow from seed, and certain types of zinnias make excellent cut flowers to take indoors for arrangements. ('Cut and Come Again' is one variety that's tried-and-true.) But zinnias have a big fault—they mildew easily in times of high humidity or frequent rains. One way to prevent mildew problems is to grow the flowers for cutting. Prepare the soil, sow ten to fifteen seeds, and three weeks later, sow more.

Cut the flowers soon after they bloom—in about four to six weeks. (That is usually before mildew has taken hold.) At the same time, make another small sowing of zinnia seeds. Space all zinnias so there's room for air circulation between the plants, and don't let water get on the plants' leaves. Small flowered "star zinnias" (*Zinnia angustifolia*) are very mildew resistant.

BULBS

You can still plant dahlia tubers the first week of the month, but obviously those planted this late won't produce as many blooms as they would have if planted earlier. Still, growers who are aiming for fall flower shows do plant late. It depends on your perspective.

All through the month, it's fine to continue planting small dahlias sold as bedding plants, since they will already be in bloom. Since all dahlias stand up

well to hot weather, they're an excellent choice to add to any flower bed that looks a bit sparse. They also do well in containers.

Caladiums already started into growth at the nursery may be added to beds or containers in shady locations. The same is true for blackberry lilies in sunny spots.

Plant spider lily (aka naked lady, surprise lily, Resurrection lily) bulbs when they become available. Remember that they're slow to become established, so don't expect too much the first year.

EDIBLES

As one vegetable crop finishes bearing, pull it up and plant another—some pattypan squash where beans have finished bearing or cucumbers where English peas grew. This lets you grow more

Watch out for mildew on some zinnias, especially in wet years. It helps to space the zinnias so there's room for air to circulate among the plants, or cut the flowers and bring them indoors soon after they bloom and sow another crop, which will quickly bloom.

TO DIVIDE BEARDED IRISES

Mid- to late July is the time to divide bearded irises, if they need it (usually every three to five years).

1. Cut the leaves in a fan shape 6 inches high. This helps prevent leaf dieback and also wind damage on newly planted rhizomes that haven't yet developed deep root systems.

2. Lift the clump with a spading fork and wash the dirt from the rhizomes with a hose.

3. Remove any part of a rhizome that's diseased, damaged, or soft. (The problem area will be dark brown or black.)

4. Using a sharp knife, cut the rhizomes into smaller pieces, each with an eye or bud.

5. Cut away and discard older growth, which won't bloom any longer.

6. Because of many fungal problems affecting irises, consider soaking the rhizome briefly in a fungicide solution or dusting it with sulfur. (Don't use sulfur when temperatures are above 89 degrees Fahrenheit.) Some gardeners mix one part liquid bleach to nine parts water and quickly dip the rhizome in the solution.

7. Replant the rhizome sections close to the surface of the soil. See page XX for planting directions. They may need some support to stay upright until new roots and growth have taken place.

8. Water well.

vegetables on less land and gives you a harvest that's more evenly spread out through the summer.

The first of July isn't too late to plant seeds of black-eyed peas or other Southern peas that mature in sixty days or fewer. No fertilizer is needed.

Indoors, you may want to start seeds of cabbage, cauliflower, and broccoli. Seeds grow poorly outside this time of year. See page 38 for tips on starting seeds.

HOUSEPLANTS

Repot houseplants anytime this month. You may also want to take cuttings (pages 97 and 163) or divide overgrown plants (page 163). July is a good time to do any of this because temperatures are warm and the plants are actively growing and will respond well.

If you took cuttings of English, grape, or Swedish ivy; heart-leaf philodendron; pothos; or wandering Jew, why not combine several cuttings in a hanging basket? Very likely you have a few of those green plastic baskets left over from previous years' purchases of petunias and other trailing annuals for the garden. Hanging baskets of houseplants are just as nice as those of annual flowers. You could place them on a screened porch or shady deck during the rest of the summer and then take them indoors in fall. By September, you'll find that those tiny rooted cuttings have grown into full plants. Repot them individually if you like.

Another way to handle vining houseplants is to plant them in a good-sized (10 or more inches in diameter) container and let them grow up a support. Cuttings root fast outdoors in the heat of July. Just keep them away from sun.

LAWNS

If you get it done before the end of the July, you can still install or renovate a new bermudagrass or zoysia lawn by sodding, sprigging, or plugging. (See directions on page 98.) This isn't an

■ *Try a basket of annuals and grow it indoors in good light or outside in a shady spot. Try to include at least one trailing plant that will trail over the edges and add interest to the sides of the basket and look good from beneath.*

ideal month, since it can be very hot and dry. But it can work if you do all the following:

- Keep the sod moist as you work. Fertilize bi-weekly to push growth.

- Don't let the new grass dry out even momentarily for two weeks.

- Provide 1 to 1½ inches of water to the lawn weekly until the end of September (provided rainfall doesn't do it for you).

PERENNIALS AND ORNAMENTAL GRASSES

Dianthus is easily propagated by layering. Move back the mulch, and place a mixture of rich topsoil and sand on the ground next to the plant to be propagated. Choose a stem that has no flowers or buds on it and—leaving it attached to the plant—strip off the bottom foliage (keep four or five pairs of leaves at the top of the stem). Use a sharp knife to cut a very small incision in the bottom of the stem. Place the cut stem on the sand-soil mixture and pin it down with a piece of wire. Water well and keep the area moist until rooting occurs. When new roots have developed, cut the rooted stem from the main plant and plant it where you want it to grow.

WATER GARDENS

Continue adding new water garden plants to your pond, if you want to. You may also divide water lilies that need it. (Sorry, you'll have to wait until next year to separate overgrown lotuses. They should be divided only in spring.)

These water plants do well in tubs:

- Dwarf lotuses

- Hardy water lilies: 'Comanche', 'Berit Strawn', and 'Indiana'

- Tropical water lilies: 'Albert Greenberg', 'Golden West', 'Green Smoke', 'Panama Pacific', 'Tina', and 'Yellow Dazzler'

- Others: dwarf cattail, dwarf papyrus, knot grass, umbrella palm, and variegated rush

CARE

ANNUALS

Sometimes the scattered thunderstorms that seem ever-present in our weather forecasts this time of year will flatten an entire bed of taller annuals. Give them a day of sunny weather to see whether they recover on their own. If they don't, then gently return the plants to an upright position. Some will need to be staked so they'll stay that way. You may want to stake very tall sunflowers now.

Your wax begonias are blooming well, the plants are looking good—so why would anyone suggest that you pinch off the tips of the stems, maybe removing some of those flowers? It's one of those gardening techniques that isn't well understood. Many annuals—coleus, geraniums, Madagascar periwinkle, and wax begonias among them—tend to grow leggy (straight up instead of outward) if left to their own devices. Occasionally pinching off the tips of the stems encourages more bushy growth; a fuller, more compact plant; and eventually, more flowers. If you don't believe it, pinch back one plant and don't pinch one of the same type growing next to it. When you assess their appearance at the end of the summer, you'll see a noticeable difference.

To prevent your mums from blooming in summer, rather than in fall, when it's most desirable, pinch off the tips of all the stems before the middle of July. It also gives the plant a busier appearance.

BULBS

Regularly weed flower beds containing summer bulbs. Competition from weeds prevents your good plants from living up to their potential.

All bulbs—with the exception of bearded and dwarf crested irises—need some mulch. About 3 inches is ideal.

If you didn't get to it last month, mark bulb plantings in some way so that you'll know where they are when fall fertilizing time arrives. Remove lily flowers from the plant when they start to wilt. Remove faded flowers from cannas and other summer-flowering bulbs. Cut off the spathelike flower stalks that develop on caladiums so the plant will continue to produce an abundance of colorful leaves.

■ *When you have fifteen minutes free, weed the lawn, flower beds, the vegetable plot—whatever needs it. Just a little at a time keeps your garden neat and relatively weed-free.*

Pinch dahlias back a few inches to encourage branching. When a dahlia produces several flower buds next to each other, you have a choice:

- Remove one or more of the buds so you have one (or two) larger blooms. This is called disbudding.

- Leave all the buds to grow and produce more—but smaller—flowers.

If you have the time, you may want to try it both ways and see which you like better.

EDIBLES

To encourage the plants to continue producing, pick cucumbers and squash when they're small. Old unharvested fruits slow or halt further production.

Harvest tip: the skin of summer squash and zucchini should be soft enough to pierce with a fingernail.

Check the garden daily, and harvest when vegetables have reached the optimum size. Corn is ripe when the silk turns brown and the kernels are plump and filled with "milk." Eggplant skin should be glossy and spring back when poked. Onion tops turn yellow and fall over. The tops of Irish potatoes begin to die back. Pick okra when the pods are 2 to 3 inches long. Bell peppers can be harvested when they're green, or they may be left on the plant until they turn red, if you prefer.

Pinch back scented geraniums, basil, mint, and oregano as needed to keep the plants compact. Continue to remove suckers on staked tomato plants. Remove diseased, damaged, or yellow leaves from vegetable or herb plants. These often attract insects if left in the garden.

LAWNS

Sometimes bare spots in the lawn are caused by people or pets cutting across the grass instead of going around. Evaluate why this is happening. You may decide to set up a barrier to prevent the traffic. Or it may be that the informal walkway makes sense, and therefore the grass should be removed and a path created.

■ *For that wonderful fresh-picked flavor—and the height of nutrients—harvest vegetables, such as peppers, as soon as they're ripe. Check the garden daily to keep up with how your crops are performing.*

Cool-season grasses usually slow their growth this month. You may have to mow them only every other week. Warm-season grasses, especially those that have been fertilized recently, will continue going strong, so they'll probably need weekly cutting.

PERENNIALS AND ORNAMENTAL GRASSES

Stake or provide support for perennials that have begun to sprawl. Cut off yellowing leaves or foliage damaged by disease or insects, especially leaf miners (which leave what look like trails in the leaves).

Pinch chrysanthemums back one last time this month—early to mid-month for those in the colder sections of the region and before the end of the month in zone 8. Mature mums that aren't pinched usually bloom in the summer—and that's a waste of flower power. Many plants bloom in the summer, but far fewer do so in the fall. Remove the tips of the stems one last time around mid-July so mum plants won't get leggy and the blooms will appear when they should—September and beyond.

Deadhead all perennials, including daylilies and especially phlox, after they have flowered. On plants such as 'Moonbeam' coreopsis, achilleas, or veronicas, you may want to use hedge shears to lop off the multitude of small flowers. Old blossoms left on the plants will form seeds. This takes energy away from the plant and also usually prevents any more blooms this year.

ROSES

Once a month, check climbing roses to see whether new growth needs to be tied to supports or if any canes tied up earlier have come loose. When winds and thunderstorms knock climbing roses down, it's quite a job to get them back up again, so it's best to see that it doesn't happen.

As you remove dead and dying blossoms at the end of a bloom cycle, you're pruning to encourage new growth and new flowers. Some growers like to cut back farther than just the first five-leaf cluster. On taller, older plants, they may go back to the second or third five-leaf cluster that's facing the outside of the bush and make a cut ¼ inch above it.

SHRUBS

Cut faded flowers from butterfly bush. This encourages the shrub to produce even more blooms. As you remove the flowers, cut the stem at a 45-degree angle just above a bud to encourage new growth.

Shear hedges when they have grown 2 to 3 inches. Start with the bottom and work up, trying to keep the bottom wider than the sides. Why? This way, the sun will be able to shine on the bottom portion of the hedge; without sun, it declines.

Caterpillars may appear on various shrubs. Unless they're doing considerable damage or the shrub is very young or not in good shape, you may want to let the caterpillars alone. They are, after all, one of the life stages of moths and butterflies. Some gardeners like to move troublesome caterpillars to other plants, where their damage won't be as obvious or won't make a difference. Or, if necessary, use Bt organic insecticide according to label directions.

TREES

If someone besides you cares for your lawn, be sure that caretaker keeps equipment—especially string trimmers—away from the trunks of any trees. Young trees are especially susceptible to damage, but older trees can be harmed too. The wound that's created is an open invitation to insects and borers. A 3-foot-wide circle of mulch around your trees will help keep lawn equipment at bay.

When any construction is taking place on your property, see that the workers know to keep heavy equipment away from the root zones of trees in the yard. You don't want it brushing up against the bark, either. Shallow trenches dug nearby can also harm a tree. Consult a tree-care professional, and rope off trees with a 10-foot safety zone to be sure they aren't harmed during construction. You may not see immediate signs of damage; it may take a tree as long as five years to die of construction damage. But once a large tree is lost, it can be replaced only by one that's much smaller. This is a loss to your landscape.

If you notice suckers—thin upright sprouts—at the base of any tree, dig them up. They steal nutrients and water from the tree and often attract insects. The same is true of water sprouts—flexible upright growth on limbs. Cut these back to their base.

VINES AND GROUNDCOVERS

Make sure that vines are attached securely to supports. On wisteria, remove leafless shoots and shorten the lateral branches by half.

Mow or use the string trimmer on groundcovers that are straying into the lawn. Consider installing edging to prevent ground covers from escaping.

WATER

ALL

Going on vacation? Ask a green-thumbed neighbor to keep an eye on your yard while you're gone. He or she can check your rain gauge to see whether your garden receives the needed 1 inch of moisture during your absence and, if it doesn't, can then turn on your soaker hoses or drip irrigation. By this time of year, all container plants need to be watered daily. You may want to group them together and pay a neighborhood teen to do the job.

Water enough to wet the soil deeply each time you water, rather than watering frequently and lightly. If only a small amount of water is applied each time, plants may develop shallow roots, which dry out faster in times of drought.

BULBS

Caladiums like lots of water. Don't let them wilt, because the plants won't grow well afterward. Water early in the morning and keep the water off the leaves, if possible, since the sun shining on wet caladium leaves can burn them.

Also keep soil moist around cannas, elephant ears, and dahlias. Water all others—except lilies—when rainfall doesn't amount to 1 inch in any week. Lilies can usually manage fine without additional water, except in droughts.

Caladiums—known for their colorful, patterned foliage--are great plants for shady areas. They need moist soil or regular morning watering. When possible, avoid getting the leaves wet.

Water dahlias at ground level. To avoid powdery mildew or other fungus diseases, don't let water or soil splash up on the leaves.

EDIBLES

The higher the temperature, the more moisture vegetables will need. Herbs typically require less watering than vegetables, but you shouldn't let them wilt.

HOUSEPLANTS

Before you go on vacation, think about what will happen to your houseplants while you're gone. If your absence is a week or less, and all your plants are indoors, you may not need to do a thing beyond watering all the plants thoroughly before you leave and keeping the air conditioning on (the temperature should be no higher than 80 degrees Fahrenheit). You may also be able to

HERE'S HOW

TO KEEP HOUSEPLANTS WATERED WHEN ON VACATION

1. Move all plants at least 5 feet away from a window. Water them till the excess runs out the drainage hole. When the saucer is empty, fill it again.

2. If you have a tub or sink reasonably close to a window, line the bottom of it with four layers of newspapers. First, remove the sink plug and the plant saucers. Then water the plants so the newspaper is soaked through. Turn on the faucet so that it drips once every thirty to sixty seconds.

3. Another bathtub technique if your bathroom has at least medium light is to line the bottom of the tub with several sheets of newspaper. Get as many bricks as you have plants (large containers may require two side-by-side bricks), and place the bricks on the newspaper. Plug up the opening and run enough water into the tub to barely cover the bricks. Remove the saucers from your pots and set the pots on top of the bricks.

4. If you have only a few small plants, poke a hole in the lid of a clean margarine tub. Fill the tub with water. Using a pencil or knitting needle, poke a piece of yarn or a wick made from pantyhose into the drainage hole and up several inches into the soil. Then poke the other end through the hole in the lid and let the rest dangle in the water. Water the plant so the wick becomes moistened; then it transfers the water from the tub to the pot.

5. Water the plant well, and remove any flowers or yellowing leaves. Place the plant inside a clear plastic bag (for big ones, use dry-cleaner bags). Use slim stakes to keep the plastic away from the leaves. Blow into the bag and seal the top with a twister tie. Place the plant in medium light but not where the sun will shine on it.

6. Ask at a nursery about a capillary mat system. These water very gently but effectively.

ask a knowledgeable gardener to water while you're gone. If not, see the tips above.

Houseplants don't generally appreciate hard water. But what's a gardener to do if that's what there is? In summer the solution may be to collect rainwater and use that to water your houseplants. They will really appreciate it.

LAWNS

Water newly sodded, sprigged, or plugged lawns enough that they stay constantly moist for the first two weeks, paying attention to the corners of sod strips, which dry out easily. After that, you can gradually cut back to daily watering, then every other day, and so forth. But keep a careful eye out for the first sign that the new grass isn't getting enough water. You have a big investment in this lawn now, and you want to protect it. When

rain hasn't fallen in seven to ten days, or less than 1 inch of rain has fallen, water an established lawn deeply (until the soil is wet 6 to 8 inches down).

PERENNIALS AND ORNAMENTAL GRASSES

If you have soaker hoses, this is the time to bring them out and weave them among your perennial plantings—especially if you're going to be away for a few days and no rain is forecast. Soaker hoses and drip irrigation can be hooked up to mechanical timers attached to an outdoor water faucet to water your plants automatically. Or you can turn the hoses on and off by hand. Just remember to leave them on long enough that they deliver enough water to soak the soil at least 8 inches deep. Measure the depth to which the soil was wet after the first time you use the hose on a new bed and note how long it took to produce the desired results. Then you know how long to leave the hose on in the future. Most two-year-old established ornamental grasses are extremely drought tolerant.

ROSES

Water deeply each time you water roses.

SHRUBS

Water at the base of shrubs to prevent potential disease problems. While it's fine to water lawns with a sprinkler, that's not the best choice for shrubs. Trickle irrigation or soaker hoses should be your first choice.

VINES AND GROUND COVERS

Tropical vines like plenty of water. That goes double for those planted in large terracotta containers.

If you're growing moss or ferns as ground covers, remember that both need moist soil and should be checked regularly to make sure they don't dry out. If moss begins to turn a bit brown, it will perk back up when you water or when rain falls.

FERTILIZE

ANNUALS

If you applied timed-release fertilizer to your flower beds in mid-April, now's the time for a second application if the product promised that it remained effective for three months. (Some last four to nine months.) Broadcast pellets on top of the soil according to package directions, and water well. Sprinkle with a thin coating of mulch. That should take care of the fertilizing needs of annuals in beds until frost.

Since constant watering washes fertilizer from the soil, pot-grown plants need feeding more often than annuals growing in beds. Weekly fertilizing with a water-soluble food may be needed from now through the middle of September. You can also reapply timed-release fertilizer pellets now to give your container-grown annuals an extra boost. If you do, you can stop using a liquid plant food for the next month.

BULBS

About twice a month, fertilize amaryllis bulbs growing in pots outdoors, since they will need more frequent watering than when they were indoors, and that washes the nutrients from the soil. Use a water-soluble fertilizer made for blooming plants. All summer-flowering bulbs will need a fertilizer boost this month.

EDIBLES

When temperatures are high, avoid fertilizing vegetables and herbs except for water-soluble fertilizers applied weekly to plants growing in containers. When you pull up a spent crop, work some compost or rotted manure into the soil if you plan to plant the area again soon. This will improve the soil's texture and provide a mild fertilizing effect.

LAWNS

Feed bermudagrass and zoysia. The third fertilizer application of the growing season should be made about the middle of July. Use 1 pound of nitrogen per 1,000 square feet. (See the chart on page 84.) Water well.

ROSES

Just as regular as clockwork, most roses bloom every four to six weeks, and after they finish, gardeners fertilize them to help them form the next set of flowers. Use a granular rose fertilizer or about 1 cup of alfalfa meal per bush. Water well.

Fertilize roses in containers about twice a month if using a granular rose food or weekly if using a liquid mixed with water.

PROBLEM-SOLVE

ALL

What is that bug? It's not helpful to you, your plants, or the environment to spray the minute you spy an insect. Take a few minutes to see what the insect is doing. Is it causing a great deal of damage, or has it just munched small holes in a couple of leaves? How many insects do you see? Are there just one or two, or are these insects covering the plants? Many insects are beneficial—they eat the bad bugs—so you don't want to get rid of them. And some bugs eat a leaf or two and then move on. But if the damage is more than minor, and the number of pests is increasing, get a description of the insect and the type of damage it's causing and check with the extension service or a knowledgeable garden center for advice on controlling them.

Sometime this month, pull back the mulch in various places about the garden and see whether drip irrigation is leaving an unbroken line of moisture along the length of the tubes. If you notice a dry spot, it probably means that one or more of the emitters is clogged and needs to be cleared.

BULBS

If the weather has been hot and dry, spider mites may be troublesome on many summer-flowering bulbs. Look for leaves that first look paler than those nearby and then begin to turn yellowish or look dirty. See page 29 for dealing with spider mites.

EDIBLES

Caterpillars on parsley, dill, and fennel are likely to be future black swallowtail butterflies. Try to keep the caterpillars confined to one or two plants. This will contribute to the development of the butterflies while not sacrificing your entire crop of herbs.

If mints develop rust spots (usually orange, but occasionally black or purple) on their leaves, cut the plants back to 1 inch high and remove the affected foliage from the garden. The new growth should be clear of the problem. Try to avoid overhead watering, and increase air circulation where possible.

You've tried to contain mint and it just hasn't worked—the plant has escaped and is taking over. A barrier must extend about 1 foot below soil level, but even then you have to watch and see that mint doesn't grow over the top of the barrier or over the rim of the container in which it is planted. Regularly pull up any plants that have rooted where you don't want them to grow. Also watch out for oregano, which spreads by underground runners.

If you see black or brown insects on squash, gourds, or pumpkins, they will likely be squash bugs, which suck plant juices. A mild infestation can often be controlled with insecticidal soap, but it's important to spray the undersides as well as the tops of the leaves. Also inspect the leaves and stems carefully, removing any egg masses by hand.

LAWNS

Herbicides come in a variety of types. There are even organic weedkillers, although most kill only the top of the plant, not the root.

PERENNIALS AND ORNAMENTAL GRASSES

Even though it's hot, keep up with any necessary weeding. Ten minutes early each morning should do it. Think of it as your fitness routine. Don't allow weeds to go to seed. If you aren't able to dig up the weeds right away, pinch off the seedheads and put them in a paper bag. Close the bag and toss it in the trash.

Should the month be relatively rainy, watch out for slugs and snails. You'll likely need to set out organic or homemade bait. (See page 108.)

ROSES

"But that's not the rose I bought!" It happens fairly frequently—a homeowner buys a lovely pink or yellow or white rose and enjoys it for a year. But when it blooms the next season, or the one after that, instead of lush flowers in the original color, the bush now produces puny red single blooms. What happened?

Most hybrid roses sold today are grafted—the top part of the bush is one rose and the roots are from another. Traditional rose root stock is very vigorous, which is good, but what happens is that sometimes it's too eager to grow. It puts out shoots at ground level and below the bud union (where the two roses are grafted together). If these aren't promptly pruned off, they will grow aggressively, eventually smothering out the less-vigorous hybrid rose. What can you do about it?

1. Keep all growth at or below the bud union (the swollen area on the trunk) cut off. This includes suckers that come up from the

ground at the base of the bush (these often have to be dug up, instead of just cut off).

2. Buy roses that are called "own root." This means that they aren't grafted. All miniatures are grown on their own roots and are hardier as a result. You'll pay more for own-root roses, but many growers think they're worth it.

SHRUBS

If a rhododendron dies this month, especially after buds have turned brown and branches have drooped, you may think it's due to lack of water. And that's certainly possible, if you didn't pay attention to the shrub's watering needs. But more likely it's rhododendron dieback, when plants are infected by the fungus *Phytophthora cactorum* or *P. cinnamomi*. Preventive steps include providing excellent drainage, not planting rhododendrons where others have already died from the disease, planting far enough apart so the shrubs have good air circulation, and not planting too deeply.

TREES

If you have Canadian hemlocks in your yard, see the Problem-Solve section in the June chapter.

HERE'S HOW

TO FIGHT AGAINST WEEDS

- Prevent them in the first place. Thick, healthy turf crowds out weeds. Cutting your grass on the tall side of the recommended mowing height helps create shade that prevents weed seeds from germinating and prevents sun-loving weeds from getting enough light to thrive.

- Prevent weeds from going to seed. Always remove the seedheads even if you don't have time to get rid of the entire weed till later.

- Dig weeds out by hand. Annual weeds are usually easier to eradicate this way than perennial weeds—especially those that spread by underground stolons. It's important to remove all the root; otherwise, the plant will grow back.

- Use pre-emergent weed control in early spring. These are products that prevent seeds from germinating. They work well to stop weeds that come up from seeds—usually annuals—but have no effect on weeds that are already in place. Ask at a garden center about an organic pre-emergent weed control made from corn gluten. Spread early in the season, it can reduce annual weeds and crabgrass considerably.

■ *Be sure to dig up the whole root when pulling dandelions and other perennial weeds.*

August

August is a month when shade comes into its own. During a prolonged heat wave, is anything more welcome in the yard than cooling shade? Just gazing at a shady area makes the temperature more bearable. Actually sitting beneath a shade tree is one of the pleasures of summer.

Imagine it's the hottest day of summer. You've just gathered the bills from the mailbox, and even that tiny exertion has you sweating. But as you sit on the patio to rest a moment, all of a sudden you feel cooler and more peaceful.

The temperature didn't change, but your perception of it did, thanks to your nearby water garden—the gurgle of the waterfall, the *ribbit-ribbit* of a frog who's made the pond his new home, the fleeting glimpse of a goldfish lazily searching for insect larvae. It's hard to tear yourself away, and after a few minutes, you decide you don't really have anything more important to do.

Welcome to the rewards of owning a water garden. It's a pleasure anyone can experience, even if you have a small yard or you've never gardened before.

A water garden may be a big pond filled with gloriously flowering water lilies, or a half barrel fitted with a small fountain and a couple of small plants. There's one for every type of outdoor area, including the sunny porches and patios of apartment dwellers, so don't think that the gurgling sounds of a water garden on a torrid August day have to remain a dream.

Still thinking of water, watering the plants in your yard may be your primary gardening activity during August. It depends on how high the temperatures climb, how much rain falls and how often, the kinds of plants you have, and the type of soil in the yard.

August is a good time to stretch out and relax in a hammock or a comfy lounge chair and think about ways to make what's often summer's hottest month more bearable. Look ahead to tree-planting time in a couple of months, and consider adding a shade tree or two to the yard if you have mostly sunny areas.

PLAN

ALL

If you've done a good job in the garden, you should have an abundance of produce this month. What will you do with all of it? Eat it, of course, and share it with friends and neighbors. But don't overlook the opportunity to do a good deed with your produce. Soup kitchens, nursing homes, and the food bank in your area would be delighted to receive your excess vegetables and herbs to distribute to the less fortunate. It will give you a good feeling to share your bounty and know that it will be put to good use. In fact, you may want to consider planting a bit extra next year just for this purpose. The Garden Writers Association has a program called Plant-a-Row® that encourages gardeners to do just that. For more information, visit http://gardenwriters.org/gwa.php?p=par/index.html, e-mail par@gardenwriters.org, or call toll-free 877-492-2727.

The dog days of August offer the opportunity to catch up on writing in your garden journal. Which vegetables and herbs have been spectacular successes, and which didn't perform up to expectations? Which varieties would you try again? What pests have you had to contend with? Write it all down so that when you're planning next year's garden, you'll remember exactly what happened this year—and you can profit from the experience.

HOUSEPLANTS

By next month, plants that have spent the summer in the yard will return to the house. Before they do, think about which will need to be repotted and what cuttings you may want to take. Prepare for these by picking up extra houseplant pots and a bag or two of your favorite potting mix the next time you're at the nursery or home store. And while you're shopping, look around to see what's new (to you, at least). You may find that moisture meter that you've been wanting to try, a small trellis to insert in the pot of a climbing plant, or different types of self-watering containers to experiment with.

If you like weeping figs and have been planning to buy one, this is a good month to do so. Weeping figs need high light levels, so moving one into your home during a month with plenty of sun gives it an opportunity to gradually get used to the shorter days that are on the horizon during fall and winter.

LAWNS

Here we go again about testing your soil. If you took care of it earlier in the year, great. You already know what your soil needs in order to grow good grass. But if you haven't had a soil test done within five years (less if soil conditions have changed during that time because you added a great deal of organic matter, topsoil, and so on), do it during August. Then you'll be ready for September—to tackle your cool-season lawn renovation or just fertilize, if that's all you have to do.

1. Ask the local Extension service for a box and form to use when sending in soil to be tested.

2. With a trowel, take ten or twelve samples of soil from various parts of your yard and mix them together thoroughly in a bucket.

3. Take a small sample of this mixture, place it in a plastic bag, and put it in the box. Be sure to mark on the form that you want recommendations for your lawn.

ROSES

Rose fragrance is often at its peak early in the day. Why not walk through your roses tomorrow morning and enjoy the enticing scents?

SHRUBS

In summer, when the family is in the yard a great deal, we notice how much privacy we have when we're entertaining or even outside by ourselves. While we may like our neighbors a lot, we don't want to feel as though we're living in a goldfish bowl—and they don't either. Privacy can be very welcome. It doesn't have to be provided by a tall fence between the two pieces of property. Instead, consider a naturalistic hedge or some sort of shrub screen that gives inhabitants in both houses something green and pleasant to look at while offering some solitude. Evergreens are a favorite choice shrub screen with most homeowners.

HOW TO USE A SOIL TESTING KIT

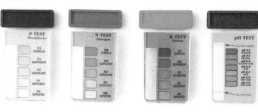

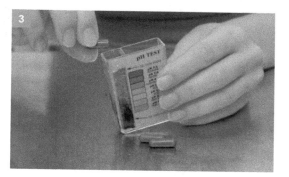

1 *You can get soil test boxes and forms from your local Cooperative Extension office. You can also purchase soil test kits at garden centers and home-improvement stores so that you can test the soil at home. These kits will allow you to test for the presence of Nitrogen-N, Phosphorous-P, and Potassium-K in the soil. Test the soil to see if anything is lacking before adding fertilizer, lime, or amendments other than compost to the garden.*

2 *Add soil to the kit from the area of the garden that you want to test. Then add water according to the instructions.*

3 *Add the indicator powder to the water in the container and shake the container to mix the soil, water, and indicator powder. (Usually the indicator powder comes in a capsule.)*

4 *Hold the container against a piece of white paper so that you can check the color of the water with the soil in it against the color key on the container. The color of the water will match one of the colors in the key on the container. The reading will tell you what is happening in the soil—acidic (low pH) or basic (high pH) soil, low nitrogen levels, or high phophorous levels. After testing, you'll know what to add (or not add) to the soil.*

TREES

This is the month when one of our most spectacular and dependable native trees becomes more visible. If you spy a flash of red as you drive by some woods, that's our native sourwood tree. If you don't have one in your yard, you owe it to yourself to consider planting one some fall, if you have room. Sourwood adds beauty to the yard in three seasons. Don't try to dig one from the woods, though; they do not transplant well from the wild. Instead, buy one grown in a container.

PLANT

ANNUALS

On the first day of August, plant zinnia seeds to provide cut flowers during September. You'll need to keep the seeds moist and the plants well watered all month. You may want to choose zinnias in fall colors—orange, gold, and yellow—or, as usual, just grow your favorite colors or those that complement the walls and furnishings indoors. It's too late to plant seeds of other annuals, except marigolds.

Children of all ages love to "help" in the yard, so ask them to do regular "chores." They especially love to see flowers and vegetables grow.

Kids bored? Grandchildren visiting? Let them help you plant marigolds in foam cups to take home with them if they live some distance away, or in a little flower bed of their own if they live nearby. Seeds sown near the beginning of the month should bloom by the end of September—sooner in warmer parts of the area and if temperatures remain high.

BULBS

Plant autumn crocus and colchicum if you can find them in local stores. They'll bloom next month. Give them a sunny location, and plant them 4 inches deep (measured from the top of the bulb) and 6 inches apart. Because the foliage (which, in the future, will come up in spring and then die back down before the flowers appear) can be dominating, a shrub border is a good place for colchicum.

If your irises didn't bloom as well this past year as they previously did, and they haven't been divided within four years, you can generally improve their performance by dividing the rhizomes and replanting pieces of them. Mid- to late July is the usual time to do this, but if you didn't get to it then, there's no reason you can't take care of it in August. It's best, however, not to wait any later than this month in order to give the rhizomes a good opportunity to become established before cold weather arrives.

EDIBLES

If you're a big fan of cucumbers or want to put up one more batch of pickles, plant seeds no later than August 1. For fall gardens, these vegetables should be planted no later than the middle of the month: seeds of bush beans, carrots, and summer squash, and plants of broccoli, cabbage, and cauliflower.

You may also sow seeds of kale, mustard, and turnip greens this month. Plant a smaller amount than usual, and follow with another planting in two weeks and a final sowing two weeks after that. That will give you a long fall harvest.

HOUSEPLANTS

This month is a good choice to repot all houseplants that have outgrown their containers. See

August is the time to plan for a fall crop of vegetables, such as kale, mustard, and turnip greens. Sow a small crop this month, another in two weeks and one more two weeks after that to ensure a long harvest throughout autumn.

HERE'S HOW

TO PROPAGATE A HOUSEPLANT BY LAYERING

A simple way to propagate trailing or vining houseplants (arrowhead plant, English ivy, heart-leaf philodendron, pothos, and so forth) is by layering.

- Fill a pot with dampened potting soil, and place it next to the plant you want to start a new plant from.

- Choose a stem, and pin it to the soil of the empty pot so that they are in direct contact.

- Keep the soil moist.

- When the portion of the plant in the new pot begins to grow, use hand clippers to remove the rooted portion from the mother plant.

page 114 for cactuses, and page 39 for orchids. Because repotting can be a little messy, it's best to repot plants when it can be done outdoors—in the shade, of course—rather than in deep winter, when it must be done inside. After repotting, give extra attention to watering—let the soil stay slightly moist except for cactuses—and keep repotted plants in bright light but away from sun until they've begun growing again.

PERENNIALS AND ORNAMENTAL GRASSES

When seed-started perennial plants growing in containers didn't get large enough to get planted in a regular flower bed, place them in a "nursery bed" of rich soil, where they can be given special attention and care until next spring when they're transplanted. In zone 6, divide peonies if they need it.

ROSES

Potted roses may still be planted the first week of the month, but not afterward. They need time to become established before cold weather arrives. Place the rosebush in the hole so that the bud union (swollen area on the trunk) is 1 inch above soil level or at soil level (the latter for zone 6 gardeners—see the map on page 226). Then mulch with 3 inches of organic material—pine straw, cocoa hulls, shredded pine bark, and so forth. Even if you don't usually give your roses winter protection, it's going to be important for roses planted as late as August.

■ *In the dog days of August, the soothing sound of a mechanical water feature will bring cooling serenity to a porch or patio.*

WATER GARDENS

When is a water garden not a water garden? When it's a water feature. A water feature has the look and sound of running water but no plants. It's an ideal way to enjoy the pleasures of water gardening without many of the cares. It's a nice solution for those who are away from home a great deal.

TO MAKE A WATER FEATURE

1. Buy a concrete planter with a drain hole in the bottom. Coat the inside with water sealer.

2. Buy a small submersible pump that will fit nicely into the pot you've selected. Select the type of nozzle you prefer: spray, jet, or bubble.

3. Remove the plug from the end of the pump's cord and then place the pump in the planter. Run the cord through the hole in the bottom of the container.

4. Leave enough of the cord inside the container to give the pump any needed height and then plug the hole (and hold the cord in place) with a cork.

5. Seal around the cork and hole (inside and outside the container) with silicone, to prevent leaks.

6. Let the silicone dry for twenty-four hours.

7. In the meantime, replace the plug you removed from the cord with a new one.

8. Place the planter where you want it to go, and place gravel in the bottom to raise the pump and adjust the height of the nozzle.

9. Fill the pot with water, and plug in the pump.

10. Enjoy the beguiling sound of cascading water whenever you want.

Are there areas beside your water garden that always remain wet? These spots are good candidates for planting marginal or bog plants such as old-fashioned flags and cardinal flower. August isn't too late to plant these moisture-loving perennials. In fact, you may find that nurseries have them on sale. Check the collection of perennial plants at regular nurseries, as well as water-garden retailers. It's fun to experiment with marginal plants to see what you like best and which combinations of plants look best around your water garden.

ANNUALS

Remove from the garden any annuals that are diseased or dying. Not only will the garden look better, but that may prevent the problem from spreading.

Deadhead at least weekly and remove damaged leaves whenever you see them. Cut back petunias that aren't blooming well or have grown leggy. They'll be reblooming well in two weeks.

BULBS

Remove faded flowers from cannas, dahlias, gladiolus, lilies, and crocosmia. This keeps the plants blooming longer. For a neater appearance, also remove dying leaves from caladiums and damaged leaves from elephant ears.

In the warmest areas of the region, pinch dahlias lightly one last time the first part of the month to encourage growth that produces additional blooms. To encourage dinner plate-sized flowers, you'll need to remove all but one of the buds in a cluster and leave fewer clusters on the plant. That gives you fewer but bigger flowers. Leaving all the buds to blossom produces many smaller blooms.

As gladiolus stalks turn brown, cut them back to the ground. Don't do it before then, though, because the leaves help the bulb gather strength for the next year.

ANNUALS, BULBS, AND PERENNIALS

Make sure that all tall plants that are prone to falling over in high winds and hard rains—dahlias, foxgloves, glads, lilies, peonies, sunflowers, and some yarrows, among others—have stakes and that you regularly tie new growth to the stakes. Sometimes a plant that's been knocked over by wind can be propped up again—but often the plant is too damaged to recover. You don't want that to happen to your favorites. If plants flop over when buffeted by rain and winds, stake them back up. Or as a preventive measure, stake taller plants that are prone to falling over.

EDIBLES

Pay attention when the greenish skin of canta-loupes begins to lighten. That's a sign they're reaching maturity. These melons are ready to be eaten when you tug the stem and it separates from the fruit. You should also be able to detect the fragrance of the fresh fruit. On watermelons, the top will become dull and the area of the skin that's closest to the ground will turn from light to bright yellow. The stem should also begin to turn brown.

If you're picking tomatoes before they're com-pletely red because birds are pecking on them don't place the tomatoes on a sunny windowsill to finish ripening. Put them on the kitchen counter instead. They'll ripen just as soon but be of higher quality.

Harvest Southern peas when the seeds are fully developed and the pods are still soft. Onions are ready to be dug when at least three-fourths of the tops have fallen over.

■ *Carefully dig up all onions planted at the same time when half to hree-quarters of their tops have fallen over.*

Remove damaged or overripe vegetables from plants and toss them on the compost pile (if you keep a "hot" pile that will kill the seeds) or in the trash. Leaving them on the plants attracts insects, which may winter over and cause problems next year.

HOUSEPLANTS

What's the humidity like inside your house this time of year? If your central air conditioning is on twenty-four hours a day, the indoor humidity may not be quite high enough for plants that crave high humidity, such as Boston fern, bromeliads, croton, English ivy, and nerve plant (*Fittonia verschaf-feltii*). If leaf tips of houseplants brown regularly and flower buds turn brown instead of opening, the air may be too dry. Try grouping a number of plants together.

Do you have a stack of empty houseplant contain-ers left over after repotting this summer? Why not clean them now? Then they'll be ready for reuse whenever you need them.

- Soak pots in a tub of water for several hours (overnight for heavily crusted containers). If pots have a lot of fertilizer salts accumulation, add vinegar to the water.

- Scrub the pots with a stiff brush, using soap and water. Rinse well.

- Refill the tub with a mixture of one part liq-uid bleach and nine parts water.

- Soak pots for thirty minutes.

- Rinse thoroughly and let dry.

■ *Before fall arrives, clean and sanitize all flower pots by soaking them in a tub of water, scrubbing then, and then sanitizing them with bleach and rinsing. They'll be ready whenever you need a clean pot.*

Mow grass when it has grown one-third higher than the recommended height for your type of grass. That means to mow tall fescue as soon as it has reached four inches tall.

Make grooming your houseplants—indoors and outdoors—a monthly ritual. Plants look better when fading leaves are removed, old flowers are snipped off, and foliage is kept clean. They'll remain healthier too.

LAWNS

It's time to sharpen your lawn mower's blade once again. Dull blades tear grass instead of cutting it cleanly. That allows disease organisms a place to enter the blades of grass.

Mow the lawn anytime the grass is one-third taller than the suggested mowing height. In hot weather, mowing high can keep the soil cooler and conserve moisture. Check the recommended mowing heights on page 79, and mow at the higher number for your type grass throughout August.

If you're going to be out of town for ten days or more, ask someone in the neighborhood to mow your grass if needed while you're gone. It'll be one less thing you have to catch up on when you return. An unmowed lawn advertises to burglars that no one's home. Besides, regular mowing, as you know, is good for the grass.

PERENNIALS AND ORNAMENTAL GRASSES

Don't let phlox drop its seed around; remove old flowers promptly. When phlox reseeds, the flowers on the new plants don't have the same color as the original—usually they're magenta. And if those are left in place and continue to reseed, soon the original planting is crowded out altogether.

To improve your garden's appearance, cut back tired-looking plants. Pinch or cut off faded flowers from all perennials. This is the basic chore in caring for perennials this time of the year. Flower beds look better when plants are quickly deadheaded, and it's best for the plants too. It prevents unwanted reseeding and allows the plant to devote its energy to top and root growth and, sometimes, to producing new flowers.

ROSES

Check climbers and ramblers to see whether canes need to be tied to fences or other supports. Remove faded roses from bushes promptly. Remove and destroy any yellowed or diseased leaves that have fallen off the bush and into the mulch. Practicing good sanitation can help prevent insect and disease damage.

Promptly prune any dead or dying (brown) wood back to where the cane is green. Seal the cut ends of the stems with white glue, shellac, or clear fingernail polish to prevent borers and other insects from getting into the canes.

Make sure your pruners are still sharp. Dull pruner blades can do quite a bit of damage to rose canes.

SHRUBS

If branches with all-green leaves appear on variegated shrubs, promptly cut them back to the main branch. If you don't, the whole shrub may revert to green, instead of having the variegation that was probably the reason you bought it.

Shear hedges one last time this month. Using hedge trimmers, cut new growth back to just above where you made your last cuts.

TREES

Don't leave fallen peaches or plums on the ground. They will attract yellow jackets.

WATER GARDENS

Use one mosquito dunk (a biological control) per 100 square feet of water surface of your pond to control mosquito larvae. If you see long strings of green algae in your water, remove them with a stick or rake.

Top off the pond when it gets ½ to 1 inch low. Those with larger, more elaborate water gardens may want to investigate automatic refill valves.

Trim off plant foliage that's covered with black spots. That's an indication of a fungus, and it's best to get it out of the water garden.

WATER

ALL

The best time to water is early in the morning. Since you may not want to be up dragging hoses about before work, consider connecting your drip irrigation or soaker hoses to a timer. It will turn the water on at a preset time (even 4:00 or 5:00 a.m., if you desire, which is actually ideal) and turn it off an hour or so later. Your plants will receive the moisture they require without any effort on your part. If you have only a few shrubs and you water by hand, do so slowly and deeply.

ANNUALS

By the time August rolls around, daily or twice-daily watering may be necessary for hanging baskets and other container-grown annuals. You may be able to lengthen the time between waterings by repotting plants into larger containers. The smaller the pot, the more often it has to be watered.

BULBS

When you go on vacation, ask a knowledgeable neighbor to water your caladiums, cannas, and dahlias deeply once during the week since they need a regular supply of moisture. Have your helper water blackberry lilies, crocosmia, and glads

if there's no rain at all during the week. Lilies shouldn't need watering.

EDIBLES

When there's no rain within a week, water deeply any vegetables that are bearing fruit. Often the plants will keep producing far into fall if given adequate moisture during late-summer dry spells.

Don't let perennial herbs go completely dry. To survive winter, they need to go into cold weather in good shape.

How are you watering? You know that most annuals planted in beds need 1 inch of water weekly—either from rainfall or supplied by you. But you may not have given much thought to the most efficient way to provide the necessary moisture. The simplest and most common technique—standing over your plants with a hose—is not only

■ *A rain gauge will show you how much precipitation has fallen in your yard, as opposed to what fell at your community's official measuring station. It's valuable information that helps you know when you do or don't need to water your plants.*

time-consuming, but often means that plants may not receive enough water or receive an uneven supply from plant to plant, and that some water is wasted because it runs off.

Now may be the time to consider drip irrigation or soaker hoses. The big advantages are that the water stays at the root level, where it's needed, and it doesn't wet the leaves, which can cause diseases.

1. Soaker hoses are relatively inexpensive and readily available at home stores, nurseries, and hardware stores. Many are made from recycled materials. They slowly deliver water at the root level, where it's most needed. They save water because it doesn't end up on walks, driveways, or the street. When new, soaker hoses may be a bit difficult to maneuver. But as you put them around your plants, just anchor them in place. Assume that soaker hoses will water the soil about 6 inches on each side of the hose.

2. Drip irrigation, sometimes called "trickle irrigation," lets you custom-design watering for all your flower beds. Water flows through flexible tubing and out of emitters. Some tubing already has the emitters installed, which is handy. But the spacing determined at the factory may or may not work well for what you grow, so many gardeners prefer to install their own emitters. It's more work, but it puts the water where you want it. Since emitters can clog up, it's worthwhile installing a filter to catch algae or dirt. Because of time and cost considerations, you may want to start with soaker hoses and see how you like them before investing in drip irrigation.

3. The thing that you'll first notice about these systems is that they water very slowly. That's good, because it prevents evaporation loss, but it means the hoses must be left on for at least an hour at a time or often for longer. About twenty-four hours after watering, insert a stick or pole into the soil to see whether the soil is damp at least 9 inches deep. If it is, you've watered the right length of time for annuals. If it isn't, leave the soaker hose or drip irrigation on longer the next time.

What about sprinklers? Use these on your lawn instead of your flowers. While sprinklers provide an even supply of water and do it relatively quickly, they have two drawbacks in the flower garden.

HERE'S HOW

TO USE HERBS

Make herb vinegars (great for gift giving) by adding one part washed herbs—leaves, whole stems, or flowers—to four parts white vinegar. Leave the herbs in the vinegar for three to six weeks, then strain. If you like, add a few sprigs of fresh herbs to the bottle before pouring the vinegar back in.

You may freeze dill, parsley, oregano, sage, tarragon, and thyme. Rinse the herbs gently, if needed, and pat dry. Place the herbs—one type to a container—in a plastic bowl or other freezer container with a tight-fitting lid. Be sure to use them within four months.

Once herbs have flowered, they're not as potent for using fresh or for preserving, but you can still get use from the plant: Cut off the flowers and use them in salads or cooking. Try basil blossoms with tomato dishes.

DROUGHT-TOLERANT TREES

Until a tree is fully established (which some-times takes up to three years), it needs to be watered during dry spells. But once some trees have developed good root systems, they are drought tolerant. Some of these trees are:

- Black gum, Tupelo (*Nyssa sylvatica*)

- Japanese zelkova (*Zelkova serrata*)

- Elm, either American (*Ulmus americana*) or lacebark (*Ulmus parvifolia*)

- Ginkgo (*Ginkgo biloba*)

- Golden rain tree (*Koelreuteria paniculata*)

- Tulip poplar (*Liriodendron tulipifera*)

- American holly (*Ilex opaca*)

- Oak (*Quercus* spp.)

- Red maple (*Acer rubrum*)

- Sassafras (*Sassafras albidum*)

■ *Ginkgo*

Instead of wetting just the soil, they wet everything they touch. And most flower beds are small or have an irregular shape. A sprinkler is likely to waste some water by depositing it on walks, the driveway, or the street.

Another idea is to water your plants automati-cally. It's easy with a timer. There are two types. Mechanical timers are inexpensive and can attach to your faucet. Set the timer to turn the water on and off, and the job will be done without any more effort on your part. Electronic timers are more expensive and must connect to your irrigation system but offer more flexibility. You can set an electronic timer to come on or turn off at different times on various days of the week and stay on for a specified amount of time.

HOUSEPLANTS

If you're planning to take an extended vacation this month, read the tips for July about how to keep your indoor houseplants watered while you're gone.

LAWNS

During drought or periods of high temperatures and no rain, cool-season grasses such as tall fescue protect themselves by going dormant. They don't look great when they turn brown, but unless the drought is severe, they revive and green up when rainfall returns. The problem is that if you occa-sionally water—thinking you're doing the lawn a favor—you will bring the grass out of dormancy and have to keep watering it.

An alternative to watering the entire lawn during prolonged dry spells is to select some areas that you will water and let the rest go. Maybe you want to keep the front lawn looking nice. Or the area visitors see when they first come to your house.

PERENNIALS AND ORNAMENTAL GRASSES

Watering during dry spells contributes greatly to the quality and number of flowers your peren-nial plants will produce. Watering often makes the difference between whether a plant lives or dies. When rainfall is less than 1 inch per week, check perennials and ornamental grasses planted

Go visiting. Take the opportunity to visit other water gardens for inspiration and ideas. These may be part of a garden tour in your own or a nearby community, they may be friends' gardens, or they can be part of public gardens in your area. It's fun to see what others have done, what plants they're using, and how they have cleverly handled little problems that have plagued you, too. Take a camera and notebook with you to record your observations. You'll enjoy looking back over them in the dead of winter.

this year to see whether they're low on moisture. Also keep an eye on perennials that need moist soil—ferns, for example. Don't let them dry out. Many mature perennials and all established ornamental grasses usually survive short dry spells without help.

When you water perennials and grasses—or any other plant, for that matter—water deeply and then don't water again until the soil has dried somewhat.

ROSES

Rosebushes need an inch or more of water per week, either from rainfall or supplied by you. But you may not have given much thought to the most efficient way to provide the necessary moisture. The simplest and most common technique—standing over your plants with a hose—is not only time-consuming, but often means that plants may not receive enough water or receive an uneven supply from plant to plant, and that water is wasted because it runs off. See Edibles (page 151) for watering options.

TREES

Whether your trees need watering, how often, and how much depends upon several factors. These include:

- Rainfall amounts (The ideal is 1 inch of water per week.)

- Temperature (The lower the temperature, the less likely you'll need to water.)

- The type of soil in your yard (Clay holds more moisture than rocky or sandy soils.)

- The species of tree (Some are more drought-tolerant than others.)

- The age and size of the tree (A newly planted tree will need watering more frequently than one that's been in your yard for five years, and in general, the larger the tree, the more moisture it requires.)

- Mulch (Between 2 to 3 inches of mulch, especially around the base of young trees—which have compact root systems easily covered with mulch—helps the soil retain moisture.)

It takes one to three years for a newly planted tree to become established. During that time—especially the first six months—you should watch the tree carefully to see whether it needs watering, particularly during the hottest days of summer and in dry spells.

How do you tell if a tree needs watering? You should test the soil by inserting a thin stick to see at what level it becomes damp. Other signs are:

- Leaves look dull instead of shiny or bright.

- Leaves look grayish instead of bright green.

- Leaves drop off.

- The tree is wilting. (When this happens, it may be too late to revive the tree.)

If you're able to water only so much—either because of local government restrictions or the size of your water bill—decide which trees will get preference. At the top of the list, put trees with sentimental value, those that were quite expensive, those that are hard to replace, and newly planted trees, which may not make it without watering.

FERTILIZE

ANNUALS

Apply a liquid or water-soluble fertilizer weekly to container plants. That keeps them blooming nonstop.

ROSES

In the parts of the region with coldest winters (zone 6), stop fertilizing the first part of the month. In zone 7, stop spreading granular fertilizer before the middle of the month, and in zone 8, before the end of the month. You want roses to slow down their growth going into winter so they won't be harmed by the first cold snap. If you plan to enter a rose show in September, use a water-soluble fertilizer once this month to help the bush produce larger blooms. (Do this no later than the middle of the month in the colder areas.)

WATER GARDENS

Do you have enough fertilizer tablets to last through the month? Water gardeners should continue fertilizing their plants at the regular rate during August. But stop fertilizing about a month before fall's first frost.

PROBLEM-SOLVE

ALL

Remove weeds by hand. If you have mulched your flower beds consistently, you shouldn't have too many weeds. And annual weeds should be easier to pull up through a blanket of mulch. Perennial weeds are the toughest to control—especially those that spread by underground runners, since, when you pull up one portion of the weed, the section that's left puts out new roots.

If you've returned from vacation to find plenty of weeds, go through the garden and snip off all the heads of the weeds, tossing them in a bag or bucket. That prevents them from setting seed. It also buys you a little time to get the weeds out of the garden.

■ *When powdery mildew appears on the leaves of roses or susceptible shrubs, pinch off the affected leaves and also remove mildewed leaves that have fallen on the ground beneath the bush and bag them up.*

LIGHTING YOUR WATER GARDEN

Hook your water garden lighting—either spotlights shining on the pool or underwater lights—to a timer so the lights come on the same time each evening and go off automatically as a preset time. Then you don't have to remember to turn the lights off every night.

Keep an eye out for insects and for signs of disease. Caterpillars are a conundrum for the ecologically minded gardener. On one hand, they can quickly destroy those plants for which you paid hard-earned money and then carefully tended. On the other, many caterpillars are butterfly larvae—and you may be trying to attract butterflies to your garden. One solution is to pick caterpillars by hand and move them onto plants in the woods or a natural area. If the infestation is severe, Bt (*Bacillus thuringiensis*) kills all types of caterpillars and what gardeners often refer to as "worms" (but which are really members of the caterpillar family).

BULBS AND PERENNIALS

A white powdery coating on leaves is a sign of powdery mildew. Dahlias are the most likely summer bulbs to be affected, but it may turn up on other plants, such as phlox and beebalm (monarda). It's a fungus and can't be cured, but may be prevented. If only a few leaves are affected, pinch them off. Keys to mildew prevention are watering at ground level and not splashing leaves when you water. Air circulation makes a difference, too—planting so that dahlias and other summer-flowering plants have plenty of room between them.

If glads aren't looking as good as they should, the problem may be fungal diseases (check the leaves for spots or markings), thrips (which suck the sap from the leaves), or aphids (which usually congregate on new growth and can be seen easily). Sometimes it takes a bit of detective work to figure out the cause, which is what dictates the remedy. You may want to cut off a leaf or other affected portion of the plant and take it to a good nursery for a diagnosis and advice on control.

HOUSEPLANTS

Ants may be a problem in houseplants outdoors, which you want to control now, so don't bring them into the house next month. First, spray the plant twice, three days apart, with insecticidal soap. Be sure you spray under the leaves. This will help get rid of any insects that are attracting the ants. Then remove the saucer and pour water through the soil repeatedly. You may have to do this several times before all the ants leave for a drier home.

LAWNS

Grass and shade are less-than-perfect partners. But if you follow these few tips, you can grow grass in moderately shady spots.

1. Choose a shade-tolerant grass. Chewings and red fescues are most available.

2. Have your soil tested, and then adjust the pH if needed.

3. Mow shaded grass higher. Grass growing in the shade needs extra leaf surface for photosynthesis, so mow it higher than grass growing in full sun.

4. Fertilize less. Feed about one-half as much as you feed the portion of the lawn growing in the sun.

5. Overseed shady-area cool-season grasses each fall—or in spring and fall, if needed.

6. Trim nearby trees or remove the lowest branches to allow more light.

If crabgrass has popped up in the lawn, one precaution you can take to minimize problems next year is to dispose of grass clippings instead of leaving them on the lawn, as usual. That will get rid of the crabgrass seeds, instead of allowing them to sprout and cause problems in the future.

FOOLPROOF HOUSEPLANTS

If you'd like to introduce someone to the pleasures of houseplants, but you're not sure how much attention the plants will get, these are the most foolproof choices: arrowhead plant, cast iron plant, Chinese evergreen, heart-leaf philodendron, spider plant, and snake plant.

PERENNIALS

If asters turn yellow and become stunted, they're suffering from a disease called aster yellows. The recommended control is to pull the plants up and destroy them. Then don't plant in that spot for the next two years.

ROSES

Powdery mildew often shows up on rosebushes in August, when humidity is high and frequent afternoon thundershowers keep leaves damp. Pinch affected leaves off the bush and remove from the ground beneath. Then fertilize and water the bush to help it grow new leaves.

SHRUBS

Azalea lace bugs may again put in an appearance in August. They suck sap from the leaves, leaving them looking dry. They may also leave shiny black-ish deposits under the leaves. Lace bugs are most likely to proliferate when azaleas are in sun. Spray with insecticidal soap twice a week for two weeks. Or ask a knowledgeable nursery professional about recommended controls and for the names of aza-leas that resist lace bugs.

By mid-month, we should finally have relief from Japanese beetles. They will have laid eggs and disappeared from sight for another year. Unfortunately, they will become grubs in the soil from now until they emerge late next spring. See page 106 for advice on long-term control of Japanese beetles, if their levels have become intolerable.

Bagworms are almost invisible on needled ever-green shrubs until one day when you notice there are many of them. The best solution is to wait till dusk, when the "worms" will have returned to the bags, and then pick them off by hand. Drop them in soapy water and dispose of them. You'll probably have to do this several times a week over a period of several weeks in order to get rid of them all. It's very easy to overlook a few each time. Then check over the shrub once a month or so after that to make sure you're taken care of them all.

TREES

If you didn't spray hemlocks with a light horticul-tural oil (sun oil), which is organic, in June or July,

■ *Bagworms, which live inside these nondescript cases attached to the limbs of shrubs, can eat the all foliage from needled evergreens quickly. Wait until early evening and pick off the cases by hand.*

do it this month. A twice-yearly spraying helps keeps woolly adelgids on hemlocks at bay.

WATER GARDENS

If, all of a sudden, your pond seems overrun by little black tadpoles, don't get concerned. They don't mean you're going to be overwhelmed by frogs. Instead they result from the eggs of toads, which lay eggs in the pond, but live on dry land once they mature.

It's true that snails do eat algae in the water garden, but only from surfaces and not as much as fish do. They also eat plants and host parasites that may affect your fish. They reproduce rapidly, so remove them by hand or in a fine net whenever you see them.

Once Labor Day is past, September has the feeling of a new beginning. Younger children have gone back to school; older ones have left for college. Some mornings there's a bit of a nip in the air. Daytime temperatures will mostly continue to be warm, with a few chillier days thrown in to remind us that Old Man Winter will be making an appearance long before we're ready for him.

Maybe this is a good time to look over your landscape plan and see whether you need any more plants, especially trees or shrubs. If beds or containers of annual flowers look tired or bedraggled at this point, mid- to late September is a great time to replace them with brightly colored mums that have begun to fill garden centers. And you'll want to pick up some pansies; what would winter in our region be without cheerful yellow, purple, or bicolored pansies? While you're at the nursery, look over the selection of spring-flowering bulbs, since you know you're going to want some to plant later in the fall.

Although it's not quite time for trees to start dazzling us with their fall foliage, September is a good time to think ahead about whether you'd like more of that autumn glory in your own yard. Shrubs and vines also produce colorful foliage in fall. And don't overlook berry-producing shrubs, much loved by birds.

Have you started a fall vegetable garden? Since you've been eating from the garden for several months now, you may think you'll postpone planting cool-season vegetables. But about the first of November, you'll regret it.

The big job in September is renovating fescue and bluegrass lawns, if they need it. While the trend today around the country is to decrease the size of lawns, or even replace them with ground covers and other plants, grass is still popular in our part of the world. Folks in Tennessee and Kentucky know that most lawns can and should be maintained without excessive fertilizer, insecticides, or weedkillers.

Take a break by attending a rose show put on by the local rose society. It's a lovely way to enjoy the best September has to offer and maybe pick up some good gardening advice at the same time.

PLAN

BULBS

Spring-flowering bulbs will begin appearing in home stores and garden centers across the area this month, but September isn't the best month to plant them. In most areas, you should wait until October or later—when the temperature of the soil is 60 degrees Fahrenheit or cooler.

But just because you're not going to plant right away doesn't mean you shouldn't plan your bulb plantings for next spring and buy many of the bulbs that you'll need. The bulbs available now are fresh and offer the best selection of the season. The main thing to remember when buying bulbs early is to store them correctly.

Look for bulbs that you haven't grown before, and consider giving one or two new-to-you species a try. There's an interesting world of selections beyond tulips and daffodils. Many bloom early or late, giving your yard a sparkle of bulb color over a longer period.

If you've become less enthusiastic about planting new bulbs because of damage by deer, chipmunks, and squirrels, buy bulbs that rarely get eaten by wildlife. Among your choices are crown imperial, daffodils, grape hyacinths, Siberian squill (*Scilla siberica*), snowdrops, Spanish bluebells, spring snowflakes, silver bells (*Ornithogalum nutans*), and winter aconite (*Eranthis hyemalis*).

PERENNIALS AND ORNAMENTAL GRASSES

What perennials besides chrysanthemums come into their own in fall? Asters, boltonia, Joe-pye weed, and sedum are a few for sunny spots. And don't overlook goldenrod just because it's so common along roadsides, or you think it causes sneezing. (It doesn't.) Many interesting goldenrod cultivars are available that provide shorter plants and bigger blooms. For fall flowers in light shade to partial sun, consider cardinal flower, Japanese anemone, toadlily (*Tricyrtis hirta*), and bugbane (*Cimicifuga racemosa*) for zones 6 and 7a, and turtlehead (*Chelone* species and hybrids) throughout the region.

■ *Don't think that because it's fall, the flower garden has to be less colorful. Sedum is a perennial plant that is outstanding in the fall garden.*

■ *To learn more about roses and how to grow specimens like these, attend a fall rose show in your area and talk to local experts.*

If you spent more time watering this past summer than you wanted to, consider grouping together plants with similar watering needs. Keep those that require moist soil in one spot and those that tolerate dry soil in another section. This simplifies watering—and is easy to do when you renovate beds or prepare new ones.

ROSES

Many local rose societies have fall rose shows. Why not check with the group nearest you to see if one is scheduled? (You can find out how to contact area rose societies on the website of the American Rose Society, http://www.ars.org.) A rose show is a wonderful place to learn a great deal about roses—and to fall in love with some new flowers. Society members are always present to give advice and answer questions, too, which can be a big help to novices and even those more experienced who still are looking for answers.

Is there any class of rose you're interested in that you haven't yet grown? Maybe you think miniature roses are cute, but you've never tried them. Or you're fascinated by the lush, romantic blooms of the English roses. This is a good time to start reading on the subject, so you'll know whether they're right for you. Some of the English roses do better in the South than others. You may want to ask for advice from a consulting rosarian in your area. The same is true of old garden roses, which have once again become highly popular. Some are better in our climate than others—and some fit into small home landscapes better than others.

SHRUBS

As we head into fall, you may be looking forward to the glorious fall color of deciduous trees—either in your yard or along the highways. But have you considered planting shrubs that have excellent fall color? They really make a yard "shine" in autumn. Berried bushes also add color—mostly red—and food for migrating birds. Ask a nursery professional about those listed here. Not all species or cultivars of each will have colorful foliage, but a professional can recommend the best.

■ *The fat clusters of purple berries make beautyberry one of fall's most attention-grabbing shrubs. This deciduous shrub is also very easy to grow. There are American and Japanese types.*

Shrubs with colorful foliage:

- Bottlebrush buckeye

- Burning bush

- Carolina allspice

- Crapemyrtle

- Deciduous azalea

- Fothergilla

- Loropetalum (zones 7 and 8)

- Redvein enkianthus

- Smoke tree

- Spirea

- Summersweet

- Viburnum

- Virginia sweetspire

- Witch hazel

Shrubs that produce berries:

- Barberry

- Beautyberry

- Chinese holly

- Cotoneaster

- Deciduous hollies

- Nandina (tall cultivars)

- Oregon grape holly (*Mahonia* species)

- Pyracantha

- Viburnum

■ *Maple trees can provide bright fall color to your yard.*

TREES

A few isolated trees may have already begun putting on their fall finery, but the big show is yet to come. Do you have plenty of trees in your yard that produce colorful fall foliage? If not, now's the time to consider some more. These are good choices:

- Black gum

- Dogwood

- Fringe tree

- Ginkgo

- Japanese maple

- Ornamental pear

- Red and sugar maples

- Sassafras

- Serviceberry

- Sourwood

- Stewartia

- Sweet gum

VINES AND GROUNDCOVERS

Did you realize that some vines also have vibrant (usually red) leaves that can really liven up your property? You might want to consider these:

- Boston ivy (*Parthenocissus tricuspidata*)

- Climbing hydrangea

- Crimson glory vine (*Vitis coignetiae*)

- Virginia creeper (*Parthenocissus quinquefolia*)

PLANT

ANNUALS

If you want to grow pansies and ornamental cabbage and kale over winter, get them into the ground as soon as they become available at nurseries. The more time they have for their roots to grow and become established before frost arrives, the better they'll weather the winter.

BULBS

Winter aconite isn't well known, but it's a worthwhile little bulb—a charming late winter–early spring bloomer with single yellow flowers that may remind you of buttercups. They often bloom through snow and emit a honeylike fragrance. And deer typically avoid them. September is the month to plant winter aconite. Soak the bulbs for twenty-four hours in room-temperature water, and plant them 3 inches deep and 4 inches apart in loose, moist soil. Because—in contrast to many other of the spring-flowering bulbs—they don't like to dry out over summer, you may want to plant them in a bed of perennials or annuals that you'll be watering regularly. (The aconite's foliage will have disappeared long before summer arrives.)

When lily bulbs become available in fall, plant them right away. See pages 71–72 for directions.

HOUSEPLANTS

Because of its mild weather, September is a good month to repot houseplants that need it. Check all your houseplants to see whether root growth has covered the plant's ball of soil. If so, it's a good candidate for repotting.

If you have a variegated snake plant (sometimes called mother-in-law's tongue) and want some more, you should divide it. Don't take cuttings, since they will yield all-green plants, not variegated plants. Division is simple:

1. Remove the plant from the pot.

2. Carefully wash most of the soil from the roots.

3. Using a sharp knife, cut the plant into sections, each with an ample amount of roots.

HOW TO PROPAGATE WITH CUTTINGS

1   *Use a sharp knife to cut off a leaf from the plant. You need at least one to two inches of "leaf stem." (The leaf stem is called the petiole. It connects the wide part of the leaf to the rest of the plant.)*

2   *Dip the leaf stem in rooting powder, which you can find at home-improvement stores and garden centers. Rooting powder is made from a natural plant hormone that stimulates root growth. You can propagate African violets without rooting powder, but they'll start growing faster with it.*

3   *Stick the stem in moist soil. Keep the soil watered and let the leaves sit for several weeks. Eventually, you'll start to see new, tiny leaves sprout from the base of the leaf that you cut off the old plant. Once the new plant has three leaves, you can gently transplant the plants into individual pots.*

4. Repot.

5. Water thoroughly.

6. On tall plants, you may need to provide a stake or light support for a few weeks until root growth takes hold.

7. Place the pot in medium light for two weeks, then move to the preferred type of light for that plant.

Other houseplants that can be easily divided include aloe, anthurium, asparagus fern, Boston fern, bromeliads, cast iron plant, Chinese evergreen, lipstick plant (*Aeschynanthus lobbianus*), mother of thousands (*Tolmiea menziesii*), orchids, peace lily, polka-dot plant, prayer plant, and spider plant.

HERE'S HOW

TO CHOOSE GRASS SEED

- Choose between cultivars, based on a discussion with an Extension agent or a knowledgeable person at your favorite garden center.

- Consider a blend—several cultivars of the same species of grass. A combination of three or more tall fescue cultivars, for instance, can be advantageous because you'll get the best quality of each grass.

- Avoid mixtures—combinations of two or more different types of grass. Often they're formulated for shade and contain grasses—creeping fescue, for example—that, while quite tolerant of shady conditions, are problematic in the warmer parts of the region because they don't perform well in hot, humid weather. The big issue with mixtures is that the various grasses in them don't necessarily need the same conditions, mowing height, and care. So it's hard to provide what they require to thrive. Also, if one is more aggressive than another, it's likely to crowd out the more timidly growing species.

If you have a sunroom, a greenhouse, or a sunny windowsill, you may want to save a few annuals to take indoors for winter:

- Good choices are wax begonias and coleus, both of which do well inside the house if they receive enough light. Geraniums often don't look great after a few months, but will survive to provide plants for next year.

- Plants already growing in pots are easiest to take indoors. But if you prefer, you can dig up small clumps of annuals and place them in pots. Do this in the first half of the month so that they become used to their new homes.

- Another method is to take 4-inch cuttings of some annuals around the first of the month, dip the ends in rooting hormone, and then place them in pots filled with packaged potting mix that's been moistened. Keep the soil damp until rooting takes place. Newly rooted cuttings will be small and manageable indoors if you don't have too much room.

If you have an empty flower bed, scatter poppy seeds on top of the soil. They will germinate in the fall and then bloom in late spring.

LAWNS

Fescues and Kentucky bluegrass may be seeded anytime in September, but earlier is better. The sooner it's done, the longer the lawn has to become established before cold weather arrives.

If your cool-season grass is just thin, you may want to overseed it. If you don't like the brown look that warm-season lawns sport all winter, overseed bermuda and zoysia with annual or perennial rye so it will look green. Do it two to four weeks before the average first frost date for your area. That could mean mid- to late September for some sections of the region. See directions for overseeding on page 73.

PERENNIALS AND ORNAMENTAL GRASSES

Peonies don't need dividing often and shouldn't be divided until they really need it, because they don't perform well for a year or more afterward.

HERE'S HOW

TO SEED A NEW LAWN

1. Have your soil tested if you haven't yet. If you did it earlier in the year, follow the recommendations it contained.

2. Remove the grass and weeds that now constitute your lawn.

3. Add organic matter to your soil if it's clay or if you've had problems in the past with grass not growing well. Spread up to an inch of fine bark, compost, well-rotted manure, sawdust, or topsoil over the lawn.

4. Till the soil 6 to 8 inches deep.

5. Remove rocks and debris. Rake the area smooth. Fill the sections that aren't level with topsoil.

6. Spread fertilizer over the soil, and lightly rake it in.

7. Sow the seed you've selected. Determine how much you'll need, according to the amount recommended on the bag for your size lawn. (Using too much is just as bad for your lawn as not seeding enough, so don't overdo it.) Then divide the recommended amount into two equal batches. Using a hand, drop, or rotary spreader, apply half the seed in one direction. Then sow the second batch at right angles to the first. This ensures even coverage.

8. Roll the lawn (lawn rollers can be found at rental equipment supply companies) to make sure the soil and seed come into firm contact with each another.

9. Mulch with a light covering of straw. You should still be able to see the ground through the straw; if you can't, it's too thick.

10. Water thoroughly.

11. Keep the soil constantly moist until the seed germinates. (But don't water so much that you create puddles.) This may mean watering several times a day for up to two weeks. It is essential that the seed not be allowed to dry out anytime after the first watering.

But when it becomes necessary, the first half of September is the time to get the job done. Leave three to five eyes or buds per division and replant no more than 2 inches deep.

This is also the month for dividing or transplanting spring- or summer-flowering perennials that need it—except hostas and ornamental grasses, which should be divided only in the spring. See March for instructions on division.

This is a good time to transplant into the garden perennials that grew in containers over the summer. They are more likely to survive in the ground than in pots, especially in zone 6 and in unusually cold winters elsewhere in the region.

Plant container-grown chrysanthemums anytime this month. Use them to fill in spots where other flowers have faded. To help the mums survive winter, avoid planting them where they're exposed to winds or where the drainage is poor. Those that survive the winter were planted the earliest.

SHRUBS

Once the weather has begun to cool from summer's torrid levels, you can begin to plant shrubs, if you like. Garden centers often get a new crop of shrubs for fall planting. Seek out a knowledgeable person at your favorite nursery and ask for advice. Describe the conditions in your yard and the type of shrub you have in mind and see what's new. Refer to page 58 for shrub planting tips.

Although fall is considered the ideal planting time for shrubs in our part of the country, I like to plant evergreen shrubs early in fall—September and October—and deciduous shrubs in November. The whole idea behind fall planting is that mild temperatures and reasonable rainfall combine to get shrubs off to a good start before they have to face the heat of summer. Even though the tops of the shrubs aren't growing, the roots will be, and that helps them to get established. Once every eight or ten years, we often have an unusually cold winter and just about any evergreen shrub planted in the previous mid- to late fall won't make it— especially broadleaf evergreens and those that are less hardy in a particular part of the region (camellias, for instance). Do you want to take a chance? The choice is yours. Usually you'll be successful.

At nurseries, shrub selection in autumn is excellent, and planting isn't such sweaty work for a homeowner. But you may not want to install an entire new landscape in fall unless the plants are guaranteed.

TREES
If you plan to move a small tree from one section of your property to another this winter, now's the time to prune the tree's roots, which will aid survival.

- First, determine the size of rootball the tree will need to survive after it's moved. Measure the diameter of the trunk 6 inches above the ground. This is the trunk caliper. Count on 12 inches of rootball for each inch of caliper. That means that if the trunk is 2 inches in diameter, move the tree with a rootball that's at least 24 inches across.

- Insert a spade into the soil 8 to 12 inches deep in a circle whose diameter you determined in the first step. This cuts roots and readies the tree for moving.

- See December for information on completing the transplanting.

VINES AND GROUNDCOVERS
Now that more moderate weather has returned or is on its way, plant perennial vines and groundcovers grown in containers and those you rooted

yourself during the summer. See pages 38, 76, and 114 for planting tips. The only difference for fall planting is don't mix fertilizer with the soil. The most important thing you can do to get your groundcover or vine off to a good start is to improve the soil before you plant.

WATER GARDENS
When a water gardening friend has too many water lilies and offers you a few hardy ones, accept them, even though it's late in the season. Keep them cool and damp, and pot them as quickly as possible. Especially if this happens early in the month, the plants will very likely have time to become established before cold weather arrives. Don't expect any blooming, though, until next year.

CARE

ALL
The end of the season seems like a good excuse to give up and learn to live with weeds. After all, frost will kill them soon. But frost won't make a difference if the weeds are allowed to go to seed. The old rule holds true: seeds one year, weeds eight years.

ANNUALS
The first of the month, pinch back ageratum so it will make a comeback with September's cooler temperatures.

ANNUALS AND EDIBLES
If your grandparents or great-grandparents were farmers or gardeners, they always collected seeds from their annuals and vegetables at the end of the growing season and saved those seeds from year to year. Today's gardener often doesn't save seeds, because most of the plants we grow are hybrids— they are a cross between two plants of the same species and usually have a name ('Big Boy' tomato, for example). Seeds of hybrids don't "come true." That is, the plant that grows from a seed saved from a hybrid plant won't produce the same kind of plant. So know which of the plants you're growing are hybrids and don't save their seeds. To save seeds of nonhybrids:

- Start checking seeds a few weeks after the flowers fade. The seeds should feel dry. Watch out for seeds that blow away: Wait a day or two too long, and they'll be gone.

- Big seeds are easier to save than little ones.

- Separate the seeds from any chaff and spread the seeds over a piece of newspaper, a couple of layers of paper towel, or a screen indoors where they'll be protected from the weather and humidity. Small seeds should be dry in seven to ten days. Larger ones may take two weeks—or longer if they weren't completely dry when harvested.

- Place the seeds in a zipper-type plastic freezer bag or in a glass jar with a screw-on lid. Baby food jars and canning jars are excellent. Close the lids securely. Label the containers with the name of the flower and the date the seeds are being placed into storage. Place the containers in a refrigerator or freezer. You may also store them in an unheated garage, but watch out for fluctuating temperatures, which harm seeds.

BULBS

If you'd like to save your caladiums for another year, wait till the leaves begin to die back—but before a frost—to dig them up. Wash the soil off the tubers, and place them in a shaded, well-ventilated area for several days to dry out. Dust with sulfur and pack in a box of dry sphagnum moss. Put the box somewhere in the house that the temperature will remain 65 to 70 degrees Fahrenheit. If caladium tubers get too cool while in storage, they're likely to rot.

Most winters, elephant ear will survive in zones 7 and 8 (and often in zone 6) if left in the ground and mulched heavily. But if you want to be sure you don't lose them to the cold, dig and store as explained for caladium.

Bring your potted amaryllis back into the house the first part of the month, if it summered outdoors. Gradually cut back on watering until the leaves begin to turn yellow, then stop watering altogether. Cut the leaves off close to the top of the bulb. Place the bulb, still in its pot of soil, in a dry, dark spot where temperatures will remain

It's easy to save seeds of some plants and grow them next year—as long as they aren't hybrids, or named plants. Big seeds are obviously easier for beginners than tiny seeds.

above freezing. The bulb will need to rest at least a month before you start it into growth again. (See page 197.)

Cut dahlia flowers in early morning. Take a clean bucket of cool water with you into the garden so the stems of the flowers can be plunged into it immediately. Cut long stems, and make your cut at a 45-degree angle, using a sharp knife or pair of garden shears.

EDIBLES

By the first of September, you should have planted collards, kale, kohlrabi, and mustard in the fall garden. By the middle of the month, plant leaf lettuce, radishes, spinach, and turnip greens. Mix 10-10-10 granular fertilizer or organic vegetable fertilizer with the soil before sowing the seeds. Water thoroughly, and keep the soil moist until seeds sprout.

To grow chives indoors over winter, insert a sharp trowel straight down into a clump of chives to remove a small portion to pot. They're handy to have in a pot in a sunny windowsill in cold weather.

To improve the soil in your vegetable plot, plant a green manure crop—also called a cover crop—in areas where the vegetables have already been harvested. These are grasses or grains that protect bare soil over winter and then are tilled under in early spring to produce valuable organic matter and add nutrients to the soil. Alfalfa, buckwheat, soybeans, and Southern peas are often sown in August, but will still improve the soil if sown in early September. Crimson clover, annual rye, and vetch may be sown anytime this month. Don't wait too late—plant seeds at least a month before your average last frost day.

Annual herbs are going to get killed by the first frost, so harvest as many as you can use this month. See page 128 to learn about drying herbs and pages 125 and 152 for advice on freezing them. If you want to harvest more than usual at one time (because a rainy spell is forecast, for instance), don't refrigerate them. (Annual herbs don't like low temperatures.) Instead, use or preserve them right away or fill a glass with water, put the cuttings in it, and keep them at room temperature for a day or two.

If you have melons, gourds, or pumpkins actively growing in the garden this month, pinch the tips of the vines. That will cause the plants to direct their energies into ripening the fruits already on the vines instead of putting on more green growth or developing tiny fruits that will never mature.

HOUSEPLANTS

Most of us tend to wait till the last possible moment before bringing houseplants back inside the house in fall. But such procrastination makes it harder for your houseplants to adapt to life indoors once again. How do you treat plants so that they adjust seamlessly to the move?

1. The ideal time to move plants is when outdoor and indoor temperatures are about the same. When nighttime temperatures begin to slip to the upper 60-degree Fahrenheit range, plan to take the plants indoors.

2. Clean them up first.

3. Make sure you don't bring any insects indoors, even worms.

4. Don't move the plants directly to the spots where they'll be spending the winter. Instead, move them to very bright light (but not where they'll be touched by direct sun).

If you saved your poinsettia from last year, bring it back into bloom by giving it 14 hours of light and 10 hours of darkness out of each 24 hours, beginning the third week in September and keep the soil moist.

5. If possible, group plants together and use pebble trays to increase humidity.

6. In two weeks, move medium- or low-light plants away from bright light into medium light.

7. After the plants have spent two or three weeks in medium light, move them to their final destinations.

8. Plants that have been gradually acclimated to indoor conditions adjust more readily and don't lose quantities of leaves or develop other problems.

Have you kept last year's poinsettia in hopes of bringing it back into bloom this year? The key is to give the plant fourteen hours of complete darkness and ten hours of light each day, beginning the third week of September and continuing until the first week of November. The options for providing the dark include:

- Place the plant in a dark closet each night, bringing it out again the next day.

- Cover the plant with a black cloth at 5:00 each afternoon and remove it at 7:00 the next morning.

- Put the plant in an unused bedroom where it will get normal light-dark cycles. Just be sure that a dusk-to-dawn light outdoors doesn't shine into the windows.

- Keep the soil moist. Also, during the day, keep the plant in bright light. Lots of morning sun is okay.

Groom all houseplants before they go back indoors. Remove all yellowed or damaged leaves and faded flowers. Clean all foliage, top and bottom. Clean splattered dirt off the pots too. If containers can't be scrubbed clean, consider new pots or hide the pots in a plastic-lined basket or a decorative container.

LAWNS

Early September is the ideal time to correct a couple of problems in cool-season lawns—getting

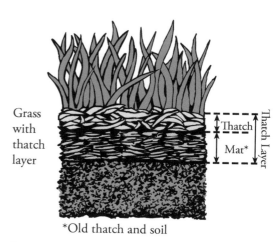

Grass with thatch layer

Thatch

Mat*

Thatch Layer

*Old thatch and soil

■ *Thatch is dead organic matter that builds up at the top of the soil and prevents water and nutrients from reaching grass roots.*

rid of excess thatch and aerating the soil (that is, allowing air to reach the soil and the grass's roots).

What is thatch? It's a layer of dead organic matter—usually grass stems, roots, and so forth—that builds up between the soil and the grass blade. A little thatch is always present, and it's not necessarily a bad thing, since it helps protect the grass's roots. It also keeps the soil from compacting. But if this layer of thatch builds up thicker than ½ inch, it can prevent water and nutrients from reaching the roots. It also provides an excellent home for insects. Because overfertilizing is one cause of thatch buildup, the problem is most prevalent with warm-season grasses that are heavy feeders—bermudagrass and zoysia among them.

Homeowners will find dethatching machines at tool rental stores. These remove the decayed layer, which is then raked up and tossed onto the compost pile. (Condo owners and others with tiny plots of grass may find a thatching rake just as convenient.)

Aeration is the process of creating spaces in the soil so that air and nutrients can get to the roots. It's often recommended for compacted soils, but is just as frequently part of the dethatching process. Aeration machines are available for rental, but manual models (about the size of a small spade, with three prongs where the shovel would go) make sense for those with small lawns.

Continue mowing lawns this month.

TREES

Harvest apples as soon as they ripen. Pick up and discard fruit that falls on the ground.

VINES AND GROUND COVERS

The time to take potted tropical vines—including allamanda, bougainvillea, and mandevilla—indoors for overwintering is when nighttime temperatures threaten to fall below 55 degrees Fahrenheit.

- Unfasten the vine from its support if it's growing on one that's outside the container.

- Spray the plant—being careful to wet the undersides of the leaves and the stem—with insecticidal soap to ensure that no insects hitchhike into the house on the vine.

- Trim back the longest shoots to the main stem or above a bud.

- Move the container to the sunniest spot in the house.

- Be careful not to overwater; once the vine is indoors, the soil won't dry out as quickly.

It's simple to save seeds of many of the annual vines you grew this year, since most are not hybrids. They will provide a free supply for the future.

Seeds should be ready within a few weeks after the flowers fade and the petals drop off. Nasturtium vine (*Tropaeolum majus*) seeds are ready when the mature fruit that holds them is dry. Harvest the seeds of morning glory when the capsule that holds the seeds is dry. Allow purple hyacinth (*Dolichos lablab*) bean pods to dry on the vine. For others, notice the changes and determine when you think the seed is dry.

- Save seeds only from vigorous, disease-free plants.

- Spread the seeds evenly on a screen so they aren't touching. Let them dry indoors for ten to fourteen days.

- Separate the seeds from any plant chaff you managed to collect.

In late September, as temperatures begin to fall, feed fish less once water temperature is less than 60 degrees Fahrenheit. Ask about fall fish food at a water garden retailer.

- Place the seeds in a plastic bag or glass jar, and seal tightly. Label the container with the name of the plant and the date.

- Store them in the freezer or a cool place.

WATER GARDENS

Cut back on fish food. When water temperature falls to 60 degrees Fahrenheit—possibly later this month—give fish less food than you may have been providing in summer and feed them less frequently (no more than once a day). Water garden suppliers have special fish food that provides what fish need going into winter.

Even though we're headed into the off-season for water gardens, you should still test the pond's water monthly, particularly if you have fish. A balanced pond that has only a little algae, no nitrates, no ammonia, and the correct pH (6.8 to 7.8) is a healthy pond. It's also a more beautiful one because the fish and underwater plants are easily seen and admired.

Cleaning out the pond is a chore that doesn't have to be done very often—maybe every four or five years—and it's one that you can postpone even longer by paying attention to keeping leaves and other debris from settling into the bottom of your pond. But eventually sludge will build up and have to be removed. Too much can be toxic to fish and encourages algae, the bane of the water garden.

1. Remove as much of the water as possible, and place the fish in a temporary tank. Consider covering containers so the fish can't jump out.

2. Remove plants from the pond and place them in the shade. Don't let them dry out.

3. Pump the rest of the water from the water garden.

4. Remove all the solids at the bottom of the pond. Do not scrub the sides of the pond or use any cleaning chemicals.

5. Return any saved water to the pond.

6. Place fish and plants back in the pond.

7. Slowly fill the round with fresh water, adding a dechlorinator and any other products you normally use to remove chemicals in your water supply.

WATER

ALL
Check emitters in drip irrigation systems to find any that have gotten clogged. Clean and replace them.

ANNUALS AND PERENNIALS
If rainfall is less than normal this month, check around your flowers to see whether the soil is dry, and then water those that need it. Since dahlias are in their prime and like plenty of moisture, see that they're watered once or twice a week if rainfall is less than an inch every seven to ten days. Keep the water at ground level to avoid getting the foliage wet and initiating fungal diseases. Water newly planted mums or asters so that their soil is moist but not soggy. This increases their chances of surviving the winter.

FERTILIZE

ANNUALS
When setting out ornamental cabbage and kale, mix granular fertilizer with the soil at the root level. On newly planted pansies, use a water-soluble fertilizer each week until frost. A high-phosphorus fertilizer (usually one that has the word *bloom* in its name) is best for pansies. It will encourage flowering now and bud production for later blooms.

BULBS
Toward the end of September and continuing through November, fertilize previously planted spring-flowering bulbs—everything from crocus to tulips. Fall is the time of year that these bulbs begin growing and need the nutrients that fertilizer supplies. It really can make a difference in the size and number of the flowers and in whether your bulbs perennialize.

But how do you know where spring-flowering bulbs located in order to feed them? Ah, that's the difficulty. You have to mark them in some way in the spring:

- Use brightly colored golf tees.

- Place thin bamboo stakes at the corners of bulb beds.

CHOOSE NEW LOCATIONS FOR ROSES

Never plant a new rosebush where another rose was removed. The new rose simply won't grow well, because of a toxic substance exuded by the roots of the first bush.

- With bulbs planted near the street, use a squirt of spray paint on the curb.

- Plant grape hyacinths or Dutch iris in all your bulb beds. Their foliage comes up in fall and marks the areas that need fertilizing.

Slow-release fertilizers made especially for bulbs—some of which are organic—will continue to feed all winter. If you'd prefer to use a granular fertilizer that you have on hand, sprinkle 8-8-8 over the bed now or next month. Then feed again when foliage has grown 1 inch above soil level next year.

EDIBLES

Fall vegetable crops need some fertilizer—especially nitrogen, which is no longer in the soil from your spring or early summer fertilizing. The fertilizer mixed with the soil at planting time may be sufficient, especially if your soil is well amended with organic matter, but keep an eye on the new plants as they sprout and grow. If they aren't growing as quickly as normal in fall, or if they aren't as green as they should be, sprinkle a handful of granular or organic slow-release fertilizer around each plant.

LAWNS

Feed all lawns on September 1. The recommended amount is 1 pound of nitrogen per 1,000 square feet of lawn. (How that translates into pounds of commercial fertilizer is explained on page 84.) This will be the last fertilizer application of the year for warm-season grasses.

PERENNIALS

Don't fertilize mums. This includes those you just bought and those that have been growing in the garden for a year or more. Late fertilizing encourages tender new plant growth, which is likely to get killed by frost. You want the plants to be developing deep, strong roots to carry them through the winter instead of new top growth.

WATER GARDENS

Hardy water lilies and marginal or bog plants need to gradually slow down their growth and get ready for winter. To help them do that, stop fertilizing four to six weeks before your first frost date.

PROBLEM-SOLVE

HOUSEPLANTS

When you bring houseplants back inside your house this month, don't let any insects hitchhike indoors. How do you prevent it?

- Mix up a tub or bucket of five parts warm water and one part insecticidal soap. Remove plants from their pots, place them in the mixture, and let the plants stand for an hour.

- Even after doing this, you may want to keep outdoor plants isolated for about a month from those that spent the summer inside. Sometimes a stray insect manages to get in anyway, or insect eggs hatch. The problem will be easier to deal with when you can keep the infestation confined to one or two plants.

PERENNIALS

Heavily sprinkling black pepper on the ground around newly planted perennials may deter squirrels and chipmunks, which can otherwise do quite a bit of damage by digging. If slugs have been a problem in your perennial garden, encourage toads to take up residence by providing "toad homes." Toads dine on the slugs.

TREES

If tulip poplar leaves yellow and begin to fall off this month, the problem is often lack of water.

Check susceptible trees for fall webworm nests. If you find some, remove them from trees with a gloved hand and destroy.

As you walk about your yard this month, keep an eye out for possible tree or shrub problems. Signs include:

- Leaves falling off prematurely

- Dying or discolored leaves

- Stem dieback

If you spot any of those signs, look closer to see whether you can determine the problem. Look for telltale signs of insects or diseases. See whether the

■ *To avoid insects hitchhiking inside the house on the foliage of houseplants that summered outdoors, carefully clean the tops and bottoms of all leaves before the plants are taken indoors.*

soil seems very dry or excess water is standing in a puddle. If you're not sure, ask an Extension agent or a knowledgeable employee at a good nursery for advice.

WATER GARDENS

By the end of the month, have leaf netting in place. It's much easier to prevent leaves from getting into your water garden than it is to remove them once they're there. But netting can also prevent damage to fish and plants by wild animals, ducks, and herons.

One day the pond is full, and the next day the water level is down considerably. If the situation continues, suspect a leak. Sometimes these are obvious—there's a wet spot beside the pool. But other cases require detective work.

- Shut off any pumps. If the water level stops falling, you've located the leak—in the

waterfall or plumbing system. Closely inspect all connections. Look for backups caused by plant material or other obstructions.

- If the water level continues to fall after you've turned off the pump, the leak is probably in the liner or edge. Drop a few drops of food-safe vegetable dye (available at grocery stores) in the water along the sides to see whether you can find where colored water is escaping the pond.

- Once the water reaches below the leak, it stops and that makes it harder to find the leak. You can add some more water (treating for chlorine and other water chemicals) and then run the dye test just described. Or you can move rocks here and there and check in the folds of the liner for the leak.

- Patching material is available to fix liner leaks.

October

October often requires the same sort of busyness in the garden that April does. But where you're gearing up for a new season in April, you're winding down in October, taking care of all the tasks that need to be done before winter arrives. Think of it as cleaning up after a successful party and pleasurably preparing for the next one.

Although frosts can arrive in October in our region, mostly the weather is excellent for working outdoors—not too cold and rarely too hot. Rain can be abundant—or not. Attendance at college football games is more likely to interfere with weekend gardening than inclement weather.

Still, most of the things that need to be accomplished in the October garden can be fit around other activities—overseeding a zoysia lawn with rye so it won't be brown till May (when the zoysia will turn green), harvesting the last tomatoes and some interesting pumpkins from the garden, enjoying a final burst of fall color from mums and asters, as well as deciduous holly shrubs and the surprising purple show put on by beautyberry (*Callicarpa* spp.).

And while you're savoring the beauty of fall, ready the garden for its six-month rest but plant bulbs to welcome a new season and set out charming pansies so everyone can enjoy the sprightly blooms all winter. Gardening is always a matter of looking forward (can't wait for those tulips to bloom!), looking back (those daylilies were so easy and so good-looking; maybe we should have more), while indulging in a little instant gratification (pansies or ornamental kale, or maybe both?).

And October is a perfect example of that. One Saturday you might be planting tulips in chicken wire boxes to outwit the small rodents that love to nosh on them. Another Saturday, you're taking down bean supports, washing them off, and storing them until they're needed again next year. And many of us will begin thinking of indoor gardening again once the weather cools. We buy new houseplants and repot some old favorites that have outgrown their containers. We take cuttings of easy-to-root houseplants so we can share our bounty with friends or at a fall festival. Yes, October is a great gardening month; you'll enjoy it.

PLAN

ALL

It can take years to get some garden soils to the point where you feel they're just right, and even then, organic matter added to soils decays rapidly in our climate. What's a gardener to do?

Keep improving the soil with a new batch of organic matter each year. That can get expensive if you buy soil amendments, but if you make your own compost, it's free. With leaves falling this month and vegetable plants being killed by frost, fall is a good time to get serious about composting. The general directions are on pages 216-218. You can go the fast route—making a layered compost pile as you would lasagna, keeping it moist and turning it regularly. Or if time doesn't matter, you can just pile everything into a bin and let it even-tually rot. In the latter case, though, you have to be careful not to toss anything with seeds into the pile (from weeds to rotten tomatoes), any diseased or insect-covered plant part, or any plant that has been treated with a chemical. Even if you choose the let-it-rot method, as most people do, you can speed the process some by cutting up in small pieces everything you add to the pile.

What about newspapers as compost? A few—shredded or torn to bits—are okay, but mostly they're better as mulch. If you don't have a compost bin, consider building or buying one in October.

ANNUALS

Find out when the first frost of fall typically hap-pens in your area. Then make a note each year of the date it actually occurs in your yard. You may also want to write down those spots that freeze sooner or much later than the rest of the yard. And keep a record of which plants withstand a couple of freezes. Sometimes this is because the plant itself withstands the cold, and sometimes it's because the location is protected. It's a handy thing to know.

As your area's first frost approaches, listen closely to the local weather forecast each night. Often the first frost is a light one, and another may not occur for several weeks afterward. It's a shame to lose your annuals when they can continue blooming for several weeks longer.

- Don't cover plants with plastic. When the sun comes up and hits it the next morning, it will burn the plants beneath the plastic.

- Old bedspreads, mattress pads, and quilts provide good protection and don't have to be removed until the day has warmed up.

- Some gardeners use nonwoven landscape fabrics for frost protection. Since they come in rolls, they're handy. But they may not provide more than 2 to 4 degrees of protection. If the temperature falls below 28 degrees Fahrenheit, plants beneath them can be harmed. Consider applying a double thickness in the afternoon to capture the warmth that's already in the soil and around the plant. Also experiment with different brands of nonwoven fabric if you like to protect plants from frost in fall and spring.

BULBS

You may be thinking that you'll have to wait till next year before you see any spring-flowering bulbs in bloom. But not so. It's easy to grow some bulbs indoors, either through forcing (see page 198) or by growing paper-white narcissus (page 209) and amaryllis. With a nice supply of bulbs available in October, this is a good time to make your selections.

Continue to plan for new beds—and buy the bulbs to go in them—all this month. Mesh bags of bulbs may seem to be a bargain, but they're usually smaller bulbs and aren't always cared for in ship-ping and in stores as carefully as individual bulbs. Remember the rule of thumb: The bigger the bulb, the bigger and more numerous the flowers growing from it.

Get out your garden notebook and write down the names of the bulbs you're planting, their color and height, where you're putting them in the yard, and where you bought them. This record comes in quite handy when you really like a particular tulip or other bulb next spring, but can't recall the name of it or even which garden center sold it to you.

PERENNIALS AND ORNAMENTAL GRASSES

While the larger types of ornamental grasses make wonderful specimen plants mixed with perennials or annuals, grasses can fill an entire border by themselves. An ornamental grass bed is intriguing in all seasons except for a few weeks in very early spring, when the grasses have to be trimmed back. If you decide to try one, put it where you can see it (and maybe even hear it, as the winds blow through the grasses) in the winter.

ROSES

Does this year's experience with roses have you dreaming about more roses for next year?

- Start collecting catalogs of rose suppliers now. Many rose nurseries accept orders in the fall for delivery at the right planting time in spring. Local nurseries that sell a lot of roses may also let you order ahead. Talk to several and see what their policies are. Also find out how they decide which roses to order for delivery in late winter or early spring.

- Check the All-America Rose Selections website (http://www.rose.org) to learn about next year's award-winning roses. AARS roses are grown for at least two years in various test gardens around the United States and Canada, where they're given ordinary care and graded on their performance. While not every rose that wins an AARS award is ideal for the growing conditions in the South, most are disease-resistant bushes that have much to recommend them. They're a good place to start your search for new roses.

- Also ask friends who love roses about their favorites. Many older roses are tried and true, and will give you no trouble.

- The selection of top-rated yellow roses is smaller than for other colors, but there are some excellent choices. If you haven't bought the American Rose Society's *Handbook for Selecting Roses*, jot a reminder in your garden notebook to get a copy of the latest edition after the first of the year.

Remember all those times this past growing season that you had to drag a hose around the yard to water your roses? Wouldn't you rather avoid that next year? Now's the time to investigate your watering options.

TREES

When you're considering a new tree for the yard, do you wonder whether you should buy a large tree and have it planted by the nursery or a small tree that you can easily handle?

- Factors that favor getting a large tree: You've moved into a new house, and this tree will be in a prominent place in the landscape. In effect, it will become a focal point while smaller plants grow. (A larger tree gives a more finished look to a landscape.)

- Factors that favor purchasing a small tree: It's cheaper and will require less watering. Because a smaller tree adjusts to being planted better than a big one, the two trees may be the same size in just a few years.

VINES AND GROUNDCOVERS

Vines can grow up walls and on fences and can climb strings. But if you're going to build or buy a trellis or arbor, it's important to match the support to the vine that's going to be growing on it. Because annual vines are relatively light, if you make a mistake when placing them, they're gone by fall; you can try them somewhere else next year. But big vines require sturdier support, and wisteria needs the strongest of all.

PLANT

ANNUALS

In our part of the country, pansies and ornamental cabbage and kale have become outdoor decorating fixtures in the autumn landscape. Plant them as early in the month as possible.

- Ornamental cabbage and kale may not make it all the way through winter, but are unusual enough that they're worth planting even if they last only till January. Place them where you need a bold accent but where they won't be missed if they're removed.

- Pansies can grow in sun or partial shade. They look much better over winter when spaced closely—about 4 inches apart. From planting until frost, fertilize weekly with a liquid fertilizer made for flowering plants.

- Firm soil gently around both kinds of plants so they won't be heaved out of the ground as the soil freezes and then thaws.

- Water thoroughly.

- Mulch with 2 to 3 inches of organic material for protection from the cold.

BULBS

Finally, the month you've been waiting for—the time to plant tulips, daffodils, hyacinths, crocuses, and a host of other spring-flowering bulbs. The photographs with the bulb bins, or in catalogs and magazines, look so appealing and colorful that you're planting dreams, too. Fortunately for the gardener, unless wildlife interferes, bulbs usually deliver on the dream.

If you plan to use a bulb planter instead of digging up a bed, be sure it's heavy-duty, or it won't last. One handy trick with a bulb planter is not to remove the plug of soil from it. As you step on the crossbar to push the tool down in the ground to dig the second hole, the first plug will be pushed out. It can then be put on top of the previous bulb. Warning: This works only for already-improved soil or light soil. It isn't a recommended technique for clay.

Use chicken wire or hardware cloth over bulbs if you've had problems with wildlife. Some people make a little basket of chicken wire and put the bulbs inside. Others plant the bulbs, then lay a straight piece of hardware cloth on top, covered by soil. The bulbs will grow through the holes.

HERE'S HOW

TO PLANT SPRING-FLOWERING BULBS

If you're planting just a few bulbs, you'll probably want to dig individual holes with a trowel, a shovel, or—for spring-flowering bulbs only—a sturdy bulb-planting tool. If you plant lots of spring bulbs—and that's how they look their best, in groups of one hundred—you'll find it easier to dig a bed.

1. Make the bed 8 inches deep or at least 1 inch deeper than the recommended planting depth of the bulbs you're planting. (I always plant tulips 12 inches deep. It seems to keep them coming back many more years than they would otherwise.)

2. Place the soil on the driveway or on a tarp.

3. Loosen the soil on the bottom of the bed, and till in some Nature's Helper™ or other fine bark and the amount of Bulb Booster™ fertilizer recommended on the package. (If you can't find Bulb Booster, use 10-10-10 granular fertilizer, or equivalent.)

4. Space the bulbs in the bed according to the suggestions on their tags or packets.

5. Mix the soil removed from the hole with one-fourth to one-half organic matter and replace half of it over the bulbs.

6. Water thoroughly.

7. Add the remainder of the soil.

8. Water again.

9. Mulch with 2 to 3 inches of shredded leaves, pine straw, or other fine mulch.

HOW TO PLANT BULBS

1. First scrape the mulch away from the planting area. Then remove the soil from the planting area to make a trench or hole that is the depth of four to six times the height of the bulbs you're planting.

2. Then, set the bulbs in the planting area. For a natural look, mix several types of bulbs together in a bucket and then scatter them on the ground. Fix the bulbs so the pointy end is up.

3. Sprinkle ground cayenne pepper on the bulbs to keep the squirrels from eating the bulbs. (They don't like the taste of the pepper.) If you have serious problems with creatures digging up bulbs, consider making a makeshift cage out of chicken wire. Plant the bulbs in the cage and bury it.

4. Cover the bulbs with soil. You'll want to cover them with enough soil so that the bulbs are buried at least four to six times their height. If you don't feel like digging, you don't have to. Scatter the bulbs and cover them with soil at least four to six times as deep as the bulbs are tall. Your flower bed will be slightly taller in the spring, but you'll have saved yourself a lot of work!

Or you can soak bulbs in bulb protectant before you plant them. (This is effective only the year of planting, though.) See page 45 for a list of bulbs that aren't usually bothered by wild critters.

EDIBLES

Plant garlic this month. Separate a bulb into individual cloves and plant each clove 2 inches deep and 4 inches apart in a part of the garden that has well-drained soil. (Garlic stays small if grown in unamended clay.) Since the garlic will remain in place until about June, place it where it won't be in the way as you till the garden in the fall or spring.

HOUSEPLANTS

Does your spider plant have lots of "babies"? (These are known as aerial plantlets.) It's easy to root them this month:

- Fill a 2- to 3-inch pot with moistened potting mix.

- Place the pot next to the spider plant.

- Pin the plantlet to the soil using a V-shaped piece of thin, flexible wire or a bent paperclip.

- Keep the soil moist.

- Remove the pin and cut the plantlet from the mother plant after it has rooted.

Or you can remove the plantlet from the parent plant in the beginning and place it in its own pot so that it's in constant contact with the moist soil.

Keep potting up houseplants that you rooted in the past six weeks. These will make nice gifts or provide you with more plants to place around the house. Once rooted cuttings have been placed in pots of soil, put them somewhere you can give them extra attention for the next three or four weeks. They may need a little more water, humidity, or light as they're adjusting to their new homes.

LAWNS

If you missed establishing a fescue or Kentucky bluegrass lawn in September, is there still time to get it done in October? Maybe. It depends on when the first frost arrives and whether temperatures remain cool after that. Obviously, you'll get more reliable results the first part of the month—cool-season grasses germinate best if the soil temperature is 58 degrees Fahrenheit or above. But if you've just completed a new house the middle or end of the month, plant grass anyway—anything that takes hold is better than bare ground. See page 165 for tips on starting a new lawn from seed.

This month is a good time to overseed with warm-season grasses such as zoysia and bermudagrass with annual or perennial rye so they will be green, not brown, all winter. See page 73 for tips on overseeding.

- When: Try to do it two to four weeks before the first-frost date for your area. But since rye germinates very quickly, you can usually sow the seed up to and just beyond the first fall frost.

- How much: Use about 10 pounds of rye seed for each 1,000 square feet of lawn.

- Fertilizer: Don't use a high-nitrogen fertilizer when overseeding warm-season grasses. That can bring the bermudagrass or zoysia out of dormancy just as cold weather begins.

- Water: The seed will need to be kept constantly moist—through either watering or rainfall—until germination.

The downside of having a green lawn all winter is the possible need for occasional mowing, especially in fall and spring. Mow when the rye gets to be about 3 inches tall and cut it to about 2 to 2½ inches high.

PERENNIALS AND ORNAMENTAL GRASSES

The cooler days of October present an excellent opportunity to prepare new beds for ornamental grasses and perennials. There several ways to prepare areas not previously used for growing plants. (See top of next page.) Choose the one that works best for you.

Once the bed is prepared, it's a good idea to cover it with layers of newspapers (held down by rocks)

HERE'S HOW

TO PREPARE ORNAMENTAL BEDS FOR PLANTING

- Method 1: Kill grass and weeds by smothering them. First, mow as close as you can. Then cover the area with a thick layer of newspaper, topped by a thick layer of mulch. An alternative to the newspaper is black plastic, which works very quickly to kill existing vegetation in hot, sunny spots. You may want to cover the black plastic with an organic mulch, so it won't look so bad. When you're ready to plant, remove the plastic and till the mulch and newspapers into the soil. Add one-fourth to one-third the volume of the soil in organic matter (aged mushroom compost, rotted leaves, compost, fine pine bark, and so on).

- Method 2: Mow the area closely. Till the soil and then water. Wait seven to ten days and then till up any weeds or grass that have sprouted. You may need to do this three more times, at ten-day intervals, to ensure that most weed seeds have germinated. (This method doesn't work well if the area contains weeds that spread by underground runners.) Then amend the soil with organic matter (see method 1) and plant or leave fallow till spring.

- Method 3: Rent a sod cutter and remove existing sod. (This can also be done by hand, with a shovel, in small areas.) Move the strips of sod wherever you need new grass. Water the area to encourage weed seeds to sprout. Kill them by method 1 or by digging them out. After the first removal of weeds, water again and remove the weeds two weeks later. Then till ample organic matter into the soil. (See method 1.)

---

or with a 3-inch layer of mulch. (Shredded leaves are good, and they're readily available this month.) This helps prevent any weeds from taking hold before spring planting.

SHRUBS

October is a perfect month for planting new or transplanting existing shrubs.

1. Wet the soil deeply at least twenty-four hours before you plan to move a shrub.

2. Dig a new hole where the shrub will be planted. Estimate the size, keeping in mind that it's better to be too wide than not wide enough. Roots must be given room to spread out.

3. Use a spading fork to gently probe the soil around the shrub, starting 4 feet out from the trunk. The object is to locate as many roots as possible, especially the major roots.

4. Dig under and around the main trunk of the shrub, at least 2 feet around.

5. Find and loosen vital roots by rocking and lifting.

6. When a shovel can fit all the way underneath the shrub, tip the rootball to one side so you can get a tarp or piece of strong burlap beneath it. Do the same to the other side.

7. Use the tarp or burlap to help lift the shrub out of the hole. This may take several people, depending on the size of the shrub. If you have to break off chunks of soil because the whole thing is too heavy, that's all right. But take care to preserve as many roots as possible. They're the secret to success.

8. Gently ease the shrub from its burlap covering into its new hole, making sure that it's at the same level it grew before, never deeper.

9. Arrange the roots so they aren't crowded.

10. Fill the hole about halfway with soil.

11. Water with a transplanting solution.

HOW TO PLANT A TREE

12. Add the rest of the soil.

13. Water again.

14. Cover with 3 inches of organic mulch—shredded leaves, pine straw, or finely shredded bark.

15. Water regularly until the ground freezes.

You may also plant shrubs from the nursery at this time, either those sold in containers or ones that are balled and burlapped. If you're planting broad-leaf evergreen shrubs, as well as deciduous shrubs, get the evergreens planted first during the month, then tackle the deciduous shrubs.

TREES

October is a good month to plant evergreen and deciduous trees, both those grown in containers and those balled and burlapped. The size of the planting hole is very important for the survival of a newly planted tree. It should be at least three times as wide as the rootball, but not any deeper.

1. Dig a hole no deeper than the depth of the rootball but at least twice as wide, preferably three or four times wider.

2. If the wrapping is real burlap, you simply have to cut and remove the fabric on top of the ball and peel the burlap down the sides so it stays below the soil line. It will eventually decompose. Synthetic burlap must be removed completely. Remove the wire basket that surrounds the root ball and burlap, if present.

3. Place the plant in the hole and adjust the hole depth so that the plant is about 1 inch higher than it was planted in the nursery to allow for settling of soil. Use a shovel handle laid across the hole to help determine the proper depth.

4. Shovel in the soil around the root ball, stopping to tamp down the soil when the hole is half full.

5. Fill the rest of the hole with loose soil and tamp down again to ensure good contact between the soil and the roots.

6. Soak the planting area with water. Once the soil has settled, build up a 2- to 3-inch basin around the plant to catch rainfall and irrigation water. However, do not build a basin if your soil is very heavy and doesn't drain well.

7. Apply 2 to 3 inches of organic mulch such as shredded bark or wood chips, keeping the mulch a few inches away from the trunk.

Never pick up or carry a tree by its trunk. Instead, handle it by its container or rootball.

Handle root systems of trees that are balled and burlapped carefully to make certain they're not damaged while being transported home, moved to the planting site, or placed in the hole. If the rootball falls apart, the tree may die. This is especially true of a needled evergreen. Also take pains not to damage the bark, since wounds leave openings for insects or diseases to enter.

Remove all tags and labels before you plant the tree. Do keep them, though, so you know the name of the tree and what type of care it needs. A good place to store these is in an envelope kept with your garden notebook.

When you choose a spot to plant a tree, be sure that it's not within 15 feet of a sidewalk. The roots of some trees can crack the sidewalk.

It's rarely necessary to wrap the trunk of a tree when it's planted. Wrapping may cause an increase in disease, insect, and water damage to the trunk.

CARE

ANNUALS

If you have pots of annuals that will spend the winter indoors—geraniums, scaveola, and wax begonias will do fine as long as there's enough light—take them in at the first of the month. It's harder for the plants to become acclimated when they've become used to temperatures in the 40-degree range and all of a sudden are placed where it's 70 degrees Fahrenheit.

Don't remove snapdragons or annual dianthus (pinks) from the garden at the end of the season. They will often live through the winters in our region, becoming perennials instead of annuals. Both begin blooming early in spring. Even when snapdragons get killed by a bad winter, they often come back from seed.

Your yard will usually look nicer if you cut down and remove frost-killed annuals. But you may want to consider leaving a few with large seeds— sunflowers, marigolds, and zinnias, for instance— because they attract birds to the garden in the fall and winter.

Encourage reseeding. Some plants—such as cleome, cosmos, and four-o'clocks—reseed readily. So don't disturb the soil too much when removing these plants; that way, the seeds will germinate next spring and provide you with free plants.

Discourage fungus diseases. If some plants had serious fungus problems during the growing season, it is a good idea to remove the mulch from the bed in which these plants grew and replace it with shredded leaves or other fresh mulch. Otherwise, the fungus is likely to overwinter in the old mulch and become a problem again next summer.

BULBS

Some gardeners like to leave certain summer-flowering bulbs in the ground over winter— blackberry lily, crocosmia, lily, lily-of-the-valley, and spider lily—to bloom again the next year. Caladiums are tropical plants that will die if exposed to temperatures below freezing, so they're always dug up and stored (see page 167) or treated as annuals.

Dahlias and cannas will often survive winter when left in the ground under an extra-thick blanket of mulch, but may not make it through an extracold winter. So if you have dahlias and cannas that are irreplaceable, dig at least some of them for storage. Most growers think gladiolus performs best the next year if the corms are dug in the fall and replanted the following spring.

1. Carefully dig up the corms, tubers, or rhizomes, being careful not to damage them.

2. Shake off the soil.

3. Remove small new gladiolus corms from the main corm.

4. Trim off any damaged or dead portions of dahlia tubers.

■ *When digging up and storing bulbs, tubers, and rhizomes of summer-flowering plants, such as dahlias, glads, and caladiums, attach labels to the clumps so you can identify them next spring.*

5. Place the corms, tubers, or rhizomes in a shady spot that's out of the weather but has good air circulation. Leave them there for about a week to dry out.

6. Brush off any soil that remains.

7. You may want to dust the corms, rhizomes, or tubers with a fungicide such as sulfur to help prevent them from rotting while in storage.

8. Store them in a shallow tray of dry peat moss or vermiculite. (Store dahlias upside down.)

9. Place the tray in a spot where you can easily check it several times during the winter. The temperature should stay below 50 degrees Fahrenheit but above freezing.

If you planted new lily bulbs last month, add 1 or 2 inches more mulch over their soil, so they will be protected from the vagaries of winter weather. Do the same for cannas, elephant ears, and glads that you plan to leave in the ground, if you didn't renew their mulch last month.

EDIBLES
Pick green tomatoes if a frost threatens, and you don't plan to protect them. Wash them carefully and place them in a single layer in a dark spot. Check them weekly, and toss out any that have rotted. Don't place them on a sunny windowsill.

Harvest winter squash before frost. The skins should be hard enough that a fingernail can't pierce them. Pumpkins should be an even color. Cut the stem from the vine, and let the squash or pumpkin dry in the garden for a week or two. Then store in as cool a spot as is available. (An ideal temperature range is 50 to 55 degrees Fahrenheit.)

Harvest vegetables regularly. This is especially important for warm-season crops that will soon be killed by frost. Besides, plants continue to produce more vegetables if they're picked regularly.

Keep an eye on cool-season vegetables such as kale, collards, and cauliflower. Harvest them as they begin to mature this month.

Remove ferny asparagus tops after they've turned yellow or been killed by frost. Mulch the plants with 2 to 4 inches of organic matter.

During a dry spell, dig sweet potatoes when the roots are about 2 to 3 inches in diameter and soil temperature is above 55 degrees Fahrenheit. Dig carefully, since the skins are thin and easily damaged. Place the sweet potatoes—unwashed—in a warm, dry spot (in a heated part of the house if temperatures outside or in the garage have gotten chilly). Avoid sun. They will need to cure for ten to fourteen days. Then store them in a single layer in a dark, cool place (but with temperatures above 50 degrees Fahrenheit—don't refrigerate). Check sweet potatoes weekly to make sure they haven't begun to rot. Remove any that have deteriorated.

As vegetable plants are killed by frost, remove them from the garden. If they suffered no disease or insect problems, break them into small sections and toss them onto the compost pile with the tree leaves you're probably adding weekly.

HOUSEPLANTS
Now's the time to begin looking ahead to Christmas—Christmas cactus, that is. (The plant with the smooth ends on the segments is the true Christmas cactus. The one with the hook- or crablike ends is Thanksgiving cactus. They're treated the same, so they're usually referred to as holiday cactus.)

To get your holiday cactus to bloom:

1. Cut back on watering the plants. That doesn't mean not watering them; just water less than usual. Let the soil dry out completely between waterings. (If leaves begin to shrivel, water lightly.)

2. Place the plants where temperatures are between 45 and 58 degrees Fahrenheit at night until buds form. Do not expose the plants to freezing temperatures.

3. Or, if you don't have a place where temperatures are within the 45 to 58 degree Fahrenheit range, move the plants to a spot where they can have thirteen hours of complete darkness and eleven hours of bright light each day. (Watch out for lamps and for street lights shining through windows.) The second part of that regimen is essential. Sometimes gardeners just place a holiday cactus in a dark closet and leave it there. But the plant needs light, as well as a period of darkness.

4. As soon as buds form, move the plants into bright light (no sun—if the foliage turns reddish, it's getting too much light).

5. Keep the soil moist and fertilize every other week until blooming is complete.

Keep an eye on houseplants that summered outdoors to see whether they are affected by lower humidity levels (flowers dropping off prematurely, leaf tips drying up, leaves curling or becoming deformed). If so, increase humidity levels where possible. Remember that misting doesn't do much more than temporarily raise the amount of moisture in the air. It's not a long-term solution.

LAWNS
If you have oak trees, you get a good crop of acorns dropping onto your lawn in fall. Usually the squirrels that live in the oaks take care of most of them for you. But some years the raining down of acorns is so heavy that even the squirrels can't keep up. Try to remove as many as you can by hand. (Or see whether you can hire a kid for this.) Acorns really mess up your lawn mower if they're left in place.

Keep mowing the grass as long as it's growing. When zoysia and bermudagrass lose their green, that's the signal to stop mowing them. But fescue and Kentucky bluegrass like cooler weather. If there's been ample rainfall, and especially if they've been fertilized this fall, they'll be growing nicely until a hard frost comes along.

PERENNIALS AND ORNAMENTAL GRASSES
Fall's first frost comes to many parts of the region this month. Be prepared to cover those plants that need protection to keep them blooming a while longer. Also plan—after the first killing frost—to take down supports and stakes, clean them off, and

store them out of the weather so they'll last longer. Some supports may need a coat of green spray paint after a year or two of use. This is a good time to take care of that so they'll be ready to put into action when needed next spring.

Deadhead asters, mums, boltonia, and other fall flowers that have finished blooming. Cut these back or not, as you prefer, after they've been nipped by frost. The ones that have seeds attract birds (especially goldfinches) to the garden. But in spots highly visible from the street or your front windows, large areas of dead perennials look messy.

ROSES
In the coldest parts of the area, consider what you're going to do with container-grown roses over the winter. Your choices include:

1. Leave them outdoors, in a protected spot, mounding organic mulch over the pot and canes. (There should be about 12 inches over the bud union.) You may use anything from shredded leaves (although they blow off rather easily), to straw, to aged mushroom compost.

2. Dig a hole big enough for the pot, place the container in the hole, replace the soil around it, and then build up a 12-inch mound of mulch over and around the bush.

3. Let the rose stay outside until after the first frost or two (as long as temperatures don't fall into the low-20 degrees Fahrenheit range). Then move the containers into an unheated garage or basement for the winter. Many gardeners choose this option for tree roses, which are hard to protect over winter.

SHRUBS
Have you been growing figs, gardenias, or lemons or oranges in containers on the patio or in the yard? Move them back indoors before the first frost. Some may have grown to such a hefty size that they require the efforts of two people as movers. Place them in as much sun as possible over winter.

Deciduous hollies develop such an enormous crop of berries that it may take your breath away. Often they completely line the branches. Cut a few branches covered with berries, bring them indoors, and place them in a vase. They'll last a very long time. When cutting the berried branches, prune back to a main branch, to the ground, or to just above a bud on the branch. Use sharp pruners and cut at a 45-degree angle.

TREES

October is leaf time in our region. So many of those wonderful trees you appreciated during the spring and fall are going to drop their leaves now. Don't think of their cleanup as a chore. Rather, think of it as the trees' providing soil amendments and mulch.

- Remove leaves at least weekly. If they get too thick, they'll smother the grass and, in mulched areas, can prevent rainfall from penetrating.

- Pile leaves onto the compost pile. If you don't have a compost pile, this is an ideal time to start one. (See pages 216–218.)

- Save some leaves (usually the last ones of the season) to shred into mulch. Spread the leaves an inch thick in a circle on the driveway. Mow over them until they're in small pieces. If you have a shredder, use that instead.

- Be careful to rake up and remove from the yard all leaves of trees that suffered disease damage during the year—leaf spots, mildew, and so on—or those that were infested with insects. Getting them away from the susceptible tree helps prevent future problems.

VINES AND GROUNDCOVERS

Remove seedpods on annual vines, and save the seeds to plant next year. See the September chapter to learn more.

■ *Save money by turning leaves into compost or leaf mold, which can be used as a soil amendment or a mulch next spring. Try to rake up leaves weekly in fall so they don't damage the grass, preventing light and water to get to it.*

OCTOBER

HERE'S HOW

TO HARVEST GOURDS

- Leave ornamental gourds on the vines until they mature. This is usually when the stems turn brown and the tendrils are completely dry.
- Remove the gourds from the vines.
- Wash them with soapy water to which a little liquid bleach has been added.
- Place the gourds on a screen or wire mesh that's several feet up in the air to dry.
- Rotate the gourds as they dry, so they won't develop any soft spots.
- The time it takes for a gourd to dry varies according the type of gourd, its size, and the thickness of the shell. A gourd is ready when it feels light and you can hear the seeds rattle inside.

Dig up the roots of the ornamental sweet potato vine after a frost has killed the leaves. Remove the leaves, and discard any tubers that were damaged when digging. Let the vine dry in a warm, dry place for twenty-four hours. Put the plant in a flat or box of peat moss, and store it in a cool, dark location. Replant next spring.

Don't let leaves smother groundcovers. Once leaves start falling heavily, blow them off evergreen groundcovers at least weekly.

Evergreen vines and groundcover plants should go into winter well watered. This helps prevent the "burning" of leaves that you sometimes see during cold weather.

WATER GARDENS

If you didn't put netting over your water garden last month to catch falling leaves, do it now. The netting should have small- to medium-sized holes. Large openings leave too much space for debris to fall through. Too many leaves in the pond will upset the balance of the water. If you've had problems with cats, raccoons, and other animals preying on your fish, the problem can sometimes get worse in cold weather, because the fish are more sluggish. In that case, you may want to leave the netting over the pond all winter to foil the intruders.

When the water temperature is between 52 and 60 degrees Fahrenheit, continue to feed the fish, but don't feed them as much as usual or more

often than once a day. A reminder for the colder parts of the state and during those years when cold weather seems to arrive early: stop feeding fish when the water temperature falls below 50 degrees Fahrenheit, and resume next spring when the temperature in the pond again climbs above 50 degrees.

As hardy water lilies fade, cut back dead and dying leaves, and sink the plants to the bottom of the pond. Do the same with marginal plants. Some of these may survive if left along the edges of the water garden, but since we don't know what winter's going to bring, it's best to put them in deep water, where their roots won't freeze.

After a hard freeze kills the foliage of tropical water plants growing in containers, here's what you need to do:

- Empty all the water from the pot.
- Store any cold-sensitive containers—ceramic, pottery, terracotta—indoors so they aren't affected by the weather.
- Consider discarding inexpensive plants such as bunches of anacharis (also called elodea).

If you'd like to try keeping tropical water lilies, there are two methods: Dig a hole in an area of the yard that has moist soil. Place the pots of plants in it and nestle some soil around the containers—it doesn't have to come up to their top rims. Just before the next predicted hard freeze, cover the pots with shredded leaves. A second technique is to place the plants—still in their pots—in a plastic tub that's kept in an unheated garage or basement. Check weekly to make sure the soil is slightly moist.

WATER

EDIBLES

Water vegetables and herbs that are still in good shape just as carefully at the end of the season as you do earlier in the year. As long as they're producing, take good care of them.

LAWNS

Four groups of grass-growing homeowners should keep watering in mind this month:

- Those with new lawns

- Those who are overseeding or have just over-seeded warm-season lawns

- Those who have overseeded cool-season lawns

- Those who live where rainfall hasn't added up to 1 inch for the past couple of weeks

Play close attention to watering new cool-season lawns that were sown last month. Until cold weather arrives, they should receive 1 to 1½ inches of water weekly, through either rainfall or your efforts.

FERTILIZE

BULBS

Fertilize spring-flowering bulbs as you plant, preferably using a slow-release bulb fertilizer. Last month, did you get around to fertilizing the previous year's bulb plantings? If not, do it in October. Follow the directions on the label, watering the fertilizer in after application.

HOUSEPLANTS

Fertilize all houseplants—except holiday cactus—one last time near the beginning of October. Then you won't need to feed most of them again until March. As temperatures cool down and light levels become less bright, many houseplants go dormant or rest through the winter. During that time, they aren't growing and therefore don't need fertilizer. If you feed plants when they don't need it, you've wasted your money and time, but more important, the excess fertilizer will build up in the soil. The exceptions to the rule are flowering plants and plants that continue to grow during winter.

■ *Fertilize all houseplants at the beginning of October and then stop feeding all but flowering plants until March. Because they won't be growing, the plants don't need additional nutrients.*

These generally need fertilizing about every four to six weeks.

LAWNS

About the middle of the month, spread 1 pound of nitrogen on tall fescue and Kentucky bluegrass lawns. (See the conversion chart on page 84 for the correct amount of the fertilizer you've bought.) Either spread fertilizer just before rain arrives or water it well after application. Fall is an excellent time to lime your lawn if a soil test shows that lime is needed.

PROBLEM-SOLVE

ALL

Keep an eye out for henbit, a pretty little weed that germinates and grows in the fall. Henbit has rounded, toothed leaves and violet flowers. It remains in the lawn over winter and is often most

noticeable in the spring. Henbit is one of several winter annual weeds that germinate in the fall and grow all winter long. Some others include annual bluegrass, common chickweed, deadnettle, speed-wells, and mustards.

BULBS

If you have had problems with voles, do not put mulch over your tulip beds. A covering of mulch gives the voles somewhere warm to spend the winter—eating your bulbs in the meantime.

EDIBLES

Cabbage loopers may still be a problem in the fall, before frost, on all cole crops (broccoli, Brussels sprouts, cauliflower, and cabbage). They may also eat holes in lettuce and in beet leaves. Handpicking works fine if the infestation is small and you can reach the caterpillars, but you may also spray or dust with Bt, an organic control.

■ *Pull up henbit, a weed that appears in the lawn and flower beds in fall and stays there over winter. It's pretty but if it isn't removed, it will continue to come back year after year and take up more space each time.*

■ *Don't give mice and voles and a warm winter sleeping area—keep the mulch off your spring bulbs.*

HOUSEPLANTS

Because tobacco mosaic virus can be transmitted from smokers' hands to plants, if you smoke, always wash your hands thoroughly with soap and water before touching or working with houseplants. Better yet, wear gloves. Once an indoor plant has developed a virus, it usually has to be destroyed.

PERENNIALS AND ORNAMENTAL GRASSES

Is your large ornamental grass standing straight and tall, or does it appear to need staking? Floppy growth on ornamental grasses is due to too much fertilizer (established grasses don't need fertilizing)

or too little light. If more sun is needed, replant it early next spring.

WATER GARDENS

If you have a fish or two living in a small potted water garden, what do you do with it during the winter? One solution is to take the fish indoors into an aquarium that's kept between 45 and 60 degrees Fahrenheit. Use an air pump to supply oxygen. You can also overwinter fish in the basement in any clean container. Count on 1 gallon of water per inch of fish. Feed occasionally. About once a month, remove one-fifth of the water and replace it with fresh water.

HERE'S HOW

TO CONTROL HENBIT

- As soon as you see henbit this month, begin pulling it out. It has shallow roots, so it's easy to control by hand. But if left in the lawn, it tends to take over areas that have thin stands of grass.

- If you've had henbit in your yard before, spread a pre-emergent control, such as corn gluten, first thing this month, before it appears again. This weed comes back from seeds, so a pre-emergent product will prevent the seeds from germinating—and break the cycle of henbit showing up in your lawn in ever-larger quantities each year.

November

This is the month for giving thanks, although, really, we ought to give thanks every day for our blessings. Some researchers think that by giving gratitude for even the mundane or ordinary events in our lives, we become happier. What are you grateful for in the garden?

You might be thankful for having a place to garden—whether it's part of a field in which to grow almost unlimited amounts of vegetables or a screened porch that's ideal for container plants.

Perhaps you're grateful for having the time and energy (or helpers) to accomplish at least part of what you want to in the garden. Your human blessings might include supporters who encourage you, garden mentors who increase your knowledge and prevent you from making mistakes, or great plant breeders who keep coming out with new plants that flower better, or produce more vegetables, and at the same time are less subject to insects and diseases.

I'm thankful for excellent garden books, magazine and newspaper articles, YouTube videos, blogs, and pictures shared by friends on Facebook and Twitter. These contain so much inspiration.

I'm also grateful for the weather. Yes, it's true that the weather in our region can be changeable, but we have a generally mild climate that is ideal for growing many different kinds of plants, from annuals to perennials and shrubs to trees. If you've ever gardened in a climate with lots of snow and low temps, or high temperatures and the sun beating down on you and your plants every day, you know what a treat a moderate climate is.

You might be thankful for being able to eat the freshest vegetables and fruits possible from your backyard. What a joy it is to know exactly where your food came from and exactly how it was grown! You're probably also thankful for all the organic products that make it easier to grow food—and all plants—without harmful chemicals.

Finally, I'm grateful for the freedom to grow what I want—especially my favorite plants. Every gardener has several—a favorite tomato, a plant that grandma grew—and the growing year wouldn't be the same without them. These are the plants that make us grateful that we're people who grow plants, even if in just a small way.

PLAN

ALL

This is the time of year when the thoughts of a dedicated flower or vegetable grower turn to greenhouses. It's always so difficult this time to give up fresh-grown produce and have to return to the pallid stuff sold at the supermarket.

Could this be the year that you break down and buy or build a greenhouse? Many growers who start plants from seed find them ideal for that purpose, as well as perfect for extending the season to almost year-round growing (depending on whether and how much you plan to heat the structure). Greenhouses come in a wide range of configurations—from plastic-covered "hoop houses" to elegant glass-walled additions to the house. Size and materials determine the cost; there's usually one for every budget and circumstance.

ANNUALS

If you have time, consider a bed of specialty annuals next year—flowers just for cutting, for example, or for drying (such as cockscomb, globe amaranth, decorative-type sunflowers, and zinnias). These could be placed in an out-of-the-way spot where it won't matter how they look when you harvest the plants. Raised beds are excellent for projects such as this, because they require no bending over, and they produce few if any weeds.

HOUSEPLANTS

Be careful when you buy houseplants this time of year. Many of them are harmed if they're exposed to cold. That means carefully covering them up so they aren't exposed to low temperatures between

■ *A greenhouse is the dream of almost every serious gardener. There are many sizes and types, from simple and inexpensive to elaborate. Often gardeners start out with a small, simple plastic structure and move up to a larger and more sophisticated structure.*

Think ahead to spring and add a few more spring-flowering shrubs to your yard, if you don't have many. November will be a good month to plant.

the store and your vehicle or between your car and the house. It also means going directly home if you've bought a plant on a day that temperatures are below 50 degrees Fahrenheit. Sitting in a cold car can harm a plant.

LAWNS

Year by year as trees grow, they cast more and more shade. With shrubs, trees, flowers, and vines, we can compensate by choosing selections that prefer (or at least will tolerate) shade. But grass is a sun-loving plant. Some grasses tolerate shade better than others, but there may come a time when you're frustrated to find that even those grasses aren't growing well, although you followed the recommendations on page 156. That's when you have a choice to make:

- Trim the trees. Remove lower limbs so that they're no closer than 10 to 20 feet from the ground (10 feet for smaller trees, 20 for tall ones). Have a professional arborist thin some of your trees so that more light will reach the lawn. Late fall and winter, when deciduous trees are dormant, is the best time to prune them or have them pruned. Never top a tree or allow someone to top your tree, even if you're trying to get grass to grow. Topping is bad for trees.

- Form an island in the lawn around groups of tall trees and replace the grass beneath them with mulch.

- Plant a groundcover. Many evergreen ground covers love medium to heavy shade as much as grass dislikes it.

PERENNIALS

If you don't grow Lenten roses, start searching the catalogs or ask your favorite nursery to order some for you next spring. They're evergreen, grow in shade (even deep shade), and bloom in late winter (sometimes as early as January, depending on the weather and where you live). Not many other plants flower that time of year, so Lenten roses are a delight. As you consider where to put them, think of a spot that you walk by daily in the winter so you can enjoy the blooms. The plant reseeds, so a neighbor who's growing Lenten roses may be willing to share. Or perhaps you can work out a trade for one of your perennials.

SHRUBS

As you look at your yard, are you pleased with the shrubs you have and how they fit into your landscape? One of the biggest trends in landscaping is four-season color—having something in the yard that's blooming or colorful at every season of the year. If you acted on the suggestions made in February, your yard will be more interesting this winter than ever before. Looking ahead to spring, do you have enough flowering shrubs? It's such a delight to welcome spring with a riot of flowers, and when those flowers are provided by shrubs, they're easy care—plant them and reap the rewards for years to come. Here are a few spring-flowering shrubs to consider:

- Evergreen azalea

- Deutzia (*Deutzia gracilis*)

- Flowering quince

- Forsythia

- Fothergilla

- Kerria

- Leucothoe

- Rhododendron

- Spirea

- Viburnum

■ *Daffodils are a good bulb to naturalize in the grass or at the edge of woods. In our region, the ones that bloom the earliest are the best choice for grassy areas. Always mow the grass very short before you plant.*

PLANT

ANNUALS

As long as the ground isn't frozen, it's not too late to plant pansies and ornamental cabbage and kale. Firm the soil around the roots of the plants; you don't want to leave air pockets that can lead to frozen roots. And be sure to mulch well after planting.

BULBS

Naturalizing bulbs is fun—just toss them on the ground and dig holes where they fall. It provides an appealing natural look. Daffodils are a good choice for naturalizing, since they return reliably each year. Often you see pictures of daffodils naturalized in lawns, but there's one problem: Cool-season grasses such as fescue and bluegrass need mowing long before the daffodil foliage has ripened and died. Crocus leaves will have ripened sufficiently

by the end of March, but they're usually too short to be seen through tall fescue or bluegrass. Better choices include naturalizing in a wildflower meadow or along the edges of the woods. This is a good way to use smaller bulbs, should you find a good end-of-the-planting-season sale.

Why not bring the beauty of bulbs indoors? There are several ways of doing this: growing amaryllis bulbs in pots of soil, placing hyacinth bulbs and crocus corms over water in special glasses, and potting up bulbs and giving them a chill in the refrigerator. All are fun. Read on to learn about all three methods.

If you plan to use your amaryllis as a temporary houseplant, tossing it out in spring, the type and size of bulb you buy isn't as important as it is if you plan to keep it for years, bringing it back into bloom each winter. As a long-term investment, buy an amaryllis bulb that's as large as you can find (about the size of a grapefruit) and a named cultivar (not just red, white, pink, and so on).

1. Start with a clean plastic flowerpot that's 2 inches wider than the diameter of the bulb.

2. Place a coffee filter or piece of screen over the drainage hole.

It's fun to grow crocus over water in small vases made especially for forcing the tiny bulbs into bloom indoors.

3. Fill the container about halfway with dampened potting soil.

4. Position the bulb on top of the soil. One-third to one-half of the bulb should be above the pot's rim.

5. Fill in around the bulb with more moist potting soil, firming it gently.

6. Water thoroughly.

7. Set the pot aside in a warm spot. It doesn't need light and shouldn't be watered again until the bulb starts growing.

8. When new growth appears, move the pot into bright light, water enough to keep the soil moist, and fertilize monthly with a houseplant fertilizer.

To bring an amaryllis from last year into bloom again, water the soil so that it's wet all the way through. Then follow the final two steps above.

Here's how to grow bulbs over water. The easiest way to grow bulbs indoors is to buy small crystal vases made especially for forcing crocus and hyacinths into bloom indoors. Fill the container with water and place the bulb in the flared top section. Keep the water at the level of the bottom of the bulb, and the roots will grow into the vase and be visible through the glass. As soon as top growth emerges, move the vase to good light and keep cool.

Grow a sweet potato vine indoors, since November is definitely the month for eating sweet potatoes. Just buy an extra one as you shop for your Thanksgiving meal. You'll need a tall glass or jar, some toothpicks, water, and a fresh sweet potato—preferably one that's home-grown or from a farmers' market (the ones at the supermarket have sometimes been treated with growth retardant).

1. Fill the glass with water.

2. Stick toothpicks around the middle of the sweet potato.

TO FORCE BULBS

The most common bulbs for forcing are daffodils, tulips, hyacinths, and crocus.

1. Buy bulbs that are marked "for forcing."

2. Buy 6-inch plastic bulbs pots, if available. These are about two-thirds as tall as the regular 6-inch flowerpots. (Hyacinths can be planted singly in 4-inch pots.) If using old containers, wash them thoroughly with soapy water, rinse, and soak briefly in a solution of one part bleach to nine parts water.

3. Moisten potting soil and—if you plan to plant the bulbs outdoors after they've been forced—mix in a small amount of Bulb Booster.

4. Fill the pot about three-fourths full of damp potting soil.

5. Position the bulbs on top of the soil so that they're not touching one another or the container. Daffodils and crocus should be covered with about 1 inch of soil. The tips of hyacinths and tulips should be showing above the soil. Place tulip bulbs so their flat side faces the outer rim of the pot; then the foliage will gracefully arch over the side.

6. Add more potting soil until it's within ¼ to ½ inch of the rim.

7. Water thoroughly.

8. Write on a plant label the name of the bulb, its color, and the date you planted it. Stick this down into the soil.

9. You may want to place the pots in large clear plastic bags to retain moisture. If so, you'll need to check occasionally to make sure that no mold is developing.

10. Put the pots in the refrigerator.

11. It takes about twelve weeks before most bulbs are ready to be brought into the house to bloom.

3. Position the sweet potato so that the bottom half is in the water.

4. Place the sweet potato on a sunny windowsill.

5. Add water several times a week so that half the sweet potato is always beneath water. Roots will develop from the bottom, and green stems and leaves from the top of the tuber.

What do you do when a tall plant such as dracaena gets too big or has dropped so many lower leaves that most of those remaining are near the top of a tall stalk? You can air layer the top portion of the plant so that it will develop roots and can be moved to a new pot.

1. Using a sharp knife, cut one-third of the way into the stem. Use a pin or small sliver of wood to hold the cut piece open.

2. Brush a rooting hormone onto the cut portion of the stem.

3. Loosely wrap a piece of plastic (cut from a dry-cleaner bag—or use plastic wrap from the kitchen) around the wound and tape it at the bottom. Leave the top open.

4. Moisten long-fibered sphagnum moss and place it inside the plastic so it covers the wound. Moss may need several hours before becoming fully moist.

5. Close the top of the plastic (with duct tape or a twist tie).

6. Don't let the moss dry out. If necessary, loosen the top of the plastic so you can water.

7. When you see a mass of roots in the plastic, cut the plant's stem below the roots.

8. Remove the plastic and the moss.

9. Plant in a new pot.

10. Keep in a warm spot with bright light for several weeks before moving the plant to its final location.

WATER GARDENS

Tropical water lilies won't survive outdoors over winter, so what do you do with them?

- Toss them out, and buy new ones next year.

- Bring them indoors as houseplants. But they'll need at least six hours of sun (or grow lights) and temperatures of 70 degrees Fahrenheit or above. Place the plants in tubs or trays that have no holes, so they may be kept full of water to keep the plants wet. Umbrella palm makes an interesting houseplant in medium light.

- After the foliage has been killed, remove the tuber from the pot and place it in a tub of slightly moist sand or peat moss. Place it in an area where the temperature stays about 55 degrees Fahrenheit.

CARE

ALL

Clean up frost-killed foliage and remove it from beds, if you haven't gotten to it earlier. You don't want to leave anything that insects or disease spores can overwinter on.

ANNUALS

After annuals fade and are removed from the containers they grew in all summer, what do you do? Much depends on the type of container—particularly the material it's made from—and how much storage space you have.

- Leave them in place. This is the easiest solution—provided your pots are not clay or terracotta (which may be harmed by temperatures below freezing) and that no neighborhood cats decide the pots make excellent litter boxes. Unless a clay container is unusual, or large and expensive, you may still decide to leave it outdoors all winter, figuring it's easier to replace it if it cracks, especially if it's several years old.

- Out goes the soil. An alternative is to remove the soil and turn the containers upside down. You have several options of what to do with the soil: To reuse for next year, place it in clean garbage cans or in heavy-duty plastic garbage bags. You may also spread it in 8-inch mounds around the bases of rosebushes, to protect them from low temperatures. Or use the soil to fill low places in the yard.

- Clean up the pots. Once you've emptied the containers, it's okay to put them in storage after you've let them stay outdoors long enough to dry completely. But that means you'll have to clean the pots next spring before you use them again—and there are so many other things you'll want to be doing in the garden then. You probably have more time on a warmish November day. So fill a tub with soapy water that's been mixed with one part household bleach to nine parts water. Try to remove most soil clods before washing. Dip or soak pots in it (depending on their size and how dirty they are), then scrub, inside and out, with a stiff brush. Rinse with clear water and let dry. Store out of the weather, and the containers will be ready to replant next spring when you're raring to get going again with annuals.

BULBS

Keep any spring-flowering bulbs that you haven't yet planted in a cool spot. Since it's getting late in the season, it's best to refrigerate tulips if you have the space in your fridge. They need a certain amount of chilling before they can bloom. Keep refrigerated bulbs away from apples and other ripening fruit, which give off a gas that may harm the bulbs.

EDIBLES

Lightly mulch all perennial and biennial herbs. Several herbs also appreciate wind protection during winter. These include chamomile, lavender, sage, and tarragon. Use row cover material to build a little three-sided box to block wind, or cover the plants with evergreen boughs.

If you didn't last month, mulch the asparagus bed during November. Remove the tops of the plants first, and toss them onto the compost pile.

Mulch vegetables that are staying in the ground over winter. Use a 6-inch-thick blanket of straw over carrots and 2 to 3 inches of hay, straw, or shredded leaves at the base of collards.

Remove all plant supports—tomato cages, bean-poles, cucumber trellises—from the garden. Clean and store them in a shed or garage if possible. They will last longer if not exposed to winter weather.

November is garden cleanup time if you haven't kept up with this earlier in the fall. Pull up all plants and compost them or till them under.

Drain all hoses, including soaker hoses, and store them in the garage or basement for the winter. Do the same with drip or trickle irrigation systems in the vegetable garden, since you'll have to till the area soon or in the spring. Store all parts of the system together indoors.

Many vegetable gardeners who like to plant crops early in the spring till the garden now, turning under all mulch and old plants. This improves the soil, helps kill overwintering insects, and readies the garden for the new planting season. Leave a few rows in furrows or in mounds 6 to 8 inches high. These will warm up and dry out first and be ready to plant sooner than the rest of the garden.

To protect the garden from erosion over winter, cover regular rows with fresh shredded leaves. Don't cover hilled-up rows, since the mulch will keep the soil cool in spring.

■ *Because English ivy can tolerate chilly temperatures indoors, both night and day, it's ideal to grow in unheated rooms. Mist the leaves occasionally to help keep spider mites at bay.*

Another way to use fall's abundance of leaves to good advantage in the garden is to pile them in the paths between rows. That prevents your feet from getting muddy when you walk in the garden, and it improves the soil when you till in the leaves next fall. Some gardeners alternate rows and paths—that is, this year's leaf-filled paths become next year's garden rows.

On a warm day, pour soil from containers into a black plastic garbage bag and wash the pots using soapy water. See pages 149 and 198.

HOUSEPLANTS

How cool do you keep your house? Some home-owners like it warm all winter, and others turn the thermostat way back (either all the time or when they're away from home). Although many plants can adjust to lower temperatures, just as people do, some really need warmth.

Plants that can tolerate temperatures of 50 to 60 degrees Fahrenheit in the daytime and 45 to 55 degrees at night include:

- Cast iron plant

- Cactuses (only while resting in winter)

- Cyclamen

- English ivy

- Norfolk Island pine

- Miniature rose

- Wandering Jew

Plants that grow well in medium temperatures: 60 to 65 degrees Fahrenheit during the day and 55 to 60 degrees at night:

- Aluminum plant

- Asparagus fern

- Bromeliads

- Flowering maple (*Abutilon*)

- Peperomia

- Piggyback plant (*Tolmiea menziesii*)

- Purple passion plant

- Schefflera

- Snake plant

Plants that are ideal in warm temperatures (70 to 80 degrees Fahrenheit in daytime and 65 to 70 degrees at night):

- Arrowhead plant

- African violets

- Bromeliads

- Chinese evergreen

- Cactuses

- Croton

- Dracaena

- Ficus

- Gloxinia

- Grape ivy

- Peace lily

- Philodendron

- Poinsettia

- Prayer plant

- Snake plant

LAWNS

Don't let falling leaves mat down on the lawn. A heavy covering of thick, wet leaves can smother the grass. Remove them once a week and dump them onto the compost pile.

When you think you've gotten to the end of the leaf season, leave ½ to 1 inch of leaves on the lawn and mow over them several times—a mulching mower works best; it chips them up into tiny pieces. This creates a topdressing of organic matter that will filter down into the topsoil. It helps prevent thatch by adding microorganisms to the soil and also increases the soil's content of organic matter.

PERENNIALS

Containers of perennials have to be protected from cold throughout the region, but especially where temperatures may fall into the teens or even to 0 degrees Fahrenheit. You may want to plan on moving large pots to protected places during the day and then take them in out of the weather if temperatures fall below 20 degrees Fahrenheit. Some people wrap the pot in insulation. All perennials or grasses in small pots (8 inches or smaller) should be stored in an unheated garage, basement, or crawlspace where temperatures remain chilly (30 to 40 degrees Fahrenheit), but above freezing.

Clean all tools and oil those that need it. If you don't have a regular place to hang your tools so you can grab them whenever they're needed, this is a good time to create one.

If you don't reuse potting soil from year to year, dump it from containers into the compost pile or an area in the yard that needs some soil. If you have too many pots—especially those black plastic gallon-sized ones—think of who might be able to use them. A gardening program at a local school? A community garden? A Master Gardener who's conducting a greenhouse program? Some garden centers have recycling programs for the pots.

Mulch perennial beds well after a hard freeze or two. Sometimes gardeners cut back perennial

■ *By the end of November, get all the fallen leaves off the lawn and into piles so they'll rot into compost. You can mow a thin layer of leaves on the lawn to make a topdressing that filters down into the soil to improve it.*

KEEPING HOUSEPLANTS CLEAN

You can keep your indoor plants clean in a number of ways. Use a damp rag or paint-brush to gently wipe the dust off the leaves. Or, to clean the whole plant at once, fill a bucket with tepid water, turn the plant upside down (with your hand over the soil) and dunk the leaves in the water.

plants in the fall, and other times they wait till late winter or early spring. There's no right or wrong way, but here are a few guidelines:

- If any perennials were attacked by insects or disease this year, cut them back now and remove them from the garden. Don't add them to the compost pile. Both actions will help prevent problems next year.

- Finish deadheading perennials in prominent locations, but leave some seeds for the birds.

- Don't cut back chrysanthemums, but do mulch mums that were newly planted this fall.

- Don't prune evergreen ferns or tender perennials.

- Leave standing anything that has an interesting appearance.

SHRUBS

If a needled evergreen is planted in a woodland site, leaves from deciduous trees frequently get caught in the needles. Often the wind blows these away, but sometimes a number of leaves remain and can kill the shrub or tree's needles by blocking the sun. This may also happen at the base of small evergreen azaleas. Remove the leaves promptly.

VINES AND GROUNDCOVERS

Pull down frost-killed annual vines, and toss the debris on the compost pile. Leaf removal is the main gardening chore in November. Don't let falling leaves smother groundcovers, especially evergreens, that are planted beneath trees. A thick, wet mat of leaves can do just that. Use a leaf blower weekly. If the plants need some winter protection, wait until all the leaves have fallen and then shred as many as needed (in a shredder or by spreading them on the driveway and running the lawn mower over them several times until they're in small pieces). Sprinkle the shredded leaves back around the ground covers. But don't let even this light material cover the crowns of the plants. If the ground cover is mulched well already, compost the leaves. Rotted leaves make an excellent soil conditioner and mulch.

VINES THAT PRODUCE BERRIES

Homeowners who want to attract birds and small wildlife to their yards often plant bushes and trees that produce berries. A few vines also produce berries or other showy fruit that attract wildlife:

- American bittersweet (*Celastrus scandens*)
- Hyacinth bean
- Pepper vine (*Ampelopsis arborea*), (zone 7 only, may become an invasive pest)
- Sweet autumn clematis (may be invasive)
- Trumpet honeysuckle
- Virginia creeper

WATER

ANNUALS

If rainfall has been less than usual, and the ground isn't frozen, your pansies and ornamental cabbage and kale may need to be watered. Don't let them wilt. Check to see whether seed-sown hardy annuals such as poppies have sprouted and need watering.

HOUSEPLANTS

Keep Christmas and Thanksgiving cactus on the dry side until buds form.

FERTILIZE

BULBS

This is the last call to fertilize spring-flowering bulbs that you planted in previous years. You'll see a noticeable difference in your bulbs next spring if you fertilize in the fall.

LAWNS

Fertilize cool-season grasses about the middle of the month with special "winter feed" which is low in nitrogen, high in phosphorus and potassium. This encourages good root growth.

PROBLEM-SOLVE

ALL

If deer pose a problem for landscapes in your county, check with your local Extension service to see whether it has a list of deer-resistant shrubs. These lists abound in books and on the Internet, but what works best in one locale doesn't always transfer to another place. It seems that deer in different areas have varied tastes. Talk with neighbors and members of local garden clubs and plant societies to find out what shrubs deer have passed by in others' yards. However, if deer populations are extraordinarily high, they will feed on any plant, even some that are not their favorites.

ANNUALS

Annuals or cuttings brought indoors for the winter need strong, bright light. If they begin to grow leggy—as though they're reaching for the light—they may need to be moved to a sunnier window or even placed under grow lights.

BULBS AND PERENNIALS

Bulbs and poor drainage don't mix. Same for many perennials. Since winter can be rainy in our region, now is a good time to walk through your yard and note areas that remain wet after a rain. Then you can correct the problems when warm weather returns.

TREES

Dogwood anthracnose is quite a problem here and can kill or weaken an affected tree. It's not always simple to tell the difference between a mild case of dogwood anthracnose and other fungal problems, but one good clue this time to year is that the leaves don't fall off as they should. If you think the disease is present, consult the Extension service for the latest research recommendations.

Spray a coating of horticultural oil on hollies and other trees affected with scale. Carefully follow the label directions concerning application during the correct temperature and weather conditions.

VINES AND GROUNDCOVERS

Deter rabbits by putting chicken wire around desirable groundcover plants, but arrange it so they can't nibble through the wire. Repellents may also keep rabbits at bay.

FRUIT TREES

Pull mulch away from young newly planted (1-2 year old planted) fruit trees and wrap trunks with hardware cloth to deter rabbits and moles. Voles may make a home in mulch layer in the winter and chew into the tender bark for sugary sap. Chicken wire also works, but do not wrap around trunk too tight. Bury wire one inch below the soil to prevent vole tunneling. (See photo page 30.)

December

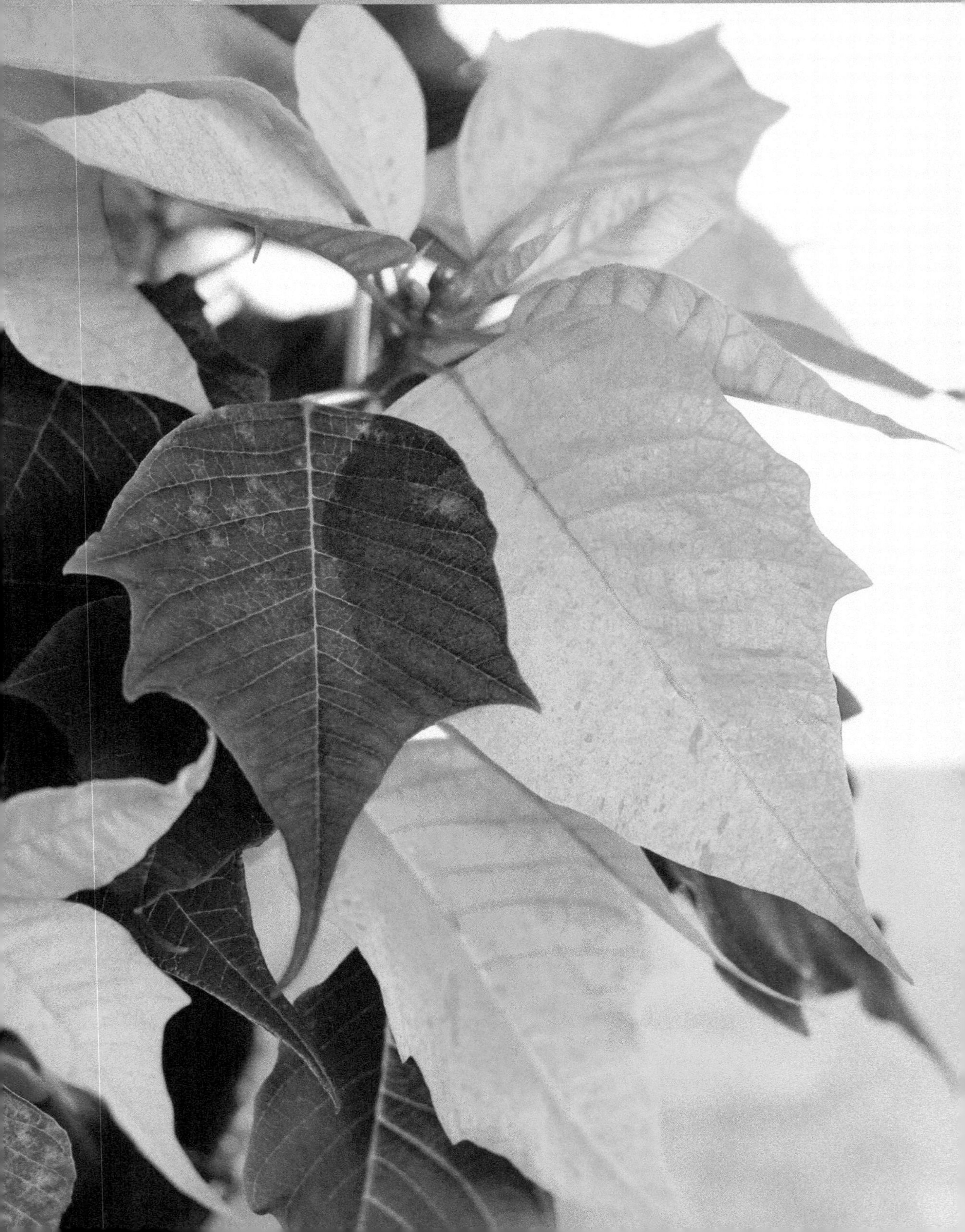

Life is so hectic in December that you may not have much time to think about gardening—except for making sure that family members know about a few must-have items you're dying to receive as gifts. As a refuge from the bustling pace of the holidays, set aside a "garden corner" in your favorite room. Have a comfortable chair, a good lamp, a study table beside the chair, and a large basket to hold a supply of garden reading. As catalogs arrive in the mail, drop them in the basket with magazines you've saved, your garden notebook, and your favorite garden books. Then read and think and make notes to your heart's content.

The nicest part of garden daydreaming is that we don't have to worry about how much time we have to plant or work in the garden, and we don't need to be concerned about whether we have enough money. The prettiest gardens always sprout in your imagination in the dead of winter. And you never know—those dreams often do come true. Maybe not right away but eventually.

This is the month of blooming holiday plants. Have you tried a poinsettia in a color other than red?

And maybe you plan to buy a live Christmas tree and plant it in the yard after the holidays. That's always a good environmental choice, and it saves money on landscaping, but it's important to care carefully for the tree indoors.

Of course there are always a few mundane things you can do in the garden, if you have the time and energy. But most can be postponed till after the holidays.

Do try to force a few bulbs, though, if you have the time this month or next. They're charming and often fragrant—and guests rarely can believe that you did it yourself.

You can even plant spring-flowering bulbs outdoors if temperatures are moderate. So many bulbs never get planted because we buy them, put them aside as we get busy, and then think it's too late to plant. As long as the ground isn't frozen this month, it's okay to get those daffodils or tulips in the ground. They'll bloom later that bulbs planted earlier, but at least they won't go to waste.

PLAN

ALL

Check over the year's notes in your garden journal to see whether they spark ideas to move toward next year. If you've noted some plants that have passed their third year in your yard without performing satisfactorily—or that always attract insects or diseases—maybe next year is the time to replace them with better plants.

EDIBLES

If you've been hankering after a cold frame, now's a good time to plan to build one. They're inexpensive and easy to construct, and they make vegetable growing much easier. Check with the Extension service or on the Internet to find plans. Cold frames are also available for sale, so you could put one on your gift list.

HOUSEPLANTS

If you're going to be away from home during the holidays for ten days or longer, plan to have someone water your plants or use the vacation watering techniques on page 138. Don't turn off the heat while you're gone; it's not good for your plants. That may make the temperature too low for many tropical houseplants. (See the November chapter for temperatures that various plants prefer.) You may also want to move plants to the room that stays the warmest in your house. Then if the power should go out because of an ice storm, the plants may still be okay.

TREES

If you've decided to buy a live Christmas tree this year and plant it in the landscape after the holidays, it's a good idea to dig the hole ahead of time, because the weather may not be suitable for hole digging when you need to plant the tree. After the hole has been prepared, fill it with leaves or mulch and cover it with a board or piece of plywood so no one accidentally trips into it.

If you've moved to property where the trees are overgrown, you know they need pruning. If this involves large trees, consult an arborist. Few homeowners are equipped to work in tall trees. The International Society of Arboriculture (http://www.isa-arbor.com) can provide a list of certified arborists (those who have passed a test on their knowledge) in your area.

■ *You can build a cold frame from scratch or build one from a kit. A cold frame allows you to extend your vegetable growing season by at least a month.*

■ *A thoughtful holiday gift would be a kit for forcing narcissus into bloom indoors. Several kinds grow quickly in trays of water, while others are placed in containers of potting soil.*

WATER GARDENS

In the warmer parts of the region, ponds don't freeze over for very long. But when we experience an extracold winter, we usually wish we'd invested in a deicer. They keep a small section of the water surface open so that oxygen can enter and gases harmful to the fish can escape. Floating on the surface of the pond, the device has a thermostat that turns on the heat when water temperature goes below 40 degrees Fahrenheit. It's an excellent investment for keeping hardy plants alive in shallow water gardens.

PLANT

BULBS

Yes, you can still plant tulips, daffodils, and other bulbs outdoors, as long as the ground isn't frozen. Try to get it done by the end of the month; otherwise, blooming may be delayed.

Paper-white narcissus, a bulb with highly fragrant white blooms, and two similar but yellow-flowered relatives—soleil d'or and Chinese sacred lily— can be quickly forced into bloom this month (or in January, if bulbs are available). There are two ways to do this:

1. Place bulbs in a shallow bowl, and gently pour decorative pebbles around them to the top rim of the bowl. Add water, and place the bowl in a spot with bright, indirect light and cool temperatures. Keep the water level just below the rim.

2. Pot up paper-whites, soleil d'or, or Chinese sacred lilies (*Narcissus tazetta orientalis*) as described in November. Leave the tips of the bulbs slightly above the soil.

3. Place paper-whites in bright sunlight and soleil d'or and sacred lilies in darkness. Both prefer nighttime temperatures of 55 degrees Fahrenheit or below.

If a rosebush needs moving to another location, mild, dry days in December or January are good for taking care of this chore. Cut canes back and then cover them with soil to protect them from cold.

4.   Keep the soil moist.

5.   Remove soleil d'or and Chinese sacred lilies from darkness after ten days, and grow them in sunlight.

6.   Fertilize monthly with a houseplant fertilizer.

7.   When blooms appear, move the plants out of the sun and into bright indirect light.

EDIBLES

If the ground isn't frozen, you could plant garlic, since it needs a long growing season, beginning in winter.

ROSES

Once a rosebush is fully dormant, you can transplant it to another location this month or next—choose a time when the soil isn't too wet or isn't frozen and the temperature is above freezing. First, cut the canes back to 3 to 4 feet high. Dig the new hole ahead of time and quickly move the rose into the new hole. After replanting, mound soil 8 to 12 inches over the canes.

SHRUBS

When the ground isn't frozen, and temperatures are above freezing, continue to plant shrubs this month, especially deciduous shrubs. But be sure that you firm the soil around the rootball and don't leave any air pockets for cold to get in. Also, spread a 3-inch mulch on top of the soil, but not touching the trunk, as soon as you finish planting.

TREES

Beginning in December and continuing through March, you may also transplant trees from one part of your property to another. For transplanting to be successful, a large number of roots must be moved with the tree. This means a fairly large and heavy rootball is necessary—so two people are generally required.

1.   You should have prepared trees for moving by root pruning three to six months ahead of time. See the September chapter.

2.   Water the tree thoroughly two days before you expect to transplant it.

3.   Dig a circle around the tree that's 4 to 6 inches outside the root pruning. This allows you to gather the new roots the tree formed after some of the old roots were severed. The depth of the rootball should be about one-half to two-thirds of the width.

4.   Don't let the rootball fall apart.

5.   Roll the rootball onto a piece of burlap that's been placed beside the tree.

6.   Fasten the burlap around the rootball.

7.   Dig a hole. See page 182.

8. Plant the tree in its new hole.

9. Water thoroughly and mulch with 3 inches of organic material.

WATER GARDENS

Place tropical water plants in tubs or decorative containers (Chinese fish bowls are attractive) filled with water, place them in a room where the temperature remains at 70 degrees Fahrenheit or warmer and where the plants can be in the sun five or six hours. What a winter delight!

CARE

ALL

Is all the plant debris cleaned up and removed from the garden or tilled under? Are supports out of the weather? Have hoses been moved to the

garage? If any of these chores are still undone, take care of them on a mild day this month. In March, you will be happy that you did.

Why not put up a bird feeder in the yard? You'll enjoy the antics of the birds, and many eat insects that you'd like to be rid of. Place a feeder near a shrub or large clump of ornamental grass to provide the birds with some nearby cover. Birds like to feel that they have a hiding place from danger, if needed.

HOUSEPLANTS

This is the month of the poinsettia—and many other flowering plants. Here's how to choose and care for a poinsettia:

1. Choose plants with stiff stems and no signs of wilting. Look for dark green leaves all the way to the base. (Lower leaves of poinsettias that have been in decorative sleeves too long

■ *Cyclamen is an appealing houseplant that's widely available this time of year. Unfortunately, it needs chilly indoor temperatures, colder than is found in most houses in our region. You may want to consider it a temporary plant.*

often turn yellow and fall off.) The tiny yellow buttonlike flowers in the middle of the bracts should be closed or barely open. If they've fallen off, the plant is past its prime.

2. If outdoor temperatures are below 50 degrees Fahrenheit, make sure the plant is protected (by being wrapped in paper or placed in a large shopping bag) before you take it from the store to your car and from the car into your house. If weather is cold, take the poinsettia straight home; don't leave it in the car while you spend a couple of hours at the mall.

3. Remove any decorative wrapping when you get home. It isn't good for the plant.

4. Poinsettias like room temperatures between 68 and 75 degrees Fahrenheit and bright indirect sunlight for at least six hours daily.

5. Avoid placing a poinsettia on top of a TV set, in front of a heating vent, near an outside door, or in front of a fireplace.

6. Water frequently enough to keep the soil slightly moist to the touch, but not soggy. Don't fertilize your poinsettia until January.

These are the conditions needed by other common holiday plants:

- Azalea: cool room temperatures, bright light, moist soil

- Calamondin orange (× *Citrofortunella microcarpa*): at least four hours of sun, average to cool temperatures. Let soil dry between waterings. Watch out for mealybugs and spider mites.

- Holiday cactus: See page 185.

- Cyclamen: chilly temperatures, bright light. Don't let the soil dry out.

- Jerusalem cherry (*Solanum pseudocapsicum*): half a day of sun, chilly temperatures, moist soil. Watch out for whiteflies.

- Kalanchoe: half day of sun, warm to average temperatures. Let the soil dry out before watering again.

- Ornamental pepper: sun, moist soil, warm temperatures in the daytime, about 60 degrees Fahrenheit at night

BULBS

Shredded leaves make good mulch, but don't pile whole, unshredded leaves onto bulb beds, since they're likely to mat down when wet and not let rain through to the soil and bulbs. They could also prevent necessary air from reaching bulb roots.

Keep unplanted bulbs in a cool spot until you can get them in the ground. Tulips should be stored at 40 degrees Fahrenheit, if possible. Store in refrigerator inside heavy duty plastic bags and not near ripened fruits.

EDIBLES

Keep brown or yellowing leaves removed from potted herbs that are overwintering indoors. The best way to keep herb plants from getting leggy is to pinch them occasionally. With culinary herbs, you're probably doing this regularly. But you may need to think about occasionally pruning herbs that you're growing indoors more for scent or decoration.

SHRUBS

Be prepared to bring shrubs growing outdoors in large containers into a garage or basement overnight if temperatures are forecast to fall below 20 degrees Fahrenheit.

TREES

If you cut needled evergreens this month to make into wreaths or to use as greenery around the house during the holidays, you don't want the material to dry out and lose its needles. The best way to prevent this is to place the greenery in a bathtub and completely immerse it in water for twenty-four hours. Let it dry, and then arrange it. Keep fresh greenery away from heat sources such as fireplaces and candles. You may also want to spray outdoor wreaths with hair spray or an antidesiccant to help them last longer.

A cut Christmas tree will last longer if you pick one that's fresh and then keep the end of the

■ *When making a wreath from greenery in your yard, place the cut greenery in a bathtub and cover it with water. Leave for eight to twenty-four hours before removing from the water, letting it dry, and fashioning into one-of-a-kind fresh decorations.*

trunk immersed in water from then on. Here are some tips:

1. Test for freshness by holding a branch between your thumb and fingers and pulling lightly toward you. If few needles fall off, the tree is fresh. If the end of a branch bends easily, that's also a sign of freshness. It's natural to have some yellowing, browning, or falling of interior needles, but this shouldn't be excessive. And if you pick up a tree a few inches and plunk it back down on the ground, needles shouldn't fall from the outside of the tree.

2. Most tree lots now cut the trunk of the tree for you. This allows for fast water uptake.

You need to get the tree home and into water quickly.

3. If you're not ready to take your cut tree indoors, place it in a bucket of water and keep it on a porch or in the garage—where it's cool but sheltered from wind and sun.

4. You may want to cut about 1 inch off the bottom of the trunk before bringing the tree indoors.

5. A tree will absorb about 1 gallon of water the first twenty-four hours. Be sure to keep the stand full. From then on, add water daily as needed.

6. Keep cut trees away from fireplaces and other sources of heat.

WATER

ALL

Have garden hoses been drained and moved out of the weather? They'll last much longer if they aren't left exposed to the cold and the elements.

HOUSEPLANTS

As weather gets cooler, indoor plants may not need water as often as before. Don't water just because it's Tuesday and that's when you usually water. Always check the soil to see whether it needs moisture. If it's still damp, wait a day or two before watering. Use room-temperature water that has stood overnight, and don't let water remain in the saucers.

FERTILIZE

BULBS

Fertilize bulbs that you plant outdoors this month. Indoors, fertilize amaryllis bulbs once a month with a water-soluble houseplant fertilizer.

HOUSEPLANTS

Fertilize orchids, African violets, and other blooming plants once this month. Most other houseplants don't need feeding until early spring.

PROBLEM-SOLVE

ALL

Wildlife damage early in the season signals that more is likely to come, so you may want to investigate what you can do to protect your valuable plants. Talk with someone at your favorite nursery or call the Extension service for advice.

HOUSEPLANTS

If your plants are growing on windowsills, foliage can be damaged if it touches cold glass when temperatures are far below freezing.

- When low temperatures are forecast, move the plants off the windowsill in the evening and put them back the next day after temperatures have climbed a little higher.

Some houseplants, such as African violets, like to be watered from below, rather than on the top of the soil, which can wet the leaves. Lightly fertilize houseplants that are blooming but not those that aren't.

HERE'S HOW

TO PLANT A LIVING CHRISTMAS TREE

A living Christmas tree—one that's planted outdoors after the holidays—is a nice tradition.

1. Choose a species that grows well in your area. Unfortunately, our hot, humid summers limit our selection to eastern red cedar, Leyland cypress, Norway spruce, pine, and—in zone 6 only—Colorado blue spruce. You may plant Frasier fir (*Abies frasieri*) if you live at an elevation above 3,500 feet.

2. Examine and feel the rootball before you buy. It should be wide and heavy and not broken.

3. Move the tree carefully to protect the rootball.

4. Have a tub or container large enough to hold the rootball.

5. Water the rootball if it feels dry to the touch when you get it home.

6. Place the tree in a basement or garage when temperatures are cool but don't drop to freezing. This allows the tree to get used to indoor temperatures gradually.

7. After three or four days, move the tree into the main part of the house. It shouldn't stay in a heated room for more than five days.

8. Use only tiny LED lights, which give off little heat and are energy saving.

9. Don't let the rootball stand in water, but keep it barely moist.

10. Move the tree back to the garage or basement for several days. Don't let the soil dry out.

11. Plant outdoors when the ground is not frozen. Dig the hole before you take the tree outside. Add 3 inches of mulch to keep ground warmer and hasten root development in its new hole.

- Place a piece of cardboard between the glass and the plants at night.

- Tape bubble wrap to the window so it provides some protection from the cold while letting through the light.

- When temperatures are very low, never close draperies or curtains over windowsills that hold houseplants.

If you're trying—but not succeeding—at bringing *Cattleya*, *Paphiopedilum*, or *Phalaenopsis* orchids back into bloom, give them temperatures that are ten degrees cooler at night than in the daytime.

PERENNIALS

Winter drainage is crucial for all perennials except those that can take wet conditions.

Keep an eye out for areas of poor drainage as you walk through the yard on nice days. You may not be able to do anything now, but if you know where the problem spots are, you can take steps to improve drainage in the spring.

ROSES

As a preventive, you may want to spray rosebushes this month with a dormant oil spray to kill overwintering insects and their eggs. Follow the temperature requirements on the label, and make sure no rain is forecast for twenty-four hours. Instead of using dormant oil, some rose growers prefer to spray lime sulfur, which should be directed to the soil around the roses, as well as onto the plants. Both products are organic and safe to use when you heed the label directions.

Composting

Think of composting as recycling for the yard. You take material that you would otherwise put out for garbage collection—grass clippings, leaves, twigs—and turn them into a free mulch or soil amendment. This saves money. At the same time, you're reducing the burden on landfills that are already crammed full. So compost is good for the homeowner and good for the environment.

Composting isn't at all difficult. You don't even need any special equipment; you can make compost in a black plastic garbage bag.

Materials that are good for compost:

- Frost-killed flowers, vegetables, and vines

- Grass clippings (Although it's best to leave them on the lawn unless the grass was so tall when cut that the clippings are in thick layers.)

- Leaves

- Excess or damaged produce from the garden

- Kitchen scraps—eggshells, vegetable and fruit peelings, coffee grounds, tea leaves

- Paper—newspaper and junk mail (Use only small amounts at a time and shred first.)

- Sawdust

- Small sticks and twigs

- Wood shavings

- Straw

- Pine needles

- Rotted chicken, cow, or horse manure

Avoid these in the compost pile:

- Animal droppings (These can harbor disease.)

- Bones (Bones don't readily break down and can attract animals.)

- Meat scraps (These attract animals.)

- Glossy magazines (Pages may contain metals.)

- Weeds that have seedpods (The seeds often germinate when you spread the compost.)

- Diseased or insect-infested leaves or plants (The pathogens may survive composting and be passed on.)

- Bermudagrass (It may not die and decompose.)

- Grass clippings from a lawn that's been treated with an herbicide.

- Wood ashes

TYPES OF CONTAINERS IN WHICH TO MAKE COMPOST

1. Small-mesh wire fencing can be fastened together to make a compost bin. If you're using only leaves, concrete reinforcing wire (often sold for tomato cages) also works.

2. Drill six to nine rows of ¼- to ½-inch holes into a 55-gallon trash can. Place the barrel on top of bricks or concrete blocks.

3. Build a three-bin structure from rot-resistant wood. Leave space between the slats for air circulation.

4. Buy a rotating compost bin or other commercial container.

5. You don't even need a bin in some cases. If you have some fallow land, or an area of the vegetable garden that's not being used, just pile the

compost materials right on the ground. Or make rows of compost between rows of vegetables.

6. The ideal size for a compost pile is 4 to 5 feet high and 3 to 4 feet wide. One that's too small won't heat up (develop the high temperature necessary to facilitate decomposition).

7. Place a compost bin where it will be convenient to use, but avoid putting it in the back forty where you don't have to look at it, but your neighbors do. A partially shady spot is ideal. (Too much sun dries out the materials and calls for extra watering.)

There are two conventional ways of making compost. One is simple and slow. The other requires more attention, but is faster.

Cold compost—or "forget it while it rots"—is the lazy gardener's friend. Pile everything in a bin and forget it. Eventually it will rot. Many homeowners do this with fall leaves. In about a year, the leaves will have rotted and created leaf mold, which is an excellent soil amendment and mulch. There are two disadvantages of this type of composting: The pile doesn't heat up enough to kill any weeds or disease organisms, and it's very slow.

The fastest decomposition depends on maintaining certain combinations of materials and activities.

- Oxygen is needed for efficient and odor-free decomposition.

- Moisture helps breaks down the organic matter.

- Temperature makes a difference, because colder air temperatures slow down rotting, while warmer temperatures encourage it.

Leaves are often thought of as the ideal compost material, but they are mostly carbon. The best microbial activity takes place with a mixture of high-nitrogen and high-carbon ingredients.

The ratio should be two to three parts carbon to one part nitrogen. The easy way to remember this is

to think "brown" for carbon (leaves, twigs, sawdust, straw, cornstalks) and "green" for nitrogen (grass, vegetable peelings, moist kitchen waste, green leaves or stems pinched or pruned from plants).

BUILDING THE PILE

An effective compost pile can be constructed in various ways. Here's one that works well:

1. Shred, cut, or break materials into small pieces so they will decompose faster.

2. Place the coarsest materials on the bottom of the pile.

3. Water.

4. Put down an 8- to 10-inch pile of organic material (both brown and green).

5. Water.

6. Add 1 inch of soil.

7. Water.

8. Sprinkle with 2 to 3 inches of manure or ⅓ cup of ammonium sulfate per 25 square feet of surface. (Or use 1 cup of 10-10-10 fertilizer for each 25 square feet of surface area.)

9. Repeat layers, watering after each addition. If you prefer, you can place brown and green materials into separate layers instead of mixing them. Just keep the ratio at 3 parts carbon or brown to 1 part green or nitrogen.

10. Make an indentation in the top layer to hold water.

11. Turn the pile with a spading fork once a month.

12. Water the pile after turning if it's very dry.

13. Bury kitchen wastes and fresh vegetables down in the pile to avoid attracting small wildlife.

How do you know when the compost is ready to use? When it has shrunk considerably and you can no longer recognize the ingredients that went into it.

WHAT ABOUT LIME?

Lime and wood ashes are generally not recommended for addition to regular compost piles. They do hurry along decomposition, but they also speed up loss of nitrogen from the pile.

But if you don't add lime, won't the compost be too acidic, especially if it contains lots of oak leaves? No; finished compost is almost always in the slightly acid to neutral range (pH of 6.5 to 7.0).

WHY DIDN'T MY COMPOST PILE HEAT UP?

- Too small

- Not enough green (nitrogen) materials

- Lack of oxygen (it wasn't turned)

- Too much moisture (Cover a newly constructed compost pile with a waterproof tarp if heavy rains or a long period of rain is forecast soon afterward.)

- Not enough moisture (The pile should be damp but not soggy.)

If you don't have space for a traditional compost bin, try composting in a barrel or in a plastic garbage bag.

GARBAGE CAN COMPOST

1. Drill holes in a plastic can or metal barrel as described on page 216.

2. Fill the container about two-thirds full with organic matter.

3. Add ¼ cup ammonium sulfate or other high-nitrogen fertilizer.

4. Sprinkle with water until the materials are moist.

5. Replace the lid.

6. Twice a week, put the can or barrel on its side and roll it around to aerate the contents.

7. Remove the lid after turning the container. Replace it if heavy rainfall is expected.

The compost should be ready in several months.

PLASTIC BAG COMPOST

1. Place one 30- to 40-gallon plastic bag inside another.

2. Layer green and brown organic materials in the bag, sprinkling lime between the layers. (Use 1 cup lime, total.)

3. Add 1 tablespoon of high-nitrogen fertilizer.

4. Add 1 quart of water.

5. Close the bag and seal tightly.

6. Place in a relatively warm place (outdoors in summer, heated garage in winter) for six months to a year.

The reason lime is used in the bag-composting method (although not in regular composting) is that it helps control excess acidity caused by lack of oxygen inside the bag.

Integrated Pest Management

You may have noticed that no chemical insecticide recommendations have been given in this book. There is a trio of reasons for that.

1. Increasingly, homeowners are turning to organic remedies, feeling that they're safer for people and the environment.

2. Recommendations change, and it's best to get the latest advice from your local Extension service.

3. Spraying with an insecticide the moment you see a pest usually isn't the best action. Frequently, you also kill the beneficial insects and organisms that may have taken care of the problem naturally. And you can harm bees and birds.

I'm a mostly organic gardener, but occasionally I turn to a method to control insects and diseases that's not completely organic but does limit use of chemicals. Integrated pest management (IPM) is the practice of using a combination of methods to keep pests from damaging or ruining good plants while minimizing environmental risks.

Here is how IPM works:

1. Walk through the garden at least once a week and check on plants, noting any problems.

2. Identify the pest or problem. You may need help from the Extension service or a good nursery to do this. Not all insects cause damage.

3. Assess the damage. Is it small enough that you can live with it, or is it likely to increase unless you do something?

4. Learn something about the life stages of the insect. It's easy to kill some pests at one stage of their lives and very difficult at others. If spraying isn't going to help, there's little point in doing it.

5. Choose a control method, starting with the least toxic method likely to do the job.

6. Implement your chosen strategy.

7. Evaluate its effectiveness.

CONTROL INSECTS WITHOUT SPRAYING

Cultural control includes techniques such as crop rotation in the vegetable garden. Insects that attack a certain plant can become established in the soil if the plant is in the same spot year after year. Also important is keeping plants growing vigorously by choosing healthy specimens, planting them in good soil, and seeing that they receive the correct amounts of light and water. Insects are more likely to attack stressed plants than healthy ones.

Mechanical control can mean picking off egg masses or bugs by hand. But sometimes you may want to put up barriers—row covers, for example, which exclude insects while letting air, light, and moisture through. Traps are available for apple maggots in trees. Yellow sticky traps catch whiteflies. Paper collars are often placed around the stems of young vegetable and flower seedlings to prevent cutworm damage. You can also wash some insects, such as aphids, off the plant with a strong stream of water from a hose.

Sanitary control means removing damaged vegetables and fruits from the plants so they don't attract insects. Keep the garden free of debris—boards, brush piles, and so on—that can provide breeding and hiding places for slugs and insects. Pinch off leaves or stems that have accumulated heavy infestations of insects or eggs and remove them from the garden.

Biological control relies on beneficial insects or other organisms to attack the pest and kill it.

Ladybugs feed on aphids, for instance. Many beneficial insects are now sold by mail order.

Chemical control includes synthetic herbicides, insecticides, miticides, and fungicides, as well as safer organic, botanical, and microbial pesticides, soaps, and horticultural oils. Botanical and biological controls persist in the garden for only a short time, which is good for the environment, but might not offer a long-enough period of protection for plants.

These controls are all used by organic gardeners. You may want to try them first:

- Sulfur, copper, and lime sulfur are natural fungicides, although they may cause problems in hot weather.

- Rotenone, pyrethrum, and Neem are insecticides derived from plants.

- Bt (*Bacillus thuringiensis*) is a microorganism that controls all types of caterpillars and "worms."

- Horticultural oil suffocates insects and eggs.

- Insecticidal soap kills soft-bodied insects by drying them out.

Whether you use an organic or chemical control, it's important to follow commonsense safety rules:

- Read the label, especially any cautions. These include time and temperature restrictions (such as advising you to spray when bees have left the garden for the day or when temperatures are below a certain level).

- Wear protective clothing, as recommended on the label.

- Mix the product according to directions. Using too much not only costs you more, but can harm the plant as well as beneficial insects.

- Never spray on a windy day.

- Keep products away from bodies of water or drains.

- Store products in a cool, dry place where children or animals can't accidentally reach them.

PREVENTING DISEASE IN THE GARDEN

The sports maxim *sometimes the best offense is a good defense* is as true in the garden as it is on the playing field. Homeowners can do many things to avoid having to deal with diseases:

- Choose disease-resistant plant varieties. Old-fashioned types of crapemyrtle are likely to mildew, but the newer ones (with the Native American tribe names) aren't. Choose tomatoes that have *VFN* after the variety name. These are resistant to verticillium and fusarium wilts, as well as nematodes.

- Buy disease-free plants. Look them over carefully before you take them home. Check the undersides of the leaves. Check bulbs carefully, too. If they feel soft, have an odd odor, have black or brown portions, or are covered with a white, fuzzy film, leave the bulb behind.

- Control harmful insects. Many of them spread diseases.

- Get rid of diseased plant parts, including those that are mildewed. If even a small plant is diseased, pull up the entire plant and remove it from the garden, so the disease won't spread.

- Remove and dispose of diseased plant debris. When leaves fall off rosebushes because of blackspot, for instance, pick up all the affected foliage and dispose of it so the disease organisms don't remain near the susceptible plant. Other plants that may need this care include apple and other fruit trees, fruit vines (such as raspberries), tomatoes, and hollyhock. Don't add diseased leaves to a compost pile.

- Rotate vegetable crops. Certain plants are members of the same family and are susceptible to the same diseases.

- Don't wet the leaves of plants that are likely to develop mildew—zinnia, bee balm, and so on. Instead of using a sprinkler or overhead watering, use drip irrigation, soaker hoses, or other methods that keep the water at the base of the plant. If you must use overhead watering, try to do it early in the day so the foliage has time to dry by evening.

- Space plants so they have good air circulation.

- Don't smoke or chew tobacco in the garden. And if you're a smoker, wash your hands thoroughly with soap and water before touching plants. This can help prevent tobacco mosaic disease.

- Fertilize adequately but don't overfertilize. A plant that's growing well is more likely to resist disease, but one that's coping with excess fertilizer may be weakened.

- Sanitize garden tools when they've been used on diseased plants. Disinfect tools easily by dipping them into Lysol (the old-fashioned, smelly kind). Afterward, rinse the tools and dry and oil them to prevent rust.

Plants for Acidic or Alkaline Soils

Most plants prefer to grow in a soil that's slightly acidic to neutral (pH of 6.5 to 7), but what do you do if your soil isn't in that range? Soils in Tennessee and Kentucky tend to be acidic (some much more so than others), but people who live near or on the site of old rock quarries have to contend with alkaline soil. Soil pH can be changed (see page XX), although it's an ongoing process to keep it that way. Many people, especially those with large properties, try to stick with plants that prefer the pH of the soil in their yard. These two lists serve as starting points so you can discover the plants that perform well in one or the other.

PLANTS FOR ACIDIC SOIL (AS LOW AS 5.5 PH)

COMMON NAME	BOTANICAL NAME	SUN OR SHADE
PERENNIALS		
Asters	*Aster* species and hybrids	Sun, part sun
Baptisia	*Baptisia* species and hybrids	Sun, part sun
Black-eyed Susan	*Rudbeckia* species and hybrids	Sun, part sun
Boltonia	*Boltonia asteroides*	Sun
Chrysanthemum	*Dendranthema × grandiflorum*	Sun
Columbine	*Aquilegia* species and hybrids	Part shade to sun
Coreopsis	*Coreopsis* species and hybrids	Sun
Lily	*Lilium* species and hybrids	Sun, part sun
Lily-of-the-valley	*Convallaria majalis*	Shade, part shade
Virginia bluebells	*Mertensia virginica*	Shade, part shade
SHRUBS		
Azaleas, deciduous	*Rhododendron* species	Part sun, part shade
Azaleas, evergreen	*Rhododendron* species	Part shade, shade
Camellia	*Camellia japonica*	Part shade
Crapemyrtle	*Lagerstroemeria* species and hybrids	Sun
Forsythia	*Forsythia* species and hybrids	Sun, part sun
Holly	*Ilex* species and hybrids	Sun, part sun
Juniper	*Juniperus* species and hybrids	Sun
Leucothoe	*Leucothoe* species and hybrids	Shade, part shade
Magnolia	*Magnolia* species and hybrids	Sun, part sun
Mountain laurel	*Kalmia latifolia*	Part sun
Rhododendron	*Rhododendron* species and hybrids	Part sun, part shade
Spruce	*Picea* species and hybrids	Sun
Summersweet	*Clethra alnifolia*	Part sun, sun
Yew	*Taxus* species and hybrids	Part sun, sun

COMMON NAME	BOTANICAL NAME	SUN OR SHADE
TREES		
Canadian hemlock	*Tsuga canadensis*	Part sun, part shade
Fringetree	*Chionanthus virginicus*	Sun, part sun
Holly	*Ilex* species and hybrids	Sun to part shade
Magnolia	*Magnolia* species and hybrids	Sun, part sun
Oak	*Quercus* species and hybrids	Sun, part sun
Spruce	*Picea* species and hybrids	Sun

PLANTS FOR ALKALINE SOIL (UP TO 8.0 PH)

COMMON NAME	BOTANICAL NAME	SUN OR SHADE
ANNUALS		
Cosmos	*Cosmos bipinnatus*	Sun
Phlox	*Phlox drummondi*	Sun
BULBS		
Bearded iris	*Iris germanica*	Sun, part sun
Canna	*Canna* species and hybrids	Sun
Crocus	*Crocus* species and hybrids	Sun
Snowdrops	*Galanthus* species and hybrids	Sun, part sun
PERENNIALS		
Baby's breath	*Gypsophila paniculata*	Sun, part sun
Dianthus	*Dianthus* species and hybrids	Sun, part sun
Globe thistle	*Echinops ritro*	Sun
Hibiscus	*Hibiscus moscheutos*	Sun
Hollyhock	*Alcea rosea*	Sun
Lenten rose	*Helleborus orientalis*	Part shade, shade
Peony	*Paeonia lactiflora*	Sun, part sun
Primrose	*Primula* species and hybrids	Part shade, part sun
Red valerian	*Centranthus ruber*	Sun, part sun
Verbena	*Verbena* species and hybrids	Sun
SHRUBS		
Mock orange	*Philadelphus coronarius*	Sun, part sun
TREES		
Black locust	*Robinia pseudoacacia*	Sun
Golden chain tree	*Laburnum × watereri*	Sun
Thornless honey locust	*Gleditsia triacanthos var. inermis*	Sun
VINES		
Clematis	*Clematis* species and hybrids	Sun
Dutchman's pipes	*Aristolochia macrophylla*	Sun to shade
English ivy	*Hedera helix*	Shade to sun
Trumpet honeysuckle	*Lonicera sempervirens*	Sun, part sun
Wisteria	*Wisteria* species and hybrids	Sun

Plants for Wet Soil

Many homeowners have clay soil, which doesn't drain well. This can be discouraging when plant descriptions say, over and over, "prefers moist, well-drained soil." While drainage problems can often be remedied, sometimes the simplest solution is to grow plants that don't mind "wet feet" (having their roots moist all the time). Here are some of the best.

COMMON NAME	BOTANICAL NAME	SUN OR SHADE
PERENNIALS AND ORNAMENTAL GRASSES		
Astilbe	*Astilbe* species and hybrids	Shade
Cardinal flower	*Lobelia cardinalis*	Any
Carex	*Carex* species and hybrids	Shade
Goat's beard	*Aruncus dioicus*	Part sun, part shade
Japanese blood grass	*Imperata cylindrica* 'Rubra'	Sun, part sun
Japanese iris	*Iris ensata*	Sun, part sun
Joe-pye weed	*Eupatorium purpureum*	Sun, part sun
Louisiana iris	*Iris* species and hybrids	Sun
Maidenhair fern	*Adiantum pedatum*	Shade
Marsh marigold	*Caltha palustris*	Sun
Rose mallow	*Hibiscus moscheutos*	Sun
Siberian iris	*Iris siberica*	Sun, part sun
Sweet flag	*Acorus calamus*	Sun, part sun
Turtlehead	*Chelone glabra*	Sun, part sun
SHRUBS		
Carolina allspice	*Calycanthus floridus*	Sun to part shade
Inkberry	*Ilex glabra*	Any
Redosier dogwood	*Cornus stolonifera*	Any
Summersweet	*Clethra alnifolia*	Part shade to full sun
Swamp azalea	*Rhododendron viscosum*	Sun to part shade
Tartarian dogwood	*Cornus alba*	Sun to part shade
Virginia sweetspire	*Itea virginica*	Part shade, shade
Winterberry	*Ilex verticillata*	Sun
Witch hazel	*Hamamelis* species and hybrids	Sun, part sun
TREES		
American persimmon	*Diospyros virginiana*	Sun
Bald cypress	*Taxodium distichum*	Sun, part sun
Black gum	*Nyssa sylvatica*	Sun, part sun
Red maple	*Acer rubrum*	Sun, part sun
River birch	*Betula nigra*	Sun
Sweet gum	*Liquidambar styraciflua*	Sun
Water oak	*Quercus nigra*	Sun
Willow oak	*Quercus phellos*	Sun

Bibliography

Ajilvsgi, Geyata. *Butterfly Gardening for the South.* Dallas: Taylor Publishing, 1990.

Armitage, Allan M. *Armitage's Manual of Annuals, Biennials, and Half-Hardy Perennials.* Portland, OR: Timber Press, 2001.

Armitage, Allan M. *Herbaceous Perennial Plants.* Champaign, IL: Stipes Publishing, 1997.

Brooklyn Botanic Garden. *The Potted Garden.* Ed. Scott D. Appell. Brooklyn, NY: Brooklyn Botanic Garden, 2001.

Brooklyn Botanic Garden. *Summer-Blooming Bulbs.* Ed. Beth Hanson. Brooklyn, NY: Brooklyn Botanic Garden, 2001.

Cullina, William. *Native Trees, Shrubs, and Vines.* Boston: Houghton Mifflin, 2002.

Cutler, Karan Davis. *Burpee's The Complete Vegetable and Herb Gardener.* New York: Macmillan, 1997.

Darke, Rick. *The Color Encyclopedia of Ornamental Grasses.* Portland, OR: Timber Press, 1999.

Dirr, Michael. *Dirr's Trees and Shrubs for Warm Climates.* Portland, OR: Timber Press, 2002.

DiSabato-Aust, Tracy. *The Well-Tended Perennial Garden.* Portland, OR: Timber Press, 1998.

Dobbs, Steve. *The Perfect Tennessee Lawn.* Nashville, TN: Cool Springs Press, 2002.

Druitt, Liz. *The Organic Rose Garden.* Dallas: Taylor Publishing, 1996.

Greenlee, John. *The Encyclopedia of Ornamental Grasses.* Emmaus, PA: Rodale Press, 1992.

Heath, Brent, and Becky Heath. *Daffodils for American Gardens.* Washington, DC: Elliott & Clark, 1995.

Heath, Brent, and Becky Heath. *Tulips for North American Gardens.* Albany, TX: Bright Sky Press, 2001.

Hodgson, Larry. *Perennials for Every Purpose.* Emmaus, PA: Rodale Press, 2000.

Lowe, Judy. *Tennessee Gardener's Guide, Third Edition.* Nashville, TN: Cool Springs Press, 2001.

McKeown, Denny. *Kentucky Gardener's Guide.* Nashville, TN: Cool Springs Press, 2000.

Noordhuis, Klaas, and Sam Benvie. *Bulbs and Tubers.* Buffalo, NY: Firefly Books, 1997.

Pleasant, Barbara. *The Gardener's Guide to Plant Diseases.* Pownal, VT: Storey Publishing, 1995.

Rice, Graham. *Discovering Annuals.* Portland, OR: Timber Press, 1999.

Rushing, Felder, and Walter Reeves. *The Tennessee Fruit and Vegetable Book.* Nashville, TN: Cool Springs Press, 2002.

Sternberg, Guy, and Jim Wilson. *Landscaping with Native Trees.* Shelburne, VT: Chapters Publishing, 1995.

Thomas, Charles B. *Water Gardens.* Boston: Houghton Mifflin, 1997.

Toomey, Mary, and Everett Leeds. *An Illustrated Encyclopedia of Clematis.* Portland, OR: Timber Press, 2001.

Turner, Carole B. *Seed Sowing and Saving.* Pownal, VT: Storey Publishing, 1998.

Utterback, Christine, with Michael Ruggiero. *The Serious Gardener: Reliable Roses.* New York: Clarkson Potter Publishers, 1997.

Walheim, Lance. *The Natural Rose Gardener.* Tucson, AZ: Ironwood Books, 1994.

Zone Map

ZONE	Average Annual Min. Temperature (°F)
6A	-5 to -10
6B	0 to -5
7A	5 to 0
7B	10 to 5

Precipitation Maps

Kentucky

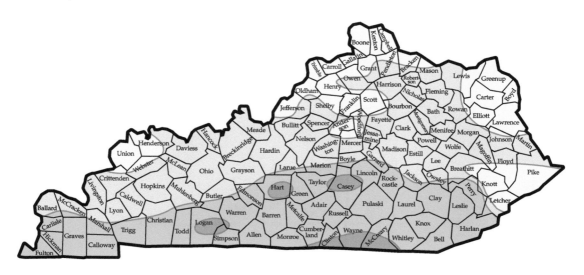

INCHES

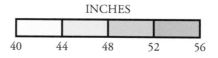

| 40 | 44 | 48 | 52 | 56 |

Tennessee

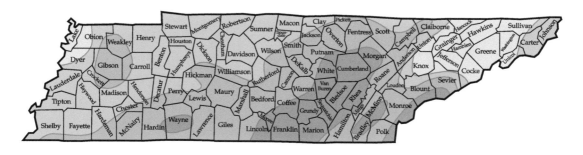

INCHES

| 44 | 48 | 52 | 56 | 60 |

Last Spring Frost Maps

Kentucky

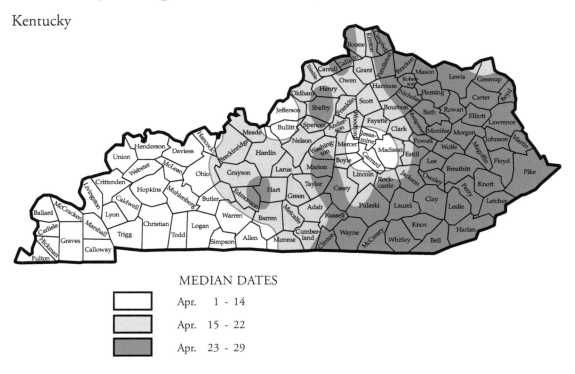

MEDIAN DATES

☐	Apr. 1 - 14
☐	Apr. 15 - 22
☐	Apr. 23 - 29

Tennessee

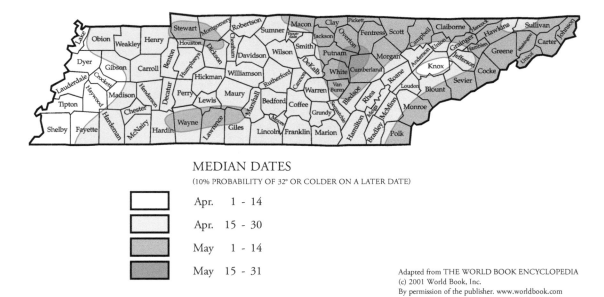

MEDIAN DATES

(10% PROBABILITY OF 32° OR COLDER ON A LATER DATE)

☐	Apr. 1 - 14
☐	Apr. 15 - 30
☐	May 1 - 14
☐	May 15 - 31

Adapted from THE WORLD BOOK ENCYCLOPEDIA
(c) 2001 World Book, Inc.
By permission of the publisher. www.worldbook.com

First Fall Frost Maps

Kentucky

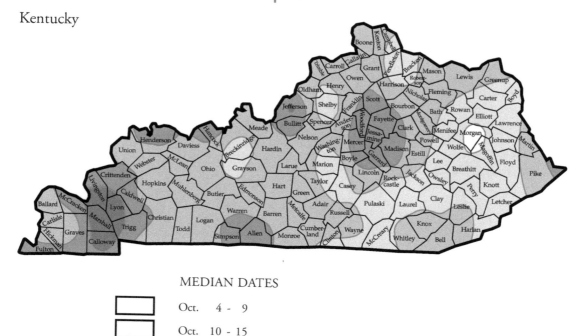

MEDIAN DATES

☐	Oct. 4 - 9
☐	Oct. 10 - 15
☐	Oct. 16 - 21
☐	Oct. 22 - 27
☐	Oct. 28 - Nov. 2

Source: The Kentucky Climate Center
at Western Kentucky University

Tennessee

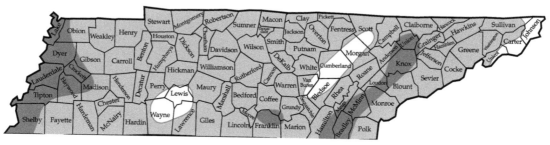

MEDIAN DATES

(10% PROBABILITY OF 32° OR COLDER ON AN EARLIER DATE)

☐	Sep. 15 - 30
☐	Oct. 1 - 14
☐	Oct. 15 - 31

Source: National Climate Data Center

Index

PHOTO CREDITS

Thomas Eltzroth: pp. 22, 31, 66, 75, 117 (left), 149 (left), 160

Katie Elzer-Peters: pp. 10, 11, 12 (all), 25, 38 (all), 41 (all), 54 (all), 73, 74 (all), 78, 81 (all), 85 (left), 86, 92 (all), 95 (all), 101, 106 (bottom), 113 (all), 118 (both), 119, 123, 135, 145 (all), 146 (right), 158, 159 (left), 163 (all), 173, 179 (all), 189, 214

iStock: pp. 18, 88, 93, 104, 142, 162, 174, 191, 192, 206

Jerry Pavia: pp. 35, 63, 69, 120, 130, 137, 161 (right), 170, 195

Shutterstock: pp. 6, 15, 20, 34, 42, 48, 50, 51, 52, 85 (right), 90, 91, 96, 106 (top), 110, 121, 126, 132, 134, 141, 146 (left), 147, 149 (right), 150, 151, 152, 153, 157, 168, 187, 190, 194, 196, 197, 200, 202, 204, 211, 213

Neil Soderstrom: pp. 32, 37, 117 (right), 133, 155, 167, 184, 208, 210

Lynn Steiner: pp. 29, 61 (all)

Meet Judy Lowe

Judy Lowe has had a lifelong fascination with gardening, starting as a child working alongside her mother, also an accomplished gardener. Later, Lowe began her garden writing career by serving as the garden editor at the *Chattanooga Free Press* and continued in that position after the paper became the *Chattanooga Times–Free Press*. Later she moved to Boston, Massachusetts, to become an editor at the *Christian Science Monitor*. Over the years, Lowe has shared her gardening wisdom and enthusiasm with countless numbers of readers.

She is a past president of the Garden Writers Association, a group consisting of nearly two thousand members of the garden writing community. Lowe's other credits and recognition include contributing articles to *Women's Day* and *Southern Living* magazines. She also appeared weekly in a gardening segment on television station WDEF-TV in Chattanooga, Tennessee.

Lowe's many awards include five Quill and Trowel Awards from the Garden Writers Association; a Special Communication Award for Tennessee Horticulture from the Tennessee Fruit and Vegetable Growers; the Exemplary Journalism for Home Gardening Communication Award from the National Garden Bureau, and many more. Lowe's proudest gardening moment occurred when a daylily was named after her.

In addition to this book for Cool Springs Press, Lowe is also the author of *Tennessee & Kentucky Garden Guide*, *Herbs! Creative Herb Garden Themes and Projects*, and *Ortho's All About Pruning*, among other gardening books. She has lived in Louisville, Kentucky, as well as several different regions of

Tennessee, and she has experienced gardening in everything from sunny sites with hard red clay to dry, shady spots with soil so rocky it ruined numerous shovels. She and her husband, Carlyle, who's known as the couple's official hole digger, currently divide their time between Tennessee and South Carolina. But no matter where Lowe lives, helping gardeners is one of her life goals.

CPSIA information can be obtained
at www.ICGtesting.com
Printed in the USA
LVHW01s0956200118
563216LV00011B/11/P